YO-EHY-550

Literary Research: Strategies and Sources
Series Editors: Peggy Keeran & Jennifer Bowers

Every literary age presents scholars with both predictable and unique research challenges. This series fills a gap in the field of reference literature by featuring research strategies and by recommending the best tools for conducting specialized period and national literary research. Emphasizing research methodology, each series volume takes into account the unique challenges inherent in conducting research of that specific literary period and outlines the best practices for researching within it. Volumes place the research process within the period's historical context and use a narrative structure to analyze and compare print and electronic reference sources. Following an introduction to online searching, chapters typically will cover these types of resources: general literary reference materials; library catalogs; print and online bibliographies, index, and annual reviews; scholarly journals; contemporary reviews; period journals and newspapers; microform and digital collections; manuscripts and archives; and Web resources. Additional or alternative chapters may be included to highlight a particular research problem or to examine other pertinent period or national literary resources.

1. *Literary Research and the British Romantic Era: Strategies and Sources* by Peggy Keeran and Jennifer Bowers, 2005.
2. *Literary Research and the Era of American Nationalism and Romanticism* by Angela Courtney, 2008.
3. *Literary Research and the American Modernist Era* by Robert N. Matuozzi and Elizabeth B. Lindsay, 2008.

Literary Research and the American Modernist Era:

Strategies and Sources, No. 3

ROBERT N. MATUOZZI AND
ELIZABETH BLAKESLEY LINDSAY

*Literary Research:
Strategies and Sources*

THE SCARECROW PRESS, INC.
Lanham, Maryland • Toronto • Plymouth, UK
2008

SCARECROW PRESS, INC.

Published in the United States of America
by Scarecrow Press, Inc.
A wholly owned subsidiary of
The Rowman & Littlefield Publishing Group, Inc.
4501 Forbes Boulevard, Suite 200, Lanham, Maryland 20706
www.scarecrowpress.com

Estover Road
Plymouth PL6 7PY
United Kingdom

British Library Cataloguing in Publication Information Available

Library of Congress Cataloging-in-Publication Data

Matuozzi, Robert N.
Literary research and the American modernist era : strategies and sources / Robert N.
Matuozzi and Elizabeth Blakesley Lindsay.
    p. cm. — (Literary research: strategies and sources ; no. 3)
Includes bibliographical references and index.
ISBN-13: 978-0-8108-6116-9 (pbk. : alk. paper)
ISBN-10: 0-8108-6116-X (pbk. : alk. paper)
eISBN: 0-8108-6237-9
1. Modernism (Literature)—United States—Research—Methodology. 2. Modernism
(Literature)—United States—Bibliography—Methodology. 3. American literature—
20th century—Research—Methodology. 4. American literature—20th century—
Bibliography—Methodology. 5. American literature—20th century—Information
resources. 6. Modernism (Literature)—United States—Information resources. I.
Lindsay, Elizabeth Blakesley. II. Title. PS228.M63M38 2008
810.9'112072—dc22

                                                                    2008015076

∞™ The paper used in this publication meets the minimum requirements of American
National Standard for Information Sciences—Permanence of Paper for Printed Library
Materials, ANSI/NISO Z39.48-1992.
Manufactured in the United States of America

Contents

Acknowledgments   vii

Introduction   ix

1   Basics of Online Searching   1
2   General Literary Reference Sources   15
3   Library Catalogs   33
4   Print and Electronic Bibliographies, Indexes, and Annual Reviews   49
5   Scholarly Journals   67
6   Contemporary Reviews   81
7   Newspapers, Periodicals, and Microforms   97
8   Manuscripts and Archives   109
9   Web Resources   123
10   Researching a Thorny Problem   135

Appendix: Selected Resources in Related Disciplines   141

Bibliography   155

Index   159

About the Authors   173

Acknowledgments

We appreciate the support of the Washington State University Libraries in granting various professional leaves that allowed us to complete this work. Thanks also to series editors Peggy Keeran and Jenny Bowers and to Scarecrow editor Martin Dillon.

Introduction

Literary history is conveniently divided into specific periods by academic convention, often as a shorthand way to summarize an era's major literary productions in terms of its genres, common themes, and linguistic innovations. Hence, the notion of "modernism" remains fluid and contested, liable to continuous revision, inflected by changing literary and historical perspectives. As a recent commentator observes, "the object of literary study called 'modernism' is a retrospective construction, largely American, post-war and academic; linked to a 'winner's history' associated with the New Criticism and a narrow canon."[1]

Moreover, access to primary literary texts and related secondary scholarly sources is evolving in a period of innovative technological development. Publishing trends and the persistence of traditional research paradigms are important parts of this story, too. In contrast to just thirty years ago, contemporary literary study has been fundamentally altered by the emergence of proprietary research databases, the Internet and the World Wide Web, and digital content; the availability of laptop computers and versatile, hand-held information appliances; and improvements in bibliographic databases, including enhanced online library catalogs. The political and academic contexts of literary theory and study also reflect the dynamism of the times, so that in the early years of the twenty-first century, scholars are faced with unprecedented opportunities and superabundant secondary resources with which to rewrite the literary and historical meaning of modernism. In this vein new and emerging information technologies mirror the tempo and sense of discontinuity associated with modernist literature and the cultural milieu that gave rise to it in the immediate aftermath of World War I. Never was the modernist aesthetic credo widely attributed to Ezra Pound—an ascription probably based on his collection of literary essays *Make It New* (1935)—more apt or inescapable than now.

Librarians, archivists, and other information specialists can provide vital guidance in this complex and rich information environment. This volume in the Scarecrow Press series, *Literary Research and the American Modernist Era* offers the scholar and researcher what we hope is a clear introduction to the best contemporary library resources and practices for researching American modernist writing from this period. We believe this exposure will enable users to improve their information skills and fluency, whether in the real or the virtual library. Even those lacking access to some of the resources described here can profit from this particular overview of literary research because it will help them frame questions, indicate where to go for answers, and demonstrate useful connections among many of the secondary scholarly sources normally consulted during the research process.

American literary modernism embraced two world wars, a brief euphoria preceding a severe economic downturn, urbanization, the rise of mass media and advertising, the efflorescence of literary journals called "little magazines," and broad cultural upheavals across all social and economic classes. Millions of immigrants had recently entered America, rapidly expanding urban populations in the 1920s and 1930s. Carnegie libraries made books and magazines widely available. Women assumed an increasingly important role in literary production and the arts, often through patronage and publishing.[2] Although primarily an urban phenomenon, modernism radiated throughout the culture in the form of fashion, music, dance, theater, architecture, and film. Influenced by European modernist literature, some American publishers began to promote work that celebrated and critiqued the tendencies of the age or that represented a decisive break with earlier values and norms.[3]

Information can be problematic if there is too much or too little that is relevant in a particular context. As indicated, the primary goal of this book is to provide the scholar of American modernism with solid research skills and an overview of current core reference tools that are focused on this field of study. Some of these resources are more general in scope than others, but all can be mined for useful information if properly assessed and utilized. The chief benefit of an efficient research methodology is that it minimizes frustration so that the scholar can devote more time to writing and reflection; in short, this reference guide will help the literary researcher separate the wheat from the chaff.

This specialized reference work mostly follows the format of others in the Scarecrow series. It provides an overview and description of selected research tools associated with the field of American modernism, including chapters on basics of online searching; general literary reference sources; library catalogs; print and electronic bibliographies; scholarly journals; contemporary reviews; period newspapers, periodicals, and microforms; manuscripts and archives; Web resources; researching a thorny problem; and a bibliographic appendix of selected resources in related disciplines. In the sections for each chapter, we have provided bibliographic citations valuable to the American modernist researcher, and have provided descriptions of selected sources throughout. At present, primary literary texts from the period of American modernism are likely not in the public domain and are virtually unavailable in digital or microform versions, although literary texts from older periods that are no longer copyrighted may be available in these formats. This situation will change in accordance with copyright law and as technology alters the availability of American modernist literary material from its early to mid-twentieth-century phase.

In today's information-saturated environment, the peculiar challenges associated with literary research are both engaging and navigable as a narrative project, this guide is worthwhile because it offers a coherent account of how contemporary research skills and resources can complement one another in helping the scholar effectively deal with typical challenges they might encounter in the course of their work on American modernist era writing. As well, this research guide will indicate some of the salient changes that have occurred in the organization and dissemination of information over the last few years, arguably the largest information explosion since the Victorian period. Hence, our pedagogic aim is not to make the literary researcher the sort of expert "who knows more and more about less and less."[4] Rather, this book describes essential scholarly tools, outlines broad approaches, and offers focused strategies that can be adapted to particular needs. We hope the resulting roadmap will facilitate the literary research process, using a wide array of media in both libraries and archives and employing both traditional and emerging information resources in literature and allied fields.

Notes

1. Tim Armstrong, *Modernism* (Malden, MA: Polity Press, 2005), 24.

2. On marginal figures in American modernist literature, see Lisa Botshon and Meredith Goldsmith, eds., *Middlebrow Moderns: Popular American Women Writers of the 1920s* (Boston: Northeastern University Press, 2003); and Steven Watson, *Strange Bedfellows: The First American Avant-Garde* (New York: Abbeville Press, 1991).

3. On modernist publishing, see Catherine Turner, *Marketing Modernism Between the Two World Wars* (Amherst: University of Massachusetts Press, 2003). On modernism in the fine and performing arts, film, architecture, and technology, see David Bradshaw and Kevin J. H. Dettmar, *A Companion to Modernist Literature and Culture* (Malden, MA: Blackwell Publishing, Ltd., 2006), more fully described in chapter 2. On modernist period fashion in the United States, Great Britain, and France, see John Peacock, *The Complete Fashion Sourcebook* (New York: Thames & Hudson, 2005). Also consult the resources in the appendix.

4. In a commencement address at Columbia University, Nicholas Murray Butler observed, "An expert is one who knows more and more about less and less." Quoted in M. J. Cohen, *The Penguin Dictionary of Epigrams* (New York: Penguin Putnam, Inc., 2001), 211.

CHAPTER 1

Basics of Online Searching

The foundation of successful research begins with knowing how to construct the most effective searches. Understanding how information is organized and how search systems work enables the construction of searches that return relevant, valuable results. Librarians often find themselves helping people who say they cannot find any results even though they have spent a great deal of time searching. In these instances, people typically use searches that consist of long strings of words, long phrases, or complete questions typed into search engines or database interfaces. This chapter discusses practical steps in constructing a search strategy to locate relevant sources efficiently, regardless of what type of source you are seeking or what type of search tool you employ.

Step 1: Formulate Research Question and Topic Sentence

Start the process with your research idea. Moving from a research question into a topic sentence can help clarify the concepts you will use for the search strategy. For example, if you want to find out about the reaction of feminists to Hemingway's works, your topic sentence could be: "I want to learn how feminist scholars have reacted to the works of Hemingway," with main concepts being *Hemingway*, *feminism*, and *literary criticism*. Another example, exploring the contemporary reaction to the Harlem Renaissance might result in a topic sentence of: "I want to discover how the works of the Harlem Renaissance were received critically at the time," with main concepts being *Harlem Renaissance*, *literary criticism*, and *reviews*.

1

Step 2: Brainstorm Keywords

Selecting and using the best keywords possible for your topic can be the most important step of the research process. This step allows you to consider multiple aspects of the topic as well as contextual concerns. Thinking of alternate words or different ways of addressing the same topic will provide a bank of keywords to use in your search. Consideration of how broad or narrow your keyword ideas are may make a tremendous impact on the number and quality of results returned in a search.

See table 1.1 for a listing of possible keywords and concepts for the sample search regarding feminist criticism of Hemingway and his themes.

Step 3: Understand the Structure of Electronic Records

Search interfaces and databases work together using a set of rules or protocols. Based on what the searcher submits as a query, the database will be searched for matching results. Although rules may vary, this is the basic structural relationship for any search tool, from *Google* to the *MLA International Bibliography (MLAIB)* to a library catalog.

A common record type, the **Ma**chine **R**eadable **C**ataloging (MARC) record, was established by the Library of Congress in 1965 and can be found in library catalogs. Most libraries use a commercial software package that presents the information to the public through the online catalog while also providing complementary modules that allow the library staff to order, receive, catalog, and maintain the materials. Common vendors are Innovative Interfaces, Endeavor (Voyager), Ex Libris, SIRSI, and Dynix.

MARC record coding allows library online catalogs to execute title, subject, author, and other searches. The MARC record includes a field and subfield organization; each piece of information about a book or journal will have a separate field. Figure 1.1 shows the MARC record for the journal *Modern Fiction*

Table 1.1.   Possible keywords for search on feminist criticism and Hemingway

Concept 1	Concept 2	Concept 3
Critique	Feminist	Hemingway
Reviews	Feminism	
Literary criticism	Women	
Analysis		

```
001     1645443
005     19950727061941.8
008     750921c19559999inuqr1p
010     56000651
022 0   0026-7724
022 0   1080-658X
050 00  PS379|b.M55
082 00  809.3
222  0  Modern fiction studies
245 00  Modern fiction studies.
246 13  MFS|f<, spring 1976->
260     [W. Lafayette, Ind.,|bDept. of English, Purdue University,
        etc.]
265     Bldg. D, South Campus Courts, Purdue University, West
        Lafayette, IN 47907
310     Quarterly
362 0   v. 1-    Feb. 1955-
510 0   Social sciences and humanities index|x0037-7899
550     Issued 1955-   by the Modern Fiction Club of Purdue
        University; <1976-> by the Dept. of English, Purdue
        University.
650  0  American fiction|y20th century|xHistory and criticism
        |vPeriodicals.
650  0  English fiction|y20th century|xHistory and criticism
        |vPeriodicals.
710 2   Purdue University.|bDept. of English.
710 2   Purdue University.|bModern Fiction Club.
```

Figure 1.1.   Modified MARC record for *Modern Fiction Studies* with tags 222, 245, 246 highlighted
Source: Washington State University Libraries catalog

Studies. The title of the journal is listed in both the 222 and 245 fields, and a variant title, the abbreviation *MFS*, is listed in the 246 field. These multiple tags allow for greater access to information in the catalog, allowing a search for *Modern Fiction Studies* or *MFS* with various types of title searches and retrieving the needed information.

Figure 1.2 provides a modified MARC record for Jane Goodman's book *Modernism 1910–1945: Image to Apocalypse*. Tags highlighted in the figure show how the author, title, and publication information are formatted. The 490 and 830 tags denote the name of the series, which allows searching by that name and retrieval of a list of all appropriate titles. The 650 fields are for subject headings, which will be discussed later in this chapter.

This brief overview illustrates how a standard structure for records allows for precise searching. Although it is not necessary to become an expert in all aspects of MARC records or other standard structures, this information helps researchers understand how search tools work.

```
001      52471380
003      OCoLC
005      20040317165819.0
008      030605s2004      enk      b      001 0 eng
010      2003054923
020      0333696204 (cloth)
020      0333696212 (paper)
050 00   PR478.M6|bG65 2004
082 00   820.9/112|221
100 1    Goldman, Jane,|d1960-
245 10   Modernism, 1910-1945 :|bimage to apocalypse /|cJane
         Goldman.
260      Houndmills, Basingstoke, Hampshire ;|aNew York :|bPalgrave
         Macmillan,|c2004.
300      xxiv, 312 p. ;|c23 cm.
490 1    Transitions.
504      Includes bibliographical references (p. 272-290) and
         index.
650  0   English literature|y20th century|xHistory and criticism.
650  0   Modernism (Literature)|zGreat Britain.
650  0   American literature|y20th century|xHistory and criticism.
650  0   Modernism (Literature)|zUnited States.
830  0   Transitions (Palgrave Macmillan (Firm))
```

Figure 1.2.   Modified MARC record for *Modernism 1910–1945: Image to Apocalypse*, with tags 100, 245, 260, 490, and 650 highlighted
Source: Washington State University Libraries catalog

Step 4: Create Your Search Strategy

One approach in creating a search strategy is to use the specific fields in a record, as discussed in the MARC record above. This type of search is useful when your information need can be met with a specific approach. An obvious example is using an author field search to locate books by a particular person. This can save time as compared to a keyword search, if you need only books by that author and no additional biographical or critical works. Other fields include publication date, title, abstract, language, and material type. At times you may need to limit your search to one of these fields, but the most flexible search strategy is the keyword approach, where the search process looks at multiple, if not all, parts of the record.

BOOLEAN SEARCHING

To use the keyword approach effectively, Boolean strategies are important for achieving efficient, relevant results. The Boolean strategy is named for George Boole, a nineteenth-century British mathematician. The design of computers and database structures is based on his work. The three Boolean operators—*and, or,* and *not*—are used to narrow, broaden, or exclude terms from a search strategy, respectively. Boolean operators are used to link the different concepts and accompanying keywords for retrieving maximum results from online search tools.

BOOLEAN "AND"

Using *and* narrows the search results. In the sample search above, you would link the three concepts with *and* to locate materials that discuss all three concepts in some way:

> *feminist* **and** *criticism* **and** *Hemingway*

As shown in figure 1.3, the area where the circles overlap represents the results that would be returned with the Boolean *and* search strategy.

The basic Boolean *and* search strategy retrieved twelve results in the *MLA International Bibliography (MLAIB)* database; one example is provided in figure 1.4.

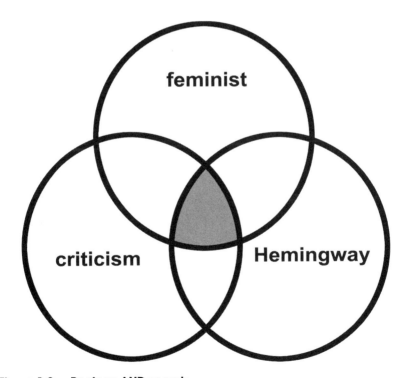

Figure 1.3.   Boolean AND search

Author(s):	Barlowe-Keys, Jamie.
Title:	"Re-Reading Women: The Example of Catherine Barkley."
Source:	The **Hemingway** Review, 12:2 (1993 Spring), pp. 24-35.
Subject Terms:	American literature; 1900–1999; **Hemingway**, Ernest (1899–1961): A Farewell to Arms (1929); novel; treatment of female characters; especially Barkley, Catherine (character); relationship to **feminist** literary theory and **criticism**.

Figure 1.4.   MLAIB record retrieved using Boolean *and* search strategy with search terms in bold
Source: MLAIB, via Gale InfoTrac

BOOLEAN "OR"

Using *or* broadens the search results. For example, you may want to ensure the most comprehensive results by searching for *America or United States*. Another example is a search for material dealing with either *fiction or poetry*.

*american fiction **or** american drama **or** american poetry*

The diagram in figure 1.5 shows that the intersection of this search strategy actually comprises all records available. Another possibility is when a writer is known by two names, such as Hilda Doolittle, who published as H. D. With *or*, records that mention any, some, or all of the words searched will be returned.

BOOLEAN "NOT"

Using *not* excludes concepts. For example, in a search for material on American literature or American history, a number of results may mention Latin America. To streamline results, you might reconfigure the search as:

*american literature **not** latin*

In figure 1.6, the results are shaded to show that the unrelated concept will be excluded. Be aware that using *not* can be extremely limiting. For example, a relevant item might have used the excluded term as part of a publisher name or author name or for a contextual or metaphorical purpose. If you use *not* and retrieve very few results when you would expect many, reconsider its use. Adding

Figure 1.5. Boolean OR search

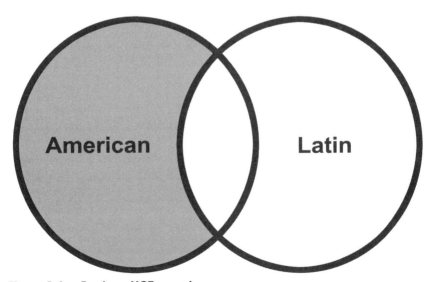

Figure 1.6. Boolean NOT search

another keyword with *and* may be a more effective way of limiting or controlling the search strategy.

TRUNCATION

In some cases, you will want results that mention all variations of a word. Truncation avoids typing a long list of words linked with *or*. For example, *litera** will retrieve *literature, literary*, and *literati* as well as *literal* and *literally*. Using *feminis** will retrieve *feminist* and *feminism* but not *feminine*. Some systems will automatically look for singular and plural forms but will not find the adjective form of the same word. Some search systems allow for sophisticated truncation, with different symbols to indicate the replacement of one or more than one letter. In some cases a different symbol is used for replacement of a letter within a word or at the end of the stem. For example, some systems will recognize *wom?n* and return the results *woman, women*, or *womyn*. The help screens in each database will clearly identify which truncation symbols are used.

NESTING

For complex Boolean searching, nesting is used to connect the terms that need to be searched together or that must be searched in a different order. For example, *American or United States and fiction or poetry* will retrieve a much different set of results than *(American or United States) and (fiction or poetry)*. Nesting is useful with several of the above topics since it allows for combination of various terms and synonyms into one efficient search strategy. One example is *Harlem Renaissance and (critic* or review* or reception)*, while another is *Hemingway and (feminis* or women) and (critic* or review* or reception)*.

PHRASE SEARCHING AND PROXIMITY OPERATORS

Phrase searching works differently from Boolean keyword approaches. In many databases, typing a long phrase achieves only results that match that specific phrase. Consider the possible differences in results between *feminis* and critic* and Hemingway* and *how feminists reacted to Ernest Hemingway*. The second search strategy will not find items that mention "feminist critique" or even the "reaction of feminists."

If the search concept is a phrase, look at the help screens in the resource to ensure correct formatting for the search. Some systems require the use of quotation marks to designate the phrase, while others employ proximity operators. Proximity operators allow more customization of phrase searches and can be particularly useful when searching for authors with multiple names who sometimes are known by a shortened form of their names.

Two typical proximity operators are *within* and *near*. *Within* (often designated by *w*) is used to indicate a word order or closeness, specifying that two words must be within some other number of words of each other. *Near* (often *n*) is used to indicate a more flexible pattern of word order. For example, *Zora w2 Hurston* will retrieve items that mention either Zora Neale Hurston or Zora Hurston; *zora n2 hurston* will also function in this way while finding references with the names inverted or in the incorrect order, such as Hurston Zora Neale or Zora Hurston Neale.

KEYWORD VS. SUBJECT SEARCHING

Starting with subject heading searches can be difficult, because the precise subject headings must be known in advance. Subject headings or descriptors are terms that are consistently used in a database or catalog; they are often referred to as controlled vocabulary. Using controlled vocabulary allows for connections in the database between items that are similar.

Knowing the precise headings in advance can be tricky. Subject headings often use inverted terms, which will not typically match people's normal usage. They may also use older nomenclature for a particular concept or group of people, such as "Afro-Americans" instead of "African Americans." To know the exact subject headings prior to searching requires looking through long lists of terms, such as the multivolume set of *Library of Congress Subject Headings*, which provides access to all of the subject headings used by Library of Congress catalogers. This work is typically available in reference departments. A keyword approach allows you to combine a number of concepts and ideas in a flexible way. Once the items are retrieved, however, it can be extremely helpful to peruse the subject headings that are provided. If you find a subject heading that captures the desired topic, that subject heading can lead to a precise, manageable set of results with the appropriate focus.

Works about authors typically have their names as a subject heading, often with the birth or death dates included. This type of heading is subdivided with additional headings, such as "Biography," "Bibliography," or "Criticism and Interpretation." It may be quicker to do a subject heading search for the name of the author you are studying and looking for the "Criticism and Interpretation" subheading than to construct and sort through the results of a keyword search.

Figure 1.7 shows the catalog record for a book about Hemingway and feminism, located using a keyword search for *feminis* and Hemingway and critic**.

This record illustrates a "contents" field that shows the complete listing of the essays included in this volume. The subject headings listed show several specific headings linked to Hemingway's name, along with general subjects, such as

Title	**Hemingway and women : female critics and the female voice /** **edited by Lawrence R. Broer and Gloria Holland.**
Imprint	Tuscaloosa : University of Alabama Press, c2002.

LOCATION	CALL NUMBER	STATUS
WSU Holland	PS3515.E37 Z6178 2002	ON SHELF

Description	xiv, 353 p. ; 24 cm.
Bibliog.	Includes bibliographical references (p. [319]-340) and index.
Contents	In love with papa / Linda Patterson Miller -- Re-reading women II: the example of Brett, Hadley, Duff, and women's scholarship / Jamie Barlowe -- The sun hasn't set yet: Brett Ashley and the code hero debate / Kathy G. Willingham -- The romance of desire in Hemingway's fiction / Linda Wagner-Martin -- "I'd rather not hear": women and men in conversation in "cat in the rain" and "the sea change" / Lisa Tyler -- To have and hold not: Marie Morgan, Helen Gordon, and Dorothy Hollis / Kim Moreland -- Revisiting the code: female foundations and "the undiscovered country" in For whom the bell tolls / Gail D. Sinclair -- On defining Eden: the search for eve in the garden of sorrows / Ann Putnam -- Santiago and the eternal feminine: gendering la mar in the old man and the sea / Susan F. Beegel -- West of everything: the high cost of making men in Islands in the stream / Rose Marie Burwell -- Queer families in Hemingway's fiction / Debra A. Moddelmog -- "Go to sleep, devil": the awakening of Catherine's feminism in The garden of Eden / Amy Lovell Strong -- The light from Hemingway's garden: regendering papa / Nancy R. Comley -- Alias grace: music and the feminine aesthetic in Hemingway's early style / Hilary K. Justice -- A lifetime of flower narratives: letting the silenced voice speak / Miriam B. Mandel -- Rivalry, romance, and war reporters: Martha Gellhorn's love goes to press and the collier's files / Sandra Whipple Spanier -- Hemingway's literary sisters: the author through the eyes of women writers / Rena Sanderson.
Subject	Hemingway, Ernest, 1899-1961 -- Characters -- Women.
	Hemingway, Ernest, 1899-1961 -- Views on sex role.
	Feminism and literature -- United States -- History -- 20th century.
	Women and literature -- United States -- History -- 20th century.
	Sex role in literature.
	Women in literature.
Other author	Broer, Lawrence R.
	Holland, Gloria, 1945-

Figure 1.7. Modified record for Hemingway and Women: Female Critics and the Female Voice
Source: Washington State University Libraries catalog

"women in literature." In some cases, a subject heading can capture the complete essence of the desired search topic, and in others, a subject heading can locate general sources to inform your research. In most library catalogs, the subject headings are active hyperlinks; clicking the appropriate heading will execute a search for that heading and retrieve a new set of results.

One advantage of the keyword search approach is that you will typically get more results, such as those in which the author in question may be mentioned in part of the book but is not central enough to the book to have been assigned as a subject heading. Keyword searching can also lead to "false drops," though, where the words you seek are included in the record, but not in the proper context.

RELEVANCY SEARCHING

Some search systems use a relevancy-ranking algorithm to display the results. In these searches, a set of criteria built into the algorithm drives the inclusion and display of results. The items deemed most relevant will display first. Relevancy ranking can take into account criteria such as:

- the presence of all keywords in the record
- the presence of some keywords in the record
- the number of times the keywords appear in the record (that is, the more often the words are repeated, the more relevant the item will be considered)
- the proximity of the keywords (that is, if the keywords are closer together, the item will be considered more relevant)
- the location of the keywords in the record (that is, if the keywords are present in the title, subject heading, or other designated fields, the item will be considered more relevant)

Some search systems allow relevancy ranking to be deactivated. Check the help screens to determine if relevancy ranking is being used and how relevancy is defined. An item that mentions a keyword seven times instead of five may not really be more useful. Relevancy searching has both fans and opponents; you will have to see how helpful it is for you.

LIMITING/MODIFYING

The ability to limit or modify searches can be a very powerful feature. In some systems, this may include being able to limit results to a particular language, date, material type, publisher, or place of publication. The material-type limit can be important in databases that offer a wide array of sources, such as books, chapters, dissertations, articles, reviews, and media items. Being able to focus on or exclude a particular type of material can make the search process much more efficient.

Step 5: Choosing a Database

After brainstorming for keywords and applying Boolean techniques, the next step is to select the appropriate search tool. You may need to alter the search strategy, depending on the tool you use. For example, if the search is primarily for books, you would choose a library catalog. Catalogs are discussed further in chapter 3, but in terms of searching, remember that catalogs do not generally contain the full text of books. Using many keywords for a library catalog search may result in few retrieved items.

For article searching, explore the search interface of the selected database. For example, access to *MLAIB* is sold to libraries by several companies. Your strategy may be different depending on whether your library subscribes through EBSCO, Gale, OCLC, or another vendor. You will be able to customize your search to look for your keywords anywhere in the record. Some article databases provide full-text access directly, which will also impact the search strategy, as illustrated in table 1.2.

The best advice is to look at the interface offered through your library and check for links to "Help" or to "Frequently Asked Questions." Reference librarians can also assist. Knowing the answers to the following questions will make your searching easier and more effective:

- Does the database require or recognize the use of Boolean operators? Are they manually entered or provided in drop-down menus? If you must type them, do they require capital letters (AND)?
- Is truncation recognized? If so, what symbols are used?

Table 1.2. List of databases and search interfaces

Database / Content	Search Interface / Access
MLAIB	EBSCO Host
	Ovid
	InfoTrac (Gale)
	First Search (OCLC)
	Wilson Web
World Cat	First Search (OCLC)
ABELL	Chadwyck-Healy (ProQuest)

- Does the database recognize quotation marks for phrase searching?
- Does the database provide or allow limits by language, date, and type of source?
- Are results displayed by date, author, or title?
- Are results ranked by relevancy? If so, how is relevance determined?

Watch for upgrades to the database interfaces. Vendors often improve search capabilities and enhance interfaces, so reviewing the features of frequently used databases is a good idea. For example, FirstSearch did not recognize quotation marks for phrase searching for many years but now provides that option. The ProQuest interface provides drop-down menus with Boolean and proximity operators in the advanced search, but in the basic search you must type the operators. In many interfaces, *and* is used by default, but in others, a string of words is treated as a phrase. The difference in results can be critical.

Step 6: Understanding Web Searching

Although the Internet contains a plethora of information, materials that are not free of charge are not widely available. Articles in academic journals are not often available online at no cost. Using *Google* or other search engines may lead to a source that lists an article but requires payment for access. If you encounter such sites, check whether the library owns the journal in question. If it does not, it can likely procure the journal through interlibrary loan services or other consortial borrowing arrangements for a minimal, or no, fee.

Search engines like *Google* can be a useful starting place to begin exploring a topic or to locate various types of sources, including identifying locations with archival and special collections or finding encyclopedia entries. An increasing number of special collections are being digitized for online access, as well. Remember, however, that items that are published for profit and protected by copyright will rarely be available at no cost online.

One notable exception is *Google Scholar*, a special service that provides information about library holdings. You may be able to find article citations as you would in *MLAIB* or other resources. Unless you are on campus or have been authenticated through your library's log-in procedures or proxy server for off-campus access, however, you will not be able to access full-text materials through *Google Scholar*.

Just as understanding the differences between library catalogs and subscription article databases is important, it is also helpful to know what Internet search engines can and cannot deliver. In most cases, a strategy that combines all three types of tools will be the most comprehensive and effective for research.

Conclusion

The techniques and strategies outlined in this chapter will be useful in a wide range of research, whether using library online catalogs to locate books, article subscription databases such as *MLAIB*, or search engines to search the Web. Use the techniques discussed above, including Boolean operators, truncation, nesting, subject searching, and proximity searching. Remember the differences between library catalogs, search engines, and article databases, and select the best source for your information need. The better your skills and understanding of online searching are, the more effective and efficient your research processes will be.

CHAPTER 2

General Literary Reference Sources

Secondary reference sources offer the researcher a helpful orientation to the area of American literary modernism, including material on crucial historical influences. Depending on the specific nature of a project, specialized and period reference sources may also provide invaluable information on more obscure aspects of a research problem. Examples of commonly used literary reference materials are concordances and bibliographies, registers, checklists and calendars, dictionaries and handbooks, specialized companions, indexes, guides, literary surveys, and encyclopedias. This chapter will briefly describe some of these reference tools, emphasizing their relevance for research in American literary modernism in different contexts. Remember to consult the notes and bibliographies in these and similar resources for additional research leads.

General Research Guides

Harner, James L. *Literary Research Guide: An Annotated Listing of Reference Sources in English and Literary Studies.* 4th ed. New York: Modern Language Association, 2002.

Harner, James L. *Literary Research Guide,* 22 May 2005, www-english.tamu.edu/index.php?id=924 (accessed 21 August 2007).

Marcuse, Michael J. *A Reference Guide for English Studies.* Berkeley: University of California Press, 1990.

(See the Library of Congress subject headings in these titles to locate similar items in your library.)

Noteworthy for its comprehensive scope, careful organization, multiple indexes, and informative annotations, Harner's **Literary Research Guide** is a standard source for literary scholars and an essential tool for advanced literary research generally. Marcuse's *Reference Guide* is perhaps less well known but is an important general source for beginning and advanced literary research, despite the fact that the cutoff date for most of its content is 1985. Harner's *Research Guide* is an evolving document, with periodic updates available on the website listed above. Since the amount of information associated with literary research is expanding daily, Harner states that in future printed editions he will excise some older content in favor of newer material. Older editions of the *Research Guide* thus remain valuable for their retrospective content and comments on editorial procedure. Both Harner's and Marcuse's guides are wide-ranging in content and exhibit a similar structure (chapters are designated alphabetically, for example), including comprehensive evaluative annotations along with publication information and detailed content notes for particular entries. Marcuse's **A Reference Guide for English Studies** has a section on individual authors, another section on English as a profession, and a hefty section on historical study and related disciplines. Both Harner and Marcuse employ a useful hierarchical arrangement as well as multiple indexes. Since Harner periodically revises and updates his *Research Guide*, it reflects the emergence of resources on the World Wide Web for literary research, offering an entire section devoted to "Internet Resources." However, because of what he calls the "unstructured, unregulated, and unstable" nature of websites generally, Harner states in the fourth edition of the *Research Guide* that he notes only those electronic resources "sponsored by an academic institution or learned society" (ix). In the case of periodicals or other irregular publications or series, however, both guides indicate supplements, updates, and revisions to bibliographic citations. Various names for the same periodical title may be correctly determined by a careful examination of the full catalog record in many online library catalogs, including *WorldCat*.

Those doing research in American modernism will be especially interested in the section in Harner's *Research Guide* covering "American Literature" and, in particular, in the subsection on twentieth-century American literature. Though many of these sources are general in nature, they offer a good starting point. Thus, the reader will find an annotated listing—arranged by genre—of abstracts and guides, encyclopedias, surveys, handbooks and dictionaries, bibliographies and biographical dictionaries, and surveys of important primary texts. All entries are numbered and contain standard bibliographic information. At the end of many entries, Harner gives the Library of Congress and Dewey Decimal call numbers for particular items, helpful for finding most of the resources held in American libraries. Interspersed are "see also" references, which indicate important supplemental material. A useful device in Harner's *Guide* that is unavailable in Marcuse's *Guide* is a running head with chapter rubrics and entry numbers for the last entry on a given page. Harner's subject index does not offer specific entries to sources on American modernism but essentially recapitulates the arrangement of the *Research Guide*.

Marcuse's *Reference Guide* treats American modernism primarily in section "R—Literature of the Twentieth Century" and section "S—American Literature." The general section on American literature is divided into subsections designated by reference material types (surveys, bibliographies, guides, etc.) and literary genres, with entries individually numbered according to Marcuse's arrangement along with standard bibliographic information and the Library of Congress call number. Some works in these sections are broad synthetic studies, and a few treat specific time periods in American literary history. Extensive annotations for reference works give the researcher a good idea of contents. In the subject index under "Modern literature," Marcuse points the reader to the entries arranged under "Twentieth-century." This section allows the user to assess the volume's potential for research in American modernism.

The general Library of Congress subject headings for American literary modernism and literary modernism (other than for geographic subheadings outside the United States or for specific time periods) are:

Modernism (Literature)—United States
Modernism (Literature)
Modernism (Literature)—English-speaking countries
Literature, Experimental
Literature, Experimental—United States
Literature, Experimental—United States—History and criticism

Specialized reference resources may be found through:

Modernism (Literature)—United States—Handbooks, manuals, etc.
Modernism (Literature)—United States—History—20th century
American literature—20th century—History and criticism
Modernism (Literature)—Encyclopedias
Modernism (Literature)—Bibliography

American Modernism Period Companions

Barbour, Scott, ed. *American Modernism.* San Diego, CA: Greenhaven Press, 2000.
Kalaidjian, Walter B., ed. *The Cambridge Companion to American Modernism.* New York: Cambridge University Press, 2005.

Mackean, Ian. *The Essentials of Literature in English Post-1914*. London: Hodder Arnold, 2005.

Specialized encyclopedias and companions (and manuals) offer in-depth, analytical treatments of a particular subject. As its name suggests, an encyclopedia tends to be comprehensive in scope for a defined subject area and usually has signed articles of varying length, while companions offer summary analytical overviews. Both of these reference works have indexes and bibliographies, though a companion is usually designed as a ready-reference source for definitions, chronologies, and biographical and factual material. Companions and manuals often contain chapters by individual authors.

In *American Modernism*, a volume in the Greenhaven Press series on literary movements and genres, Barbour situates modernism in his introductory overview as the period 1910–1940. Featuring five thematic chapters consisting of two to five essays and a brief chronology, the volume reprints previously published material on different facets of modernism. Individual essays reveal the historical and literary context of modernism and point to significant works and the linguistic aspects of American modernist prose and poetry. Other chapters assess the cultural legacy of American modernism, including its political and aesthetic engagements and contested relations with contemporaneous American writers and literary movements that paralleled it. This Greenhaven Press Companion to literary movements also provides chapters on regional modernist movements, emphasizing the Harlem Renaissance and the South.

The *Cambridge Companion to American Modernism* aims to "provide a comprehensive and authoritative overview of American literary modernism from 1890–1930." Arranged into chapters under the broad headings of "Genre," "Culture," and "Society," twelve scholars of American modernism offer in-depth thematic treatments of the cultural and social developments specific to the literature of this era. Fiction, poetry, drama, and literary criticism are covered, along with the visual arts and cinema. Other chapters discuss the Harlem Renaissance, jazz, regionalism, and contemporary themes on the role of gender and sexuality in American modernism. Each yearly chronology records major historical and cultural events and provides a short list of significant literary publications. The *Cambridge Companion* offers suggestions for further reading conveniently keyed to the volume's individual chapters. An introductory chapter titled "Nationalism and the Modern American Cannon" offers a useful analysis relating emergent visions of national identity to canon formation in American modernism and the important role played by the little magazines in publishing and disseminating modernist texts, examining the *Little Review* as an illustrative case study.

In *The Essentials of Literature in English Post-1914*, editor Ian Mackean notes, "the purpose of this book is to provide an introduction to literature in

English of the modern period—approximately 1914 to the present day—from around the world" (vii). Multiple thematic approaches offer coverage arranged around nationality, time period, and gender. "Part 1: Major Modern Authors A–Z" consists of compact treatments of a writer's output, brief biographies, and a list of selected works and sources for further reading. Scholars of American modernism will be especially interested in the section in "Part 2: Major Themes in Modern Literature" on modernism as a global literary phenomenon, including modern drama, and the section in "Part 3: Regional Influences in Modern Literature" that treats American literature. "Part 4: Reference Materials," provides an extensive time chart for the period 1914–2003, a short glossary of terms, and chronological lists of major English literary awards. The time chart offers year-by-year summaries arranged under "A selection of publications," "Historical and political events," and "Social history, popular culture, science and technology." The chronological notes emphasize the American and European contexts, although major international events are also noted. Cross-indexes cue the reader to sections that further define key concepts and terms employed throughout the book.

Modernist Period Encyclopedias, Literary Companions and Surveys, and American Literature Encyclopedias

Bercovitch, Sacvan, ed. *The Cambridge History of American Literature. Volume 5: Poetry and Criticism 1900–1950*. New York: Cambridge University Press, 2003.

———. *The Cambridge History of American Literature. Volume 6: Prose Writing 1910–1950*. New York: Cambridge University Press, 2002.

Bradshaw, David, and Kevin J. H. Dettmar, eds. *A Companion to Modernist Literature and Culture*. Malden, MA: Blackwell Publishing, 2006.

Bruccoli, Matthew J., and Judith S. Baughman, eds. *Modern African American Writers*. New York: Facts on File, 1994.

———. *Modern Women Writers*. New York: Facts on File, 1994.

Elliott, Emory, ed. *Columbia Literary History of the United States*. New York: Columbia University Press, 1988.

Encyclopedia of American Literature. 3 vols. New York: Facts on File, 2002.

Levenson, Michael, ed. *The Cambridge Companion to Modernism*. New York: Cambridge University Press, 1999.

Middleton, Tim, ed. *Modernism: Critical Concepts in Literary and Cultural Studies. Volume I: 1890–1934*. New York: Routledge, 2003.

Poplawski, Paul, ed. *Encyclopedia of Literary Modernism*. Westport, CT: Greenwood Press, 2003.

Roberts, Neil, ed. *A Companion to Twentieth-Century Poetry*. Malden, MA: Blackwell Publishers Ltd., 2001.

Serafin, Steven R., and Alfred Bendixen, eds. *Encyclopedia of American Literature*. New York: Continuum, 1999.

Wimsatt, Mary Ann, and Karen L. Rood, eds. *Southern Women Writers: Flannery O'Connor, Katherine Anne Porter, Eudora Welty. Dictionary of Literary Biography, Documentary Series*, vol. 12. Detroit: Gale Research, Inc., 1995.

Witalec, Janey, ed. *Harlem Renaissance: A Gale Critical Companion*. 3 vols. Detroit: Gale, 2003.

Many of the titles in this section testify to the range and complexity of literary modernism. Broad trends in cultural and historical contexts, significant linguistic innovations, themes and influences, modernist publishing, and major works are covered by various scholars in the field of literary studies. Although scope and emphasis vary depending on format, scholars of American modernism will be able to use these resources to assess most of the major critical statements and find basic biographical information on prominent American modernist writers and critics. The structure of these companions and encyclopedias follows a typical format, including an alphabetical arrangement in the encyclopedias. Volume editors provide an overview of contents. Signed articles or longer essays offer short bibliographies and notes in addition to suggestions for further reading. All these titles have indexes.

Two titles from the Blackwell *Companions to Literature and Culture* series, *A Companion to Twentieth-Century Poetry* and *A Companion to Modernist Literature and Culture*, offer the researcher in-depth treatments of modernist literature, both as a specific genre among other poetic forms and as an artistic movement in a broader cultural context. Such reference sources often enable the scholar to establish new connections between writers, works, and the larger milieu from which they emerged. These companions are similarly structured. The **Companion to Twentieth-Century Poetry**, although broader in scope than American modernism, has chapters that emphasize modernism. Part 1, "Topics and Debates," for example, offers two essays on modernism as a transatlantic phenomenon and an essay on the roots of modernist poetry; another chapter in Part 2, "Poetic Movements," discusses imagism. Part 4, "Readings," offers compact analyses of significant American modernist poets such as Eliot, Stevens, and Williams. A check of the index indicates that material on modernism is scattered throughout the volume. Short bibliographies accompany each article. The **Companion to Modernist Literature and Culture** is, as its title indicates, a focused treatment of modernism and modernist culture, with American modernism as a subset. Researchers may consult this title to access a broad array of topical and thematic treatments relating to modernist literature and allied literary and artistic movements; more contemporary critical concerns emphasize queer modernism, modernism and race, modernism and gender, postcolonial modernism, and global modernism. Part IV, "Readings," has chapters on major American modernist writers and significant literary works. The references and further readings that conclude each article consist of both up-to-date and older critical material. This volume is also valuable for its chapters on modernism in the fine and performing arts, architecture, the physical and social sciences, and the humanities.

Though each volume is relatively short, the Facts on File series *Essential Bibliography of American Fiction* offers researchers a valuable introduction to the writers selected for these specialized monographs, which are updated and revised versions of material that previously appeared in the Facts on File *Essential Bibliography of American Fiction, 1918–1988* (1991). Each volume has been carefully structured by the series editors to promote a balanced presentation and assessment of the authors selected for inclusion in *Modern African American Writers* and *Modern Women Writers*. Where possible, a complete checklist of primary works is provided, along with a wide range of selected secondary research resources, including archival collections, a short list of specialized scholarly journals, bibliographies, secondary articles, and book chapters. Volumes also have separate introductions and signed chapters, a "Checklist for Students of American Fiction" with sequentially numbered bibliographic entries arranged in sections according to types of reference resources, and an index for quick access to a variety of resources for literary research. Authors covered in the *Modern Women Writers* volume include Willa Cather, Gertrude Stein, Katherine Anne Porter, Carson McCullers, and Edith Wharton, among others.

The *Cambridge Companion to Modernism* is another title in their series on literary genres and cultural periods. Nine signed scholarly articles with notes are supplemented by a bibliography of suggested readings. An annual literary chronology for the period 1890–1939 provides a short list of selected literary publications and snapshots of related historical events. A helpful aspect of this *Cambridge Companion* and similar reference material is the suggestive way in which it contextualizes modernist themes and literary genres along with parallel artistic and social developments. Thus, chapters on film, the visual arts, and gender supplement articles on modernist poetry and prose. The scholar of American modernism will find the index a useful guide to specifically American topics and themes.

Besides its comprehensive scope, the five-volume Routledge series *Modernism: Critical Concepts in Literary and Cultural Studies* is a convenient source of primary critical statements on modernism and related cultural trends originally published during the emergence and elaboration of modernism between 1890 and 2001. The chronological arrangement of articles thus offers a contemporaneous and retrospective treatment of modernism from a variety of perspectives, or "a snapshot of the history of modernism in Anglo-American literary criticism from the 1890s to the present day" (1.1). The first two volumes of *Modernism* cover the period from 1890 to 1970 with articles on the emergence of American modernism by T. S. Eliot, Harry Levin, Frank Kermode, William James, and Ezra Pound. The introductory editorial overview in volume 1 offers suggestions for further reading, and most articles in the series have notes. The general thematic and topical index in volume 5 allows the researcher to identify and trace particular trends in American modernism over time and through a variety of critical responses. A "Chronological Table of Reprinted Articles and Chapters" in volume 1 allows the researcher to identify the writer, the sources from which reprinted pieces are taken, and their placement according to volume and chapter number in the Routledge *Modernism* series.

According to the editor, the Greenwood Press's **Encyclopedia of Literary Modernism** is a ready-reference tool that is "designed to fill the gap ... by providing a comprehensive and accessible source of quick reference to the key authors, works, movements, theories, places and events commonly associated with literary modernism" (vii). To date, this is the only such genre encyclopedia available in English, with entries on the "The New Woman," "Futurism," "The War," "Film and Modernism," "Technology and Mechanization," and "Thought, Language, Aesthetics, and Being 1900–1940," among many others. The alphabetical arrangement of the *Encyclopedia* offers signed articles of varying lengths, with selected bibliographies and extensive cross-indexing indicated by bolded text. The volume's "Selected Bibliography" identifies special issues of scholarly periodicals devoted to modernism. The index highlights text in bold type that sends the reader to the main *Encyclopedia* entry for a particular person or topic, a useful device in a work that is international in scope. Researchers of American modernism can thus easily locate and assess information of interest through the *Encyclopedia*'s concise entries. Key cultural events and works are described alongside parallel developments in the arts and society (see, for example, the entry for "Stravinsky, Igor: *The Rite of Spring*," a seminal modernist musical composition). Although biographical entries vary in approach, all offer at least brief discussions of key works, influences, and impact (for example, the entry for "Faulkner, William" links his work with formal experimentation, the cinema, realism, and Hispanic American writing).

The Modernist period literary histories, available in two volumes from the recent multivolume **Cambridge History of American Literature**, offer a contrast to the other sources described in this section. Recognizing the "centrality of aesthetic modernism" in American literature from the early to mid-twentieth century, the scholars responsible for these essays provide in-depth treatments of prominent and less well-known works in modernist poetry and prose. Both volumes have indexes, ample bibliographies, and yearly chronologies for the period emphasizing significant events in American literary publishing and selected national and world events. Chapter titles in volume 5, *Poetry and Criticism, 1900–1950*, suggest their potential interest for the scholar of modernism: "Modernist Lyric in the Culture of Capital" and "Poetry and the Machine Age" are supplemented by a concluding chapter on the emergence of American literature as an academic discipline during the rise of modernism. The forty-six articles in volume 6, *Prose Writing 1910–1950*, offer a broad examination of modernist themes, focusing on "the intricate interweavings of text and context … how social, political, economic, and technological transformations informed and embodied the emergence of aesthetic modernism in the United States" (xvii).

Featuring more than three hundred signed contributors, the Continuum *Encyclopedia of American Literature* is designed to be an extensive single-volume treatment covering colonial times to the present, "with a cross-section of topical articles pertaining to genre, period, ethnicity, and discipline …" (vi). Author entries provide vital dates, biographical information, a critical overview of selected works, and a selective bibliography. A comprehensive index is supplemented by a useful "Guide to Topical Articles," where the reader will find a compact essay on this subject along with the other literary topics treated in the Continuum *Encyclopedia*.

The *Columbia Literary History of the United States* "is an examination of the emergence of a national literature, the particular nature of that literature, the extraliterary factors that have been significant in its formation, and the practice of the literary arts in various forms by writers and speakers" (xv). Signed articles are arranged chronologically and emphasize movements, individual authors, and the social context of literary production. Scholars will find material in "Part Four 1910–1945" especially useful for its thematic treatment of modernism in various literary contexts. The index allows the researcher to trace modernism and related topics throughout the volume.

The three-volume Facts on File *Encyclopedia of American Literature* set is arranged in chronological and thematic periods, concluding with "The Modern and Postmodern Period from 1915." A yearly chronology summarizes selected historical events and significant publications. Volumes are arranged alphabetically and include an index. The researcher of modernist American fiction might find the brief descriptions of fictional characters and individual literary works beneficial.

Associated with the literary movement known as the Southern Renascence, volume 12 in Gale's *Dictionary of Literary Biography, Documentary Series Southern Women Writers: Flannery O'Connor, Katherine Anne Porter, Eudora*

Welty treats modern American authors whose works have come to be associated with the theme of the South as distinctive region and culture. Narrative chapters have copious illustrative material, including facsimile copies of original manuscripts and photographic portraits of each writer. Biographical and critical materials are supplemented by lists of major books, lectures and letters, author interviews, and bibliographic citations to secondary books and articles and contemporary book reviews. The cumulative indexes to additional titles in Gale's literature series are present, and each chapter in *Southern Women Writers* is prefaced with cross-references to supplemental material on each writer in Gale's literature reference sets.

Clear in organization and layout, the three volumes in **Harlem Renaissance: A Gale Critical Companion** offer the researcher a concise overview of significant aspects of the Harlem Renaissance, fully illustrated and indexed. The first volume is divided into five topical areas, including "Overviews and General Studies," "Social, Economic, and Political Factors that Influenced the Harlem Renaissance," and "Publishing and Periodicals During the Harlem Renaissance" that might be relevant to the literary researcher. The overview section offers material that was originally published during the period as well as more recent scholarly studies, with full bibliographical citations. The other two volumes are devoted to thirty-three authors associated with the Harlem Renaissance, such as Helene Johnson, Nella Larsen, W. E. B. DuBois, and Jessie Fauset, with entries arranged in alphabetical order. Each volume in *Harlem Renaissance: A Gale Critical Companion* has a literary and historical chronology from 1890 to 1937, with selected highlights from the movement. The biographical volumes give birth and death dates and a picture of the writer, along with a list of principal works in chronological order, excerpts from the author's works printed under the heading "Primary Sources," general commentaries on the author's works and annotations on individual titles, essay references, and suggestions for further reading. Some entries list archival holdings of an author's manuscripts.

Biographical Sources

American Writers: A Collection of Literary Biographies. New York: Scribner, 1974–.
Dictionary of Literary Biography. Detroit: Gale, 1978–.
Garraty, John A., and Mark C. Carnes., eds. *American National Biography.* 24 vols. New York: Oxford University Press, 1999. Available online via subscription from Oxford University Press, www.anb.org/articles/home.html.
Parini, Jay, ed. *The Oxford Encyclopedia of American Literature.* 4 vols. New York: Oxford University Press, 2004.

The sources described in this section offer summary biographical material on many American writers, are widely available as reference sets, and provide a good starting point to get basic biographical information on modernist writers. The multivolume set from Scribner, *American Writers: A Collection of Literary Biographies*, has been issued under different editors and began as a series of monographs originally issued from 1959 to 1972 under the title *The Minnesota Pamphlets on American Writers*. Including supplements to the original four volumes issued to date, *American Writers* now contains biographical information on more than three hundred authors from the earliest period to the present. Each volume is alphabetically organized, with a cumulative name and title index to the entire series in Supplement XII. Signed entries are designed "to provide introductory criticism that treats the developing career of each writer in the context of his or her circumstances" and contain a selected bibliography of primary and secondary works and an analysis of key texts (v. XII, xiii).

Although similar in structure to the Scribner set described above, *The Oxford Encyclopedia of American Literature* has a brief chronology for the period 1607 to 2003 consisting of "Literary Works and Authors," "Historical Context," and "Topical Outline of Articles." The stated aim of this multivolume set is to "provide a comprehensive discussion of literary practices within the United States . . . [including] discussions of individual authors, notable texts, and literary movements, institutions, and—for lack of a better term—aggregations (such as the academic novel or the production of 'little magazines'" (v. I, xiii). The modernist scholar will find useful discussions in the topical outline as well as access to material on "modernism" and "modernity" in the comprehensive index located in volume 4 of the *Oxford Encyclopedia* set.

The result of massive editorial collaboration, the 17,500 biographies in the twenty-four-volume *American National Biography* (*ANB*) is the successor to the *Dictionary of American Biography* that was originally published between 1926 and 1937. Broadly inclusive in scope, the *ANB* covers all the professions, disciplines, and socioeconomic classes, with an American defined as someone "whose significant actions occurred during his or her residence within what is now the United States or whose life or career directly influenced the course of American history" (v. 1, xvii). In addition, biographical subjects have been placed in broad categories such as "Occupations and Realms of Renown" to augment the expanded searching capabilities of the periodically updated electronic version of the *ANB*, which is only available by subscription from Oxford University Press <http://www.anb.org/articles/home.html>. The entries are alphabetically arranged, and information is presented chronologically around the significant achievements or noteworthy activities of the subject (including vital dates) in signed articles that range from 750 to 7,500 words. Entries offer a concluding section on secondary sources and, in some cases, repository information indicating holdings of primary source material. The multiple indexes in volume 24 (all presented in simple alphabetical lists) are by "Subjects," "Contributor," "Place of Birth in the United States," "Place of Birth Outside the United States," and "Occupations and Realms of Renown." Those researching biographical information on American modernist writers will find a wealth of material in the *ANB*. The entry on T. S. Eliot, for example, indicates where important collections of his manuscripts and papers are located. Modernist writers may be found in the *ANB* by surname as well as in the "Occupation" index under particular literary genres such as fiction writers and poets. In addition to the ANB, the eight volume set of *The African American National Biography* (2008), edited by Henry Louis Gates, Jr. and Evelyn Brooks-Higginbotham, offers concise and authoritative biographical information about African American authors from the era of American modernist writing.

The monumental ***Dictionary of Literary Biography*** (***DLB***), begun in 1978 and now comprising more than 320 volumes, has repeatedly been a *Choice* outstanding academic book and a valuable resource for literary scholars. In thousands of entries, the *DLB* covers literature and thought from all time periods, emphasizing genres, national literatures, coteries, schools, publishing history, and individual works and authors. Author entries contain a list of publications, a biography with narrative coverage of major works, bibliographical notes, and informative illustrative material. Topical volumes in *DLB* have chronologies. Though printed volumes are issued by subject, all volumes incorporate a cumulative numbered index of titles published to date as well as a cumulative name and topical index cross-referenced to the entire *DLB* series to date. The *DLB* is supplemented by the *DLB Yearbooks* and the *DLB Documentary Series*. Various volumes in the *DLB* series published to date might be of interest to the researcher of American modernism, such as the volume on John Dos Passos, described below, and *American Expatriate Writers: Paris in the Twenties*; *American Prose Writers of WWI*; *F. Scott Fitzgerald's Tender is the Night* and the *DLB* volumes on *The Great Gatsby*; *American Poets 1880–1945*; *American Writers in Paris 1920–1939*; and *American Novelists 1910–1945*.

The commercial online edition of the *DLB* from Thomson-Gale at http://www.gale.com/world/ allows for enhanced searching capabilities by author name, titles, subjects, nationality, ethnicity, birth and death dates, and full text. The electronic version is updated and expanded regularly for currency and accuracy, though it doesn't contain all the illustrative material in the *DLB*'s printed edition. For convenience, researchers should consult the Thomson-Gale *Literary Index* at http://www.galenet.com/servlet/LitIndex. This resource allows author, title, and custom searches across content in the Gale literature series, providing citations to articles (some in different volumes and sets) and lists of works by primary authors.

Chronologies

Burt, Daniel S., ed. *The Chronology of American Literature: America's Literary Achievements from the Colonial Era to Modern Times.* Boston: Houghton Mifflin, 2004.

Rogal, Samuel J. *A Chronological Outline of American Literature.* New York: Greenwood Press, 1987.

In addition to the period chronologies described in other resources in this chapter, Greenwood Press's *A Chronological Outline of American Literature* is designed to "assist scholars, students, and general readers of American literature in determining the extent of literary activity and of events related to literature in the United States during a specific year, decade, or even century" (vii). The volume covers thousands of entries spanning the period 1507–1986. Where information is available, the *Chronological Outline* divides each year into "Births," "Deaths," "Literature," and "Events," with selected listings in each category arranged alphabetically by surname or event name. The heading for literature contains all the major literary genres as well as sermons, prayers, meditations, etc. Canonical and obscure works by both genders and minorities are represented. The modernist writers are covered chiefly in the section for 1900–1940. The index of authors and events allows the user to trace a writer's publications over time and situate these works alongside other writers, works, and historical events.

The more recent *Chronology of American Literature: America's Literary Achievements from the Colonial Era to Modern Times* is well designed to present through some eighty-four hundred works and five hundred authors a broad comparative record of obscure and canonical American writers. The *Chronology* is intended to allow the reader "to correlate literary expression with historical and social developments that affected literature. …" (1). Arranged into five sections according to prominent stages in American literary history, each section contains an introduction as well as a list of births and deaths, bestsellers, and awards and prizes. Yearly chronological heading entries contain some or all of the literary genres and nonfiction as well as selected "Publications and Events," "Essays and Philosophy," and "Literary Criticism and Scholarship." These succinct overviews of works and authors are supplemented by illustrations and many photographs. Scholars of the era of American modernism—"one of the richest and most crucial in American literary history"—will be particularly interested in the sections on "The Birth of Modernism 1915–1949" and "Modernism and Postmodernism 1950–1999." The *Chronology* has author and title indexes.

Individual Author Sources

Croft, Robert W. *A Zora Neale Hurston Companion*. Westport, CT: Greenwood Press, 2002.

Curnutt, Kirk, ed. *A Historical Guide to F. Scott Fitzgerald*. New York: Oxford University Press, 2004.

Dawson, J. L., P. D. Holland, and D. J. McKitterick. *A Concordance to the Complete Poems and Plays of T. S. Eliot*. Ithaca, NY: Cornell University Press, 1995.

Peck, Charles A., and Robert W. Hamblin. *A Companion to Faulkner Studies*. Westport, CT: Greenwood Press, 2004.

Pizer, Donald, ed. *John Dos Passos's U.S.A.: A Documentary Volume*. Vol. 274 of the *DLB*. Detroit: Gale Group, 2003.

Tryphonopoulos, Demetres P., and Stephen J. Adams, eds. *The Ezra Pound Encyclopedia*. Westport, CT: Greenwood Press, 2005.

White, Ray Lewis. *Gertrude Stein and Alice B. Toklas: A Reference Guide*. Boston: G. K. Hall & Co., 1984.

Secondary sources on individual authors range from in-depth biographical works and specialized studies in scholarly periodicals to bio-bibliographies and the information found in general reference tools such as those previously listed in this chapter. The choice and type of reference source depend on the needs of the researcher. This section will examine some of these works.

The electronic version of the *MLA International Bibliography* (*MLAIB*) is the most comprehensive research database currently available to locate secondary scholarship on American modernism and the writers and works associated with this era. In 2006, the online version *MLAIB* was updated with enhanced retrospective subject indexing, making all of its pre-1963 print content searchable electronically from 1926, including citations from the *PMLA* in the nineteenth century. The current version of the online *MLAIB* also provides electronic links to selected full-text articles through *JSTOR* and will eventually provide the similar access to selected full-text articles through *Project MUSE* and to digitized monographs.

Typically, online library catalogs and bibliographic databases such as the recently merged *WorldCat–RLIN* catalog offer access to records about a particular writer or topic according to Library of Congress (LC) subject headings, which also work in traditional card catalogs using the LC classification system. Below are examples of LC subject headings for William Faulkner and specialized reference works on him:

Faulkner, William, 1897–1962

Faulkner, William, 1897–1962—Criticism and interpretation—Handbooks, manuals, etc.

Faulkner, William, 1897–1962—Bibliography

Often the easiest way to search for reference material on an author in an online library catalog is by using a keyword search query such as *william faulkner* or *faulkner and interpretation*. The type and variety of secondary material available on an author partly depend on the author's stature and on the researcher's access to material through their local library holdings. As a general rule, online searching with simpler keyword queries generates more results than specific LC subject searches, and the use of truncation in searching (using the * symbol after a search string) will usually expand the search results. For example, in the online *MLAIB* the keyword query *modern* and america** retrieved 31,866 citations, in contrast to the keyword query *modernism and american*, which retrieved 2,002 citations at the time of this writing. It is worth reiterating that specificity in online searching (such as controlled subject searches) normally produces a smaller retrieval set, or number of "hits," than a more general search. Following are some examples of LC subjects for author-specific reference works:

Eliot, T. S. (Thomas Stearns), 1888–1965—Concordances
Pound, Ezra, 1885–1972—Encyclopedias
Fitzgerald, F. Scott (Francis Scott), 1896–1940—Knowledge—History
Hurston, Zora Neale—Handbooks, manuals, etc.

Robert Croft's *A Zora Neale Hurston Companion* consists of a brief chronology of her life and works; a list of abbreviations used throughout the volume; a short historical overview of Hurston's published work; a specialized dictionary with alphabetized entries on Hurston's writings, fictional characters, and literary themes and techniques; and "further reading" sections after selected entries. A useful appendix describes institutions holding Hurston manuscripts, with contact information and an item-level listing of the archives held in each repository. A bibliography of primary works and a bibliography of Hurston criticism round out the contents in this companion.

The editor of *John Dos Passos's U.S.A.: A Documentary Volume* notes that the guide is designed "to make *U.S.A.* more accessible to readers of all kinds by offering a body of documentary material bearing on various areas of importance and interest in the trilogy" (xvii). A biographical introduction is supplemented by a chapter on the historical context of the novel's formation called "The Education of the Camera Eye" and other chapters on "*U.S.A.*—Conception and Method," "Backgrounds and Sources: American Society 1900–1930," and "Publication and Critical Response." *John Dos Passos's U.S.A* contains signed articles, a checklist for further reading, and helpful illustrations from historical and archival material that are an important aspect of the *DLB* documentary series.

As its title suggests, *A Historical Guide to F. Scott Fitzgerald* is designed to "call attention to the cultural and intellectual crosscurrents of the 1920s and 1930s that circulate below the surface of his prose" (13). A brief biography of

Fitzgerald is supplemented by five articles by different scholars relating to Fitzgerald and war, jazz-age culture, authorship, consumer capitalism, and intellectual context. Articles have notes and select bibliographies. Noteworthy is an illustrated chronology of Fitzgerald's life, with personal and family photographs as well as reproductions of original dust-jacket illustrations from his books set alongside a column of contemporary historical events. The Fitzgerald researcher should consult the bibliographic essay in the *Historical Guide* for publication information on Fitzgerald's literary output and various published editions, as well as a short bibliography of the secondary literature and selected reference sources, journals, and websites pertaining to Fitzgerald.

Scholars of modernist American poetry and literature in general should consider using concordances as part of their research. As the editors of *A Concordance to the Complete Poems and Plays of T. S. Eliot* observe, a concordance has "a peculiar magic in their consequential revelations, a way of transforming our sense of the text" (viii). Concordances tabulate systematically all the instances of significant word usage by an author, conveniently arranging these words under alphabetized headings indexed to a particular edition of an author's works. The editors note that this "key word in context" format omits 53.20 percent of all the words contained in Eliot's complete poems and plays, and the resulting list in the Eliot *Concordance* gives thousands of instances of essential word usage, from "Art" to "Zurich," allowing the researcher to gain a coherent sense of Eliot's literary diction. The page layout of printed concordances promotes serendipity and precise comparison, and this *Concordance* facilitates such use with a technical introduction, notes on bibliographic conventions, a statistical ranking list of word forms, and a reverse index of word forms.

Greenwood's *A Companion to Faulkner Studies* offers essays by thirteen scholars on different kinds of Faulkner scholarship. Each essay examines the assumptions and evolution of a particular critical paradigm and analyzes selections from Faulkner's works in light of that critical theory by way of significant examples excerpted from the critical literature. Essays are accompanied by notes, and the *Companion* is especially useful for the scholar of American modernism by including a glossary of technical terms and a selected bibliography of films and other reference resources.

The editors of *The Ezra Pound Encyclopedia* seek "to provide materials to help orient new readers of Pound and Modernism, but also to refresh even experienced readers" (xvi). The *Encyclopedia* achieves this in hundreds of alphabetized signed articles on themes, topics, works, and people associated with Pound and his era. Generally concise entries have a short bibliography supplemented by a selected, classified bibliography. A general index covers topics, people, and the titles of Pound's works. The researcher in American modernist literature will find the abbreviated scope of this and similar resources helpful because it provides a good starting point for research without being overwhelming. Another benefit of specialized encyclopedias consists in establishing important links between subjects and themes that might not be apparent in the early stages of research.

The G. K. Hall *Gertrude Stein and Alice B. Toklas: A Reference Guide* offers students of these important modernist figures a summary introduction to their lives and works, including a chronological list of published works and an annotated, chronologically arranged bibliography of secondary criticism, with entries in each year alphabetized and numbered accordingly. This arrangement results in a precise name and title index since references carry the year and the bibliographic item number from that year's list. A running chronological header in the secondary bibliography facilitates use.

Conclusion

The general reference sources described in this chapter offer a basic overview of some of the tools available to begin literary research in American modernism. Thematic, biographical, and critical sources provide access to the writers and works associated with American modernism. Through acquaintance with the format and content of these specialized secondary tools, the researcher can locate a broad continuum of information, from bibliographical lists, specific factual information, and summary statements to in-depth historical, critical, and cultural treatments of authors and works, along with secondary material in research and bibliographic databases as well as holdings in manuscript and archival collections. The choice of what to use depends on the scope of the research and the intended audience for the work. Remember that research formats cover printed books and indexes alongside online databases and electronic indexes with associated full-text, digitized content. Some secondary resources can make literary research more efficient and more focused, suggest additional research possibilities, and help clarify and contextualize important themes and events connected with American modernist authors and writing. Many of the tools and resources described in this chapter suggest a variety of interconnections with the reference resources and research tools treated elsewhere in this book. In this vein, the scholar should remember that literary research is a holistic process that requires basic skills and knowledge and the ability to navigate effectively in a dynamic and sometimes-complex information landscape.

CHAPTER 3

Library Catalogs

In humanities research, books remain a key information resource. This chapter will discuss the best methods of searching the online catalog at your college or university library as well as using other library catalogs, such as national library catalogs, national union catalogs, and cooperative catalogs provided by library consortia, including OCLC (the Online Computer Library Center, a national consortium), and the Orbis Cascade Alliance, a regional consortium of libraries in Washington and Oregon.

Just as in many other areas of information access and retrieval, library catalogs have undergone radical changes since the 1980s. A growing number of people may never have used a traditional card catalog, but online library catalogs are a relatively new development. Many large research universities are still converting older collections into the online catalog environment, and special collections may also be accessed differently. Check with a librarian to ensure that all of the collections are included in the online catalog. To conduct comprehensive searches, you may need to move beyond your library's online catalog to online catalogs with a larger scope or to print-based catalogs.

Library catalogs identify materials available in your local university library as well as across the United States and even across the world when looking for specific editions of a work or rare materials. In addition to access points that were available in card catalogs, namely author, title, and subject, online catalogs allow keyword searching across all parts of the record, along with targeted field searching by periodical title, ISBN/ISSN, call number, language, date, publisher, and series title. Most catalogs allow printing, e-mailing, and downloading records, and a growing number feature formatting by citation style and personalized services, such as saved searches or saved preferences.

Online library catalogs from different institutions may vary, depending on the software programs employed. However, the records in online library catalogs will be consistent across the United States, Canada, and the United Kingdom. Cataloging standards are based on the use of the Anglo-American cataloging rules, standardized vocabulary for subject heading assignment, and coding records in MARC (Machine Readable Cataloging) format, discussed in chapter 1. Most libraries in the United States use the Library of Congress subject headings, which allow for a standardized vocabulary to describe the topics covered in the work. Author names are also subjected to authority control, a process to ensure that one consistent form of the name is used.

There may be major variances in how online library catalogs search. For example, some may require phrases to be placed in quotation marks, and some may require Boolean operators to be typed out explicitly. Also, given the rapid changes in technology, online catalogs may have features or improvements that were not available at the time this book was written. Use this as a guide to good searching strategies, and ask a librarian for assistance with identifying or using the catalogs that are available at your library.

Author Searches

To locate works by a particular author, the author search approach seems the most efficient. The formatting of names may vary in the catalog, particularly with older works, though most authors will have an authoritative heading consisting of last name, first name, and dates of birth and death. For example, the following are the authoritative headings for some modernist authors:

Faulkner William 1897 1962
Fitzgerald F Scott Francis Scott 1896 1940
H D Hilda Doolittle 1886 1961
Millay Edna St Vincent 1892 1950

These headings may seem odd at first glance, but they provide not only the name under which the author publishes but also his or her complete name and birth and death dates. For example, for Fitzgerald, the entry begins with "Fitzgerald, F. Scott," as he is commonly known, but then follows with the full name and dates. H. D.'s heading is similar, starting with the initials she used to publish her works, followed by her full name and birth and death dates.

Although the goal is to have one form of the name for authority control, changes in Library of Congress policies on naming conventions have led to situations where two or more forms of an author's name are present in a catalog. For example, Rebecca West has two headings in the catalog:

West Rebecca Dame 1892
West Rebecca 1892 1983

The first was the original heading used for West, when she was alive. Although the Library of Congress does not always change headings simply to add the death date, it decided to remove titles such as *Dame* from the authority records. Updating local catalogs is costly in terms of money and time. Our library pays for authority record updating every few years; in the meantime, when cases like this are found, our cataloging staff updates our holdings to reflect the new heading. Depending on your library's policies, similar cases may exist in which one author has multiple headings in the catalog.

If you are unsure how to search for an author's name, the catalog can assist. For example, searching for Edna St. Vincent Millay as "St. Vincent Millay, Edna" results in a "See" reference with a link to the proper order of names as shown above. Figure 3.1 shows another example, with the results for an author search on *fitzgerald f.*

The first listing shows the complete heading for Fitzgerald, while item 5 shows another form of Fitzgerald's name, and the other items refer to other authors with the last name Fitzgerald and first initial "F."

If your author search provides no results but there clearly exist no spelling errors or other technical issues, try a keyword search for the author's name. In the case of lesser-known or less prolific writers, there may be collections that feature their work along with other writers' works. Anthologies that include many writers do not typically have cataloging records that list every contributor as an author. They do, however, provide the table of contents in a notes field that is accessible via keyword searching. Figure 3.2 illustrates this concept. The collection comprises essays or excerpts of works by a number of Modernist-era writers, such as William Faulkner, F. Scott Fitzgerald, Upton Sinclair, and Vachel Lindsay. Searching for any of them as an author would not locate this item because

Item	Heading
1	Fitzgerald F Scott Francis Scott 1896 1940
2	Fitzgerald F Stop
3	Fitzgerald Frances 1940
4	*Fitzgerald Frances Scott* -- See Smith, Scottie Fitzgerald
5	*Fitzgerald Francis Scott Key 1896 1940* -- See Fitzgerald, F. Scott (Francis Scott), 1896-1940
6	Fitzgerald Frank
7	Fitzgerald Frank T

Figure 3.1.   Modified catalog results for author search *fitzgerald f*
Source: Washington State University Libraries, Griffin Catalog (Innovative Interfaces)

Title   **Writing Los Angeles : a literary anthology / edited by David L. Ulin.**

Imprint   New York : Library of America : Distributed to the trade by Penguin Putnam, c2002.

LOCATION	CALL NUMBER	STATUS
WSU Holland & Terrell	PS572.L6 W74 2002	ON SHELF

Description   Xix, 880 p. : ill. ; 25 cm.

Bibliog.   Includes bibliographical references.

Contents   from Echoes in the City of the Angels / Helen Hunt Jackson – The land / Mary Austin -- from The rules of the game / Stewart Edward White -- from Sixty years in Southern California 1853-1913 / Harris Newmark -- **California and America / Vachel Lindsay** -- from Laughing in the jungle / Louis Adamic -- Los Angeles. a rhapsody / Aldous Huxley -- Sister Aimée / H.L. Mencken -- **from Oil! / Upton Sinclair** -- from Queer people / Carroll & Garrett Graham -- from God sends Sunday / Arna Bontemps -- The City of Our Lady the Queen of the Angels / Edmund Wilson -- Paradise / James M. Cain -- **Golden land / William Faulkner** -- Pacific village ; A thing shared / M.F.K. Fisher -- from Promised land / Cedric Belfrage -- Red wind / Raymond Chandler -- from Ask the dust / John Fante -- The day of the locust / Nathanael West -- from Diaries / Christopher Isherwood -- **Last kiss / F. Scott Fitzgerald** -- from Autobiography Hollywood / Charles Reznikoff – A table at Ciro's / Budd Schulberg

Subject   American literature -- California -- Los Angeles. Los Angeles (Calif.) -- Literary collections.

Other author   Ulin, David L.

ISBN   1931082278

Figure 3.2.   Catalog record for *Writing Los Angeles: A Literary Anthology*
Source: Washington State University Libraries, Griffin Catalog

the names appear only in the content notes areas, not as authors of the works. However, this could certainly be an important source for your research.

Depending on your library's catalog and how the name appears in various cataloging records, results may differ for keyword searches with names in different orders or using quotation marks. For example, consider the results of various searches for Vachel Lindsay in table 3.1.

This example illustrates the particular rules of our library catalog. Without the quotation marks, the order of words makes no difference. Searching as an exact phrase with the quotation marks illuminates further differences. The results show that there are forty-two items that are either primary works written by Lindsay or are secondary works focused enough on Lindsay to have his name as a subject heading. Nine additional items have Vachel Lindsay's name in the record exactly, such as the book about Los Angeles shown above. There are also two items in the catalog that contain the words Vachel and Lindsay, but they are not adjacent to each other. Those two items may be "false hits," or items that have the right words in the record but not in the context desired. However, "Vachel" is an unusual-enough name that

Table 3.1. Results for Vachel Lindsay Searches

Search Strategy	Results
K = vachel lindsay	53
K = lindsay vachel	53
K = "vachel lindsay"	51
K = "lindsay vachel"	42

the two items may be relevant. As you examine the catalog records, you will typically see the searched words highlighted in some way.

Duplicate types of searches ensure that you are locating all possible materials, such as facsimiles, standard editions, or various formats. Depending on research needs, you may benefit from viewing a facsimile of a manuscript that shows the author's notes and editing. You may also need to use a standard edition, or you may want to compare various editions. With twentieth-century authors in particular, the notion of a standard edition may be contentious or evolving. Some may insist that the standard edition be based on the galleys, the manuscript, or the first edition. For instance, William Faulkner's novels were edited by Malcolm Cowley and published by Vintage and for many years were considered the best editions of Faulkner. Recently, however, the Library of America has been reissuing Faulkner's works. Those reissued works may be considered by some scholars to be the new standard for Faulkner studies. Another example is found in Matthew Bruccoli, a major Fitzgerald scholar, who has done extensive work on comparing and correcting editions of *The Great Gatsby* in addition to writing numerous monographs on Fitzgerald and the Modernist era and editing a variety of volumes of correspondence.

When perusing results, you may also find critical editions of various works. These are often used in teaching literature and include a definitive version of the text, along with various supplementary materials that deal with biography and literary criticism. If a standard or critical edition is not needed, is not recommended, or does not exist for your author, consider issues such as the authority of the publisher or editor, the publication date, and the place of publication in determining the particular text's value. For assistance in locating primary documents, see chapter 8, which deals with archives and special collections. Reproductions of primary works are often available on microfilm or microfiche and, increasingly, electronically via the Web or subscription databases. See chapter 9 for more information about locating and using Web resources.

Title Searches

As with author searches, title searches can be efficient when looking for a specific item. Consider the way the catalog works. For example, some catalogs require you to omit leading articles, such as *a*, *an*, and *the*, in any language. Other catalogs can interpret the search with those leading articles. Titles and subtitles may appear in unexpected ways, depending on the edition. If results seem too few or are otherwise unsatisfactory, double-check the catalog by running a keyword search.

Sometimes title searching will provide more results than expected. In figure 3.3, a title search for *The Great Gatsby* retrieves the work by Fitzgerald as well as several books about *The Great Gatsby* that use the source title as part of their book titles.

In the first link, there appear to be nineteen copies of *The Great Gatsby*, one copy of a manuscript facsimile (link 2), one film version (link 7), and five works of criticism that use the title (links 3, 4, 5, 6, and 8). Clicking into the first title to view the nineteen items uncovers a greater variety of materials than expected. In figure 3.4, the first twelve items are listed. In addition to actual editions of the work, there are a concordance, a musical score, other film versions, and several other critical works.

In addition to locating specific works, title searches may also be used to look for series titles, journal titles, and audiovisual materials, for example,

T= f scott fitzgerald review
T= modern fiction studies
T= dictionary of literary biography
T= norton critical edition

If the more precise approach does not offer the desired results, try a keyword search. For example, a professor may mention critical editions as being useful for

Num	Titles	Year	Entries
1	Great Gatsby		19
2	Great Gatsby A Facsimile Of The Manuscript : Fitzgerald, F. Scott	1973	1
3	Great Gatsby A Study : Hoffman, Frederick John.	1986	1
4	Great Gatsby And Fitzgeralds World Of Ideas : Berman, Ronald.	1997	1
5	Great Gatsby And Modern Times : Berman, Ronald.	1994	1
6	Great Gatsby And The Good American Life : Berman, Ronald.	2001	1
7	Great Gatsby Motion Picture 2000	2000	1
8	Great Gatsby The Limits Of Wonder : Lehan, Richard Daniel,	1990	1

Figure 3.3.   Modified catalog results for title search *The Great Gatsby*
Source: Washington State University Libraries, Griffin Catalog (Innovative Interfaces)

1	A Concordance To F. Scott Fitzgerald's The Great Gatsby, compiled By Andrew T. Crosland. Crosland, Andrew T. Detroit, Gale Research Co. [1974]
2	The Fitzgerald Reader. Edited By Arthur Mizener. Fitzgerald, F. Scott (Francis Scott), 1896-1940. New York, Scribner [1963]
3	Fitzgerald's The Great Gatsby: The Novel, The Critics, The Background. Piper, Henry Dan. New York, Scribner [1970]
4	Gatsby Etudes John Harbison. Harbison, John. [New York, N.Y.] : Associated Music Publishers ; Milwaukee, Wis. : distributed by H. Leonard, c2000.
5	The Great Gatsby Stephen Matterson. Matterson, Stephen. Houndmills, Basingstoke, Hampshire : Macmillan, 1990
6	The Great Gatsby. Fitzgerald, F. Scott (Francis Scott), 1896-1940. New York, Scribner [1958, c1953]
7	The Great Gatsby by F. Scott Fitzgerald. Fitzgerald, F. Scott (Francis Scott), 1896-1940. New York : Collier Books, 1986, c1925.
8	The Great Gatsby. Foreword And A Study Guide By Albert K. Ridout. Fitzgerald, F. Scott (Francis Scott), 1896-1940. New York, Scribner [1961]
9	The Great Gatsby F. Scott Fitzgerald ; Edited By Matthew J. Bruccoli ; Textual Consultant, Fredson Bowers. Fitzgerald, F. Scott (Francis Scott), 1896-1940. Cambridge ; New York : Cambridge University Press, 1991.
10	The Great Gatsby [By] F. Scott Fitzgerald. Fitzgerald, F. Scott (Francis Scott), 1896-1940. [Harmondsworth, Middlesex] Penguin Books [1961]
11	The Great Gatsby by F. Scott Fitzgerald. Fitzgerald, F. Scott (Francis Scott), 1896-1940. New York : Scribner, c1953.
12	The Great Gatsby [Videorecording] / An A&E Network And Granda Entertainment Production In Association With Travellers New York : New Video, [2000]

Figure 3.4.   Catalog record for the item _Great Gatsby_
Source: Washington State University Libraries, Griffin Catalog (Innovative Interfaces)

your research. One major series is the _Norton Critical Edition_ series. The series title is not actually part of the individual record titles, so searching for _norton critical edition_ as a title will retrieve all the items in the series that your library owns. Even if a particular work is part of the series, a title search may not work. For example, searching for Edith Wharton's _The Age of Innocence_ may prove tricky: a search for _T=age of innocence norton critical edition_ will result in zero hits. A keyword search on the same phrase returns the item sought, since the keyword search looks for any of the words in any order (see figure 3.5).

Subject Searches

In addition to using keyword searching, a subject heading search can often locate materials about a writer, as discussed in chapter 1. Works about major writers are almost always cataloged with the author's name as a subject heading. Searching the name with last name first as a subject search will result in a listing of headings, including subheadings that can quickly lead to the needed materials. Two examples of subheadings are "biography" and "criticism and interpretation." Following these links will retrieve focused lists of books about the author's life and books that analyze and discuss their works (see figure 3.6).

Author	Wharton, Edith, 1862-1937.
Title	**The age of innocence : authoritative text, background and contexts, sources, criticism** / Edith Wharton ; edited by Candace Waid.
Publisher	New York : W.W. Norton & Co., c2003.
Edition	1st ed.

Other author	Waid, Candace.
Description	xx, 524 p. : ill., maps ; 24 cm.
Series	**Norton critical edition**
L.c. subject	Wharton, Edith, 1862-1937. Age of innocence.
	Triangles (Interpersonal relations) -- Fiction.
	Upper class -- Fiction.
	Married people -- Fiction.
	New York (N.Y.) -- Fiction.
Note	Includes historical documents and passages from other publications contemporary with the featured work.
Bibliography	Includes bibliographical references (p. 517-523).
Genre/form	Domestic fiction.
	Love stories.
ISBN	0393967948 (pbk.)
LCCN	00026408
LC CALL NO.	PS3545.H16 A7 2003

Figure 3.5.   Catalog record for critical edition of Wharton
Source: Washington State University Libraries, Griffin Catalog (Innovative Interfaces)

Number	Save	SUBJECTS (1-12 of 52)	Year	Entries 110 Found
1		Cather Willa 1873 1947		27
2		Cather Willa 1873 1947 Aesthetics	2002	1
3		Cather Willa 1873 1947 Appreciation Sweden	1995	1
4		Cather Willa 1873 1947 Bibliography		3
5		Cather Willa 1873 1947 Characters Artists	1996	1
6		Cather Willa 1873 1947 Characters Children	1975	1
7		Cather Willa 1873 1947 Characters Immigrants	1995	1
8		Cather Willa 1873 1947 Characters Men	1999	1
9		Cather Willa 1873 1947 Characters Women		2
10		Cather Willa 1873 1947 Childhood And Youth	1975	1
11		Cather Willa 1873 1947 Childhood And Youth Juvenile Literature	1997	1
12		Cather Willa 1873 1947 Correspondence	1986	1

Figure 3.6.   Catalog search results for subject cather willa
Source: Washington State University Libraries, Griffin Catalog (Innovative Interfaces)

Figure 3.6 replicates the first screen of results in the catalog search. It indicates that there are fifty-two subjects related to Willa Cather, with a total of 110 items. The screen shows the subheadings and how many entries are available. If only one item exists, the date of that item will also display in this particular catalog.

As you become familiar with typical subheadings, subject searching will be more comfortable. Remember, however, that most records for authors will include birth and death dates and also may feature more complete or alternate forms of the authors' names. Searching for *Fitzgerald F Scott — criticism and interpretation* will result in zero items, because the complete subject heading is "Fitzgerald F Scott Francis Scott 1896 1940," matching the author headings as discussed above. Unlike an author search, however, where you will likely see the complete name in a list of possibilities or be pointed to the complete name form by a "see" reference in the catalog, all of the date and name information must be in place before the subheadings are added in order for subject searches to execute properly. If that information is omitted, the subject search fails.

Subject headings have changed over time, and innovations in technology and cataloging practices have led to increased numbers of headings being applied to items. Older materials may have very brief headings, such as "Criticism" or "American literature," without any subheadings. Until recently, works of fiction had no subject headings assigned whatsoever. The following is a sampling of subject headings from books about various authors or issues in American modernism:

American literature—Indian authors—History and criticism
American literature—20th century—History and criticism
American fiction—20th century—History and criticism—Theory, etc.
Modernism (Literature)—English-speaking countries
Modernism (Literature)—United States
Modernism (Aesthetics)
Art and literature—United States—History—20th century
Modernism (Art)—United States
National characteristics, American, in literature
American fiction—African American authors—History and criticism
Religion and literature—United States—History—20th century
American fiction—20th century—History and criticism
American drama—20th century—History and criticism
Race in literature
Literature, Modern—20th century—History and criticism
American poetry—Women authors—History and criticism
Women and literature—United States—History—20th century

American literature—Minority authors—History and criticism
Politics and literature—United States—History—20th century

Subject headings may be used to create keyword searches. Sometimes one subject heading will perfectly capture your search needs. When that is not the case,
draw upon the useful elements of the subject headings to create a complex keyword search.

Union Catalogs

*National Union Catalog, Pre-1956 Imprints: A Cumulative Author List Represent-
ing Library of Congress Printed Cards and Titles Reported by Other American Libraries.* 754 vols. London: Mansell, 1968–1981.
WorldCat. Dublin, OH: OCLC. www.oclc.org/firstsearch
Open WorldCat. Dublin, OH: OCLC. www.worldcat.org

After a library catalog search, union catalogs, with their broader scope and
wider content, are the next step. Union catalogs offer a combination of various
libraries. A union catalog can range from the joint catalog of a regional consortium in which your university participates to a cooperative catalog of national or
international scope. Large union catalogs such as *WorldCat* contain useful information about the widest possible range of materials. These sources are helpful for
exploring an array of materials, but access to some union catalogs may be costly
in terms of time and fees. The University of Washington is currently testing the
use of *WorldCat* to replace its local catalog.

WorldCat has more than 85 million bibliographic records, including items
in formats ranging from popular fiction to unique archival materials. It features
records from 112 countries, and many records are enhanced with tables of contents, cover art, links to related websites, and reviews. *WorldCat* is searchable via
OCLC's FirstSearch interface and offers a robust selection of search types, such
as corporate authors, series titles, and specialized multimedia formats. Searches
can also be limited by audience, genre, and format, such as juvenile, biography,
and Braille. The advantages of searching many collections simultaneously are obvious, but there are limitations in union catalogs like *WorldCat*. Because so many
libraries contribute to the catalog, multiple records for an item may exist. *World-
Cat* also includes materials such as dissertations and theses, although dissertations may be difficult to obtain and college theses may not be the best sources to
use. Scholars must be vigilant in examining *WorldCat* records.

For example, a search for Willa Cather as author retrieves 1,817 results. The
results screen alerts you that 1,514 of those results are in English. With each

item, there is a link to search for other versions of the work, which can be helpful when tracking down various editions of a work. Consider Cather's novel *Shadows on the Rock*. Numerous entries exist in *WorldCat* for this novel, including two entries for the 1931 edition, along with separate entries for the 1959, 1971, 1995, and 2005 editions and one for the 1983 large-print edition. In the case of the two entries for the 1931 original edition, one record shows the call number as PS 3505, which is the number assigned to Cather, while the other offers a PZ call number, meaning that at least one library classed the novel as young adult. The PZ record is the first item returned in the search, whereas the record with the correct PS classification is ninth on the list. Figures 3.7 and 3.8 illustrate how crucial a close look at results can be.

Note the detailed information about the book and its content, such as language, description, references, and notes.

Most libraries will provide an online subscription to *WorldCat*, but OCLC has created a free version called **Open WorldCat**. *Open WorldCat* does not have the full range of options that *WorldCat* provides, but it offers an adequate range of search types, including keyword, title, author, and ISSN/ISBN. Limiting by language, publication date, and format is also available. *Open WorldCat* offers a "find in a library" feature that allows input of a zip code or place name to see a listing of libraries holding the item sought.

Figure 3.9 contains much less information than the full *WorldCat* record. For example, the *Open WorldCat* record omits some of the subject headings, all of the notes for geographic places and named persons, and the notes and genre designations. Depending on your needs, the *Open WorldCat* record may be lacking in necessary data. In many cases, however, the records are adequate for source gathering.

A similar, short-lived product called *RedLightGreen* from Research Libraries Group (RLG) received a great deal of notice upon its 2004 debut, and you may still see references to *RedLightGreen* in various sources. In 2006, RLG merged with OCLC. Due to the similarities between OCLC's *Open WorldCat* project and RLG's *RedLightGreen*, OCLC decided to not maintain both projects. As of November 2006, *RedLightGreen* was no longer available, and today you should use *WorldCat* or *Open WorldCat* as a substitute tool.

If you need to search exhaustively for every work or every edition of a work by a particular author, you may need to consult the **National Union Catalog, Pre-1956 Imprints (NUC)**. This is a massive work, comprising 754 volumes that consist of facsimiles of catalog cards from American and Canadian libraries. The work is primarily arranged by author, with some entries for editors of anthologies and title entries for anonymous works. Due to variances in cataloging practice, some titles may have multiple cards represented, just as *WorldCat* has multiple records for various editions; thus, as you track down materials, remember

Shadows on the rock.

Willa **Cather**

1931

English   Book : Fiction   Internet Resource 4 p., l., 3-280 p., 1 l. 20 cm.
New York, A.A. Knopf,

Frontenac must negotiate for his control of Quebec.

GET THIS ITEM

Access: http://www.unl.edu/Cather/

Availability: **FirstSearch indicates your institution owns the item.**
- Libraries worldwide that own item: 2265   Washington State University
- Search the catalog at Washington State University Libraries

External Resources: • **Find It! at WSU Libraries**

FIND RELATED

More Like This: Search for versions with same title and author | Advanced options ...

Find Items About: Shadows on the rock (7); Cather, Willa, (max: 1,503)

Title: **Shadows on the rock.**

Author(s): Cather, Willa, 1873-1947.

Publication: New York,; A.A. Knopf,

Year: 1931

Description: 4 p., l., 3-280 p., 1 l. 20 cm.

Language: English

Standard No: **LCCN:** 31-27212

Abstract: Frontenac must negotiate for his control of Quebec.

Access: http://www.unl.edu/Cather/
http://www.teenreads.com/authors/au-cather-willa.asp

SUBJECT(S)

Descriptor: Fathers and daughters -- Fiction.
Pharmacists -- Fiction.
Physicians -- Fiction.
Littérature américaine -- 20e siècle.

Named Person: Frontenac, Louis de Buade, comte de, 1620-1698 -- Fiction.

Genre/Form: Historical fiction.

Geographic: Canada -- History -- To 1763 (New France) -- Fiction.
Québec (Québec) -- Fiction.
Canada -- Histoire -- 1713-1763 (Nouvelle-France) -- Romans, nouvelles, etc.

Note(s): At head of title: By Willa Cather./ "First edition."

Class Descriptors: **LC:** PZ3.C2858; **Dewey:** 813/.52

Vendor Info: Baker and Taylor (BTCP)

Material Type: Fiction (fic); Internet resource (url)

Document Type: Book; Internet Resource

Date of Entry: 19740212

Update: 20061123

Accession No: **OCLC:** 167912

Database: WorldCat

Figure 3.7.   WorldCat record for Willa Cather's *Shadows on the Rock* classed as a juvenile book
Source: WorldCat

Shadows on the rock /

Willa **Cather**

1931 **1st ed.**
English ◆ Book : Fiction [8], 280, [2] p. ; 24 cm.
New York : Alfred A. Knopf,

GET THIS ITEM

Availability: **Check the catalogs in your library.**
- Libraries worldwide that own item: 106
- 🌐 Search the catalog at Washington State University Libraries

External Resources: ·   Locate Document
- ➋ Cite This Item

FIND RELATED

More Like This: Search for versions with same title and author | Advanced options ...
Find Items About: **Shadows on the rock** (7); Cather, Willa, (max: 1,536)

Title: **Shadows on the rock /**
Author(s): Cather, Willa, 1873-1947.
Publication: New York : Alfred A. Knopf,
Edition: 1st ed.
Year: 1931
Description: [8], 280, [2] p. ; 24 cm.
Language: English
References: Hutchinson, P.M. NYPL Bulletin,; v. 60, no. 6, p. 275; Crane, J. Cather,; AI7.a.i

SUBJECT(S)

Geographic: Canada -- History -- To 1763 (New France) -- Fiction.
Note(s): "Of the first edition ... one hundred ninety-four copies ... have been printed on Shidzuoka Japan vellum. Each copy is signed by the author."--P. [2]./ "Set up, electrotyped, printed and bound by The Plimpton Press, Norwood, Mass."--P. [282].
Class Descriptors: LC: PS3505.A87; Dewey: 825
Responsibility: by Willa Cather.
Material Type: Fiction (fic)
Document Type: Book
Entry: 19850722
Update: 20040909
Accession No: OCLC: 12288448
Database: WorldCat

Figure 3.8.   WorldCat record for Willa Cather's *Shadows on the Rock* classed as an adult novel
Source: WorldCat

Shadows on the rock.

by <u>Willa Cather</u>

- **Language:** English **Type:** ● Book : Fiction ● Internet Resource
- **Publisher:** New York, A.A. Knopf, 1931.
- **OCLC:** 167912

> <u>Cite this Item</u>

- **Subjects:** <u>Canada -- History -- To 1763 (New France) -- Fiction.</u> | <u>Frontenac,</u> <u>Louis de Buade, -- comte de,</u> | <u>Fathers and daughters -- Fiction.</u> | <u>More ...</u>

- **Web Resources:** <u>unl.edu</u> | <u>teenreads.com</u>

Figure 3.9.   Open WorldCat record for Willa Cather's *Shadows on the Rock*

that a single work may be shown on multiple cards in the *NUC*. The *NUC* remains a useful tool for exploring collections at institutions that do not yet have complete online catalogs.

National Library Catalogs

Bibliotheque Nationale de France, www.bnf.fr (accessed 12 June 2007).
British Library Integrated Catalogue, catalogue.bl.uk (accessed 18 February 2007).
Library of Congress Online Catalog, catalog.loc.gov (accessed 18 February 2007).

National library catalogs are an important research tool. National libraries typically hold one copy of all books published in the country. For the purpose of studying American modernism, the key national library will be the Library of Congress. Searching the vast holdings of the British counterpart, the *British Library Integrated Catalogue,* may also be useful for gaining information about the breadth and depth of British works about American literature. There may be interesting information in other countries' national libraries about American authors who were very popular in those countries. One example is a search for materials held uniquely in France on Gertrude Stein or other expatriate writers. Seeing what sources a French library deems as essential may also be illuminating. France's national library, the Bibliotheque Nationale de France, hosts a French union catalog, the **Catalogue Collectif de France**, located at http://ccfr.bnf.fr. The interface is in French; scholars can search the catalog by selecting "recherche globale" and then performing searches by author or title.

The ***Library of Congress (LOC)*** is one of the largest libraries in the world, with more than 130 million items, including books, pamphlets, maps, manuscripts, and a variety of audiovisual formats. The *LOC* may provide a final step after using local catalogs and union catalogs in exhaustive searches, or an initial step to gather a comprehensive list of materials to check for local access. The *LOC* online catalog offers basic and guided searches that allow searching by title, author or creator, subject, keyword, Library of Congress call number, ISBN/ISSN, and series title. The guided search provides additional search parameters, such as corporate name, geographic place name, and international standard numbers, as well as menu options for using Boolean search techniques.

The *LOC* is a rich resource for digital collections as well. Of particular interest is the *American Memory* project, which includes collections in literature, culture, African-American history, performing arts, and women's history, among other topics. The literature section of American Memory includes plays by Zora Neale Hurston, photographs of writers taken by Carl Van Vechten, and plays from the Federal Theatre Project.

The ***British Library*** serves as the depository library for the United Kingdom and Ireland and includes holdings of more than 150 million items comprising books, manuscripts, maps, scores, artworks, patents, and stamps. The main website allows users to peruse the collections and select from various catalogs. The main online catalog, the ***British Library Integrated Catalogue***, offers access to information about 13 million items. The British Library's website states that a number of digitization projects are in progress to increase access to a variety of materials. Of potential interest to scholars is the digitization of British newspapers.

Conclusion

The development of online catalogs has greatly enhanced researchers' access to materials held all around the world. Search technology has also increased the ways to access items in a catalog. No longer tied to just author, title, and subject access, researchers can use keyword approaches and additional field-searching techniques to pinpoint needed items in catalogs that offer national holdings, like *WorldCat*. Online catalogs are also providing features for users based on new technologies, such as social networking tools like tagging, viewing ratings from other users, and saving personalized search preferences. These tools allow users to add comments, add their own subject headings or descriptors, and save their preferences, making a catalog search much more like searching an online bookseller. Online catalogs will provide those interested in American modernism with increased options for locating and using myriad books, primary sources, journals, indexes, and multimedia materials for conducting new research in the field.

CHAPTER 4

Print and Electronic Bibliographies, Indexes, and Annual Reviews

This chapter will discuss bibliographies, indexes, and annual reviews, all of which provide access to lists of resources. The tools discussed here are generally useful for researching literary topics from all periods, genres, and nationalities, although some will be specifically geared toward American literature or modernism.

These types of tools lead to specific items available for your research. They can be presented in both print or electronic formats and feature a variety of indexing methods or searching interfaces. Typically, these resources will offer basic data about the items so that a wide array of materials, including primary sources such as manuscripts and letters and secondary sources such as journals, books, articles, dissertations, book reviews, and magazines, can be located. In some cases, annotations describing the content or quality of the sources will be provided.

Certain bibliographies are designed to serve as catalogs of particular collections. This is often true with bibliographies that chronicle the holdings of a special collection of primary materials. Other bibliographies are more inclusive, serving to provide access to all possible materials published. To be manageable in scope, these bibliographies are often focused on one particular author, genre, literary style or movement, nation, or time period. Examples are discussed below.

Other projects are more comprehensive, offering information about all materials published during a certain time. Many scholars identify the *MLA International Bibliography* (*MLAIB*), which is technically both a bibliography and an index, as the primary tool for literary research. Other indexes include the *Annual Bibliography of English Language Literature* (*ABELL*), which also fully addresses American literature, and the *Humanities Index* and *Humanities and Social Science Index Retrospective*, which are available from H. W. Wilson and provide access to journal articles, reviews, and other essays, with articles dating back to 1907 in the retrospective file.

Many of these resources have been made available electronically, although subscription prices can be expensive. Almost all academic libraries can offer access to *Humanities Index* and to *MLAIB* through one of the vendors mentioned in chapter 1, but the cost of *Literature Online* (*LION*), which includes *ABELL*, is prohibitive for some libraries. Overall, vendors are offering increased access to full-text materials online, and many libraries have instituted a linking service so that online versions of articles, even those cited in indexes that do not contain direct full-text access, are easily located. For example, your library may provide links to the full-text versions of articles cited in *MLAIB* made available through a product like *JSTOR* or *Project MUSE* or through a general article database like *ProQuest Direct* or *Academic Search Premier*.

Given the amount of materials available, *JSTOR* and *Project MUSE* are worth greater discussion. *JSTOR* is an online archive of journals. The aims of the project involve building a reliable and comprehensive archive of journals and increasing access to them, filling gaps in physical library collections, and contributing to the preservation of the scholarly record. *JSTOR* currently offers access to approximately five hundred journals in the arts, humanities, and social sciences, and the journal is working to expand its collections in business and the sciences. *JSTOR* provides full-text journals back to their first volumes, but due to agreements with the publishers, or *embargos*, it will not provide the most recent three to five years of published journals. *JSTOR* can be directly accessed and searched, but it is not a complete bibliography or index, since it offers only a certain set of journals and does not have the most recent issues.

Project MUSE is similar, providing access to a specific set of journals from specific publishers. Originally a project linked to the Johns Hopkins University Press, *Project MUSE* has included other publishers since 2000. It currently offers access to approximately three hundred scholarly journals in the arts, humanities, and social sciences. *JSTOR* is a very stable product, but journals have been added and deleted from *Project MUSE* over the years because of the vagaries of publishers. To ensure finding the most comprehensive set of materials on your topic, use a resource like *MLAIB* as your primary tool and utilize full-text archives like *JSTOR* or *Project MUSE* to access the journal articles indexed within.

A third type of resource available is the annual review, which offers an overview of materials published within a particular year. Annual reviews typically are focused on secondary sources, featuring information about literary criticism, reviews, critical editions of primary works, anthologies, new reference books, and other items. Annual reviews are often arranged by time period or genre, or sometimes even by specific authors. However, there are some resources with "yearbook" or "annual review" in the title that do not meet the definition. One example is the *Yearbook of Comparative and General Literature*, which publishes a series of essays on various topics, often dealing with an annual theme, but not offering a true overview of all scholarship in the field for a given year.

General Literature Bibliographies and Indexes

Annual Bibliography of English Language and Literature (ABELL). Leeds: Modern Humanities Research Association, 1921–. Annual. Available online via subscription as part of *Literature Online (LION)* from Chadwyck-Healey, collections.chadwyck.com.

Humanities Index and *Humanities and Social Science Index Retrospective*. New York: Wilson, 1907–. Available online via subscription from H. W. Wilson, www.wilsonweb.com.

Modern Language Association International Bibliography of Books and Articles on the Modern Languages and Literatures (MLAIB). New York: Modern Language Association, 1921–. Annual. Available online via subscription from many vendors.

Literary researchers may be familiar with some of the tools listed above. The best known in the United States is likely **Modern Language Association International Bibliography** (**MLAIB**), considered to be the key American source for bibliography in literary studies. *MLAIB* currently indexes books, journals, and dissertations that cover modern languages, literature, folklore, and linguistics. Until 1969, it was published annually by the Modern Language Association as part of *PMLA: Publications of the Modern Language Association*, and it was called *American Bibliography* from 1921 until 1955. In 1969, the *MLAIB* was launched as a separate publication with a broadened scope, as evidenced by its four sections covering English and American literature from all periods; European, Asian, African, and Latin American literatures; linguistics; and foreign language pedagogy. Folklore was added as a fifth category in 1981. The earlier years were reprinted as separate indexes; most research libraries offer the *MLAIB* in print volumes dating back to 1921.

There are still five categories in the print volumes, but they now represent British, Irish, Commonwealth, English Caribbean, and American literatures; European, Asian, African, and Latin American literatures; linguistics; general literature, humanities, pedagogy, and rhetoric and composition; and folklore. There is a comprehensive subject index, and within broad sections such as "American literature/1900–1999," one can find listings by author and genre.

Descriptors, another word for subject headings as discussed in chapter 3, are created by the Modern Language Association and vary widely in scope and precision. Fully explore the possibilities to avoid missing important sources. For instance, perusing subject headings connected to various records for Langston Hughes shows broad terms such as "American literature; 1900–1999," "Modernism," and "Hughes, Langston (1902–1967)," along with "treatment of miscegenation," "relationship to anticommunism," "as children's literature," "Harlem Renaissance," and "relationship to African American culture."

Until 2006, the online version of *MLAIB* was limited to coverage from 1963 to the present. The Modern Language Association has digitized the content from 1926 through 1962, and that material is now available as part of the standard database. Depending on your library's vendor and its default interface, the appearance or placement of the search options may vary slightly. For a comparison of features across various vendors, see http://www.mla.org/bib_dist_comparison.

MLAIB offers a sophisticated range of options for customizing searches. These limits include being able to search by particular languages, dates, journal names, source types, and subject descriptors. A newer feature allows searching for author name as subject or as article author, which will be discussed in more detail. Given the expanded content of the database, this feature is helpful for pulling primary sources such as essays written by various authors about their contemporaries. Among the gems you may find are Willa Cather's "Stephen Crane Is a Superior Descriptive Writer" and writings by Langston Hughes about a variety of Harlem Renaissance figures.

Figures 4.1 and 4.2 provide sample records from *MLAIB* showing the different subject terms that are assigned to articles dealing with issues of race in Langston Hughes' works.

The British Modern Humanities Research Association creates a similar bibliography entitled ***Annual Bibliography of English Language and Literature (ABELL)***. Also initiated in 1921, it offers coverage of books, journals, critical editions, essay collections, book reviews, and dissertations. *ABELL* includes more types of materials than *MLAIB*, most notably book reviews. Although *MLAIB* selectively indexes review articles that compare multiple works and also

Soto, Isabel. "Boundaries Transgressed: Modernism and Miscegenation in Langston Hughes's 'Red-Headed Baby'." *Atlantic Studies: Literary, Cultural, and Historical Perspectives,* 3:1 (2006 Apr), pp. 97-110.
Subject Terms: American literature; 1900-1999; Hughes, Langston (1902-1967): "Red-Headed Baby"; short story; treatment of miscegenation; relationship to displacement; African diaspora; modernism.

Language:	English
Document Type:	Journal article
ISSN:	1478-8810
MLA Update:	200602
MLA Sequence:	2006-1-13050
MLA Record Number:	2006871025
Source Database:	© *MLA International Bibliography.* New York: Modern Language Association of America, 1963- .
Gale Record Number:	N2812234433

Figure 4.1.   Isabel Soto Sample Record from *MLAIB*
Source: *MLAIB* via Gale

Baldwin, Kate A. "The Russian Connection: Interracialism as Queer Alliance in Langston Hughes's The Ways of White Folks." *MFS: Modern Fiction Studies*, 48:4 (2002 Winter), pp. 795-824.

Subject Terms:	American literature; 1900-1999; Hughes, Langston (1902-1967): The Ways of White Folks (1934); short story; role of travel; to U.S.S.R.; relationship to race; sexuality.
Language:	English
Document Type:	Journal article
ISSN:	0026-7724
Peer Reviewed:	Yes
MLA Update:	200201
MLA Sequence:	2002-1-18014
MLA Record Number:	2002298136
Source Database:	© *MLA International Bibliography*. New York: Modern Language Association of America, 1963.
Gale Record Number:	N2811781712

Figure 4.2.   Kate Baldwin's Russian Connection record from *MLAIB*
Source: *MLAIB* via Gale

indexes articles from sources such as *The New York Times Book Review*, *MLAIB* does not have book reviews that focus on a single work. *ABELL* provides book reviews that appear in the journals it indexes. *ABELL* addresses materials about literature written in English from the United Kingdom, the United States, Canada, Australia, Asia, and Africa and covers research done in languages other than English.

Many libraries will offer the print volumes of *ABELL*. Using the index is crucial for picking up all the possible entries needed because of the complex and varied subject headings that are used by the volunteer indexers. *ABELL* is offered electronically as part of *Literature Online (LION)*, a product comprising other collections, ranging from Gale reference books such as the *Dictionary of Literary Biography* to *MLAIB* itself. Libraries can subscribe to the entire *LION* package or to selected parts. Within *LION*, you can search just *ABELL* or all the parts of *LION* to which your library subscribes. *LION* may differ in content from library to library.

In *LION*, there are many ways to search the various contents. A "quick search" feature across the entire collection gives an overall result list for all possible materials, ranging from texts of primary works to website links. Searching *ABELL* via *LION* for Langston Hughes highlights some of the differences in coverage between *MLAIB* and *ABELL*. A simple keyword search in *MLAIB* for Langston Hughes retrieved 601 items, including the two sample records shown above. Searching Hughes' name as "Author as Subject" (also called "Primary Subject Author" in *MLAIB* via EBSCO) retrieved 503. A "quick search" in *LION* offers 557 items of criticism, along with links to websites, essays written by Hughes, and online reference works.

In *LION*, selecting the "Criticism and Reference" search type takes you to *ABELL*. Within that search type, there are two options: one for author/subject and one for keyword searching. *ABELL* returns results counted as both "entries" and as "hits," which correspond to actual items and the total number of times the word or phrase is mentioned anywhere. Searching "Hughes, Langston" in *ABELL* as an author/subject search retrieved five hundred items of criticism, while a keyword search for "Langston Hughes" returned 1,328 items of criticism. This means that there are 828 items that mention Langston Hughes in some way but are not primarily about him. Some of these results will certainly be less relevant than the items in the more precise subject search.

LION also offers a "Browse Author Name" function, which provides an overview of biographical details, a portrait if available, links to biographical and bibliographical materials, and links to all the results within *LION*, organized by various categories of criticism and texts.

For example, the Isabel Soto article from *MLAIB* noted above is not included in *ABELL*, but the Kate Baldwin item is present. Figure 4.3 illustrates the differences between the information offered by the two databases.

To further illustrate the differences between the two tools, consider the first twenty results in each search described above. *MLAIB* returned six dissertations,

Author:	Baldwin, Kate A.
Title:	The Russian connection: interracialism as queer alliance in Langston Hughes's *The Ways of White Folks.*
Publication Details:	Modern Fiction Studies (48:4) 2002, 795-824.
Publication Year:	2002
ISSN:	00267724
Subject:	English Literature: Twentieth Century: Authors: Hughes, Langston
	English Literature: Twentieth Century: Authors: Du Bois, W. E. B.
	English Literature: Twentieth Century: Authors: Lawrence, D. H.
Reference Number:	2002:15029; 2002:14149; 2002:15519
Additional Search Terms:	Homosexuality
	Miscegenation
	The Souls of Black Folk
	The Ways of White Folks
	The Lovely Lady
	Soviet Union

Figure 4.3.   Kate Baldwin's Russian Connection record from *ABELL*
Source: *ABELL* via LION

four book chapters, one book, and nine journal articles. *ABELL* yielded five book reviews, one book, one book chapter, and thirteen journal articles. Of the forty items, only five overlapped—all journal articles. Given the advantages of locating various sources and types of sources, both *ABELL* and *MLAIB* should be consulted for comprehensive research.

For situations where quick access to recent scholarship is necessary, use of both *MLAIB* and *ABELL* may be frustrating, since their comprehensive scope means that many materials will not be available in your library, even in print. Consider **Humanities Index** (also sometimes called *Humanities Abstracts*) as an alternative when you need a fast overview of a particular theme or author before embarking on exhaustive research. Published by H. W. Wilson, *Humanities Index* is much more limited in scope, but it covers the major American literature journals, such as those discussed in chapter 5. If your library has online access to the full text of journals indexed in *Humanities Index*, it may offer a link directly to the article or the journal. *Humanities Index* does not offer full-text materials but links to another subscription database, such as *ProQuest Direct, Academic Search Premier, Project MUSE,* or *JSTOR.* This is accomplished through OpenURL, a framework that works behind the scenes to connect various resources to find the article needed, regardless of where the search began. With many key American literature journals, your library may offer several online versions of the same articles. Talk to a reference librarian about how to find the full text of articles listed in the databases you use, since article-linking practices vary from institution to institution.

A keyword search for Langston Hughes in *Humanities Index* and **Humanities and Social Sciences Index Retrospective** retrieved 214 items. Of the first twenty results, three items overlap with the first twenty results in *MLAIB* and *ABELL,* while three additional items are among the first twenty in *ABELL.* The unique items in this database are in music journals, bringing a different flavor to potential research. Figure 4.4 provides the record for the Baldwin article on Langston Hughes from *Humanities Index.*

When searching different article databases, remember that although some similarities exist between *Humanities Index* subject headings and those in *MLAIB* and *ABELL,* none match exactly—unlike searches in different library catalogs that all use the Library of Congress subject headings. For example, consider the three terms used to address the issue of homosexuality in Hughes' work. *MLAIB* uses "sexuality" and *ABELL* employs "homosexuality," while *Humanities Index* uses a compound subject heading of "communism and homosexuality." Three terms are also used to represent the issue of race in the works. *MLAIB* uses "relationship to race"; *ABELL* uses "miscegenation," a term that has some troubling connotations in American English; and *Humanities Index* uses "race relations in literature." Given this broad range of labels for the same article, keyword

Author(s): Baldwin, Kate A.
Title: The Russian Connection: Interracialism as Queer Alliance in Langston Hughes's "The Ways of White Folks".
Source: *Modern Fiction Studies* v. 48 no4 (Winter 2002) p. 795-824
Journal Code: Mod Fict Stud
Additional Info: United States
Standard No: ISSN: 0026-7724
Details: bibl.
Language: English
Review: R
SUBJECT(S) Descriptor: Americans — Soviet Union.
Race relations in literature.
Communism and homosexuality.
Named Person: Hughes, Langston 1902-1967 American poet, novelist, short story writer and playwright—Ways of white folks.
Accession No: BHUM03102112

Figure 4.4.   Kate Baldwin's *Russian Connection* record from *Humanities Index*
Source: *Humanities Index* via WilsonWeb

searching should be your first recourse unless you have identified the correct subject headings or descriptors for the particular database in advance.

Locating the official subject headings can be accomplished by consulting the thesaurus for the index, which may be available in print or embedded within the online database. This is another example of a feature that will vary among database vendors. At the beginning of research, using a keyword search to uncover the subject headings may be more effective and efficient than studying the thesaurus.

American Literature Bibliographies

In addition to the major indexes described above, there are several print bibliographies devoted specifically to American literature and to the first half of the twentieth century. These reference tools can be beneficial for searching in a different way. Sometimes surveying a wide array of materials, rather than focusing on certain names or keywords, can be more productive. These sources provide that different point of access and may also feature additional materials that were not indexed by *MLAIB* or *ABELL*.

Bibliography of American Literature. New Haven: Yale University Press, 1955–1991. Available online via subscription from Chadwyck-Healey, collections.chadwyck.com.

Bibliography of American Literature: A Selective Index. Comp. Michael Winship. Golden, CO: North American Publishing, 1995.

Bibliography of American Literature: Epitome. Comp. Michael Winship, Philip B. Eppard, and Rachel J. Howarth. Golden, CO: North American Publishing, 1995.

Brier, Peter A., and Anthony Arthur. *American Prose and Criticism, 1900–1950.* Detroit: Gale, 1981.

Gohdes, Clarence, and Sanford E. Marovitz. *Bibliographical Guide to the Study of the Literature of the USA.* 5th ed. Durham: Duke University Press, 1984.

Spiller, Robert E., Willard Thorp, Thomas H. Johnson, and Richard M. Ludwig, eds. *Literary History of the United States: Bibliography.* 4th ed. New York: Macmillan; London: Collier, 1974.

Nilon, Charles H. *Bibliography of Bibliographies in American Literature.* New York: Bowker, 1970.

Woodress, James. *American Fiction, 1900–1950: A Guide to Information Sources.* Detroit: Gale, 1974.

The ***Bibliography of American Literature* (*BAL*)** project was begun by Jacob Planck and completed by Michael Winship and Virginia L. Smyers. The final ninth volume of this encyclopedia was published in 1991. *BAL* provides bibliographic essays for almost three hundred individual authors from the American Revolution to 1930. Planck defined the end date as excluding people who died after 1930. Given this date constriction, this set will be useful only for early modernist writers.

Winship also created a selective index and a condensed version of the work, the ***Bibliography of American Literature: A Selective Index*** and ***Bibliography of American Literature: Epitome***, respectively. These two resources are of assistance particularly in determining whether a specific author was included or excluded from a work. The selective index does not provide exhaustive coverage of subject terms, but the authors are indexed completely.

The Brier and Arthur work, ***American Prose and Criticism, 1900–1950***, is part of a Gale series called the *Information Guides*, published from 1974 to 1983. This bibliography provides information about sources by and about humorists, essayists, and literary critics. Authors include E. B. White, Dorothy Parker, and James Thurber. Brier and Arthur offer brief expository essays with embedded discussions of sources. Of particular interest is the section on literary criticism. There are concise, informative entries on radical criticism as a reaction to New Humanism, along with coverage of New Criticism, psychological criticism, and mythological criticism. These new critical schools emerged during the American Modernist era and can greatly inform interpretation of scholarship produced during the era.

The first edition of Gohdes' ***Bibliographical Guide to the Study of the Literature of the USA*** was published in 1957 and was the first of this type of source to focus on American literature directly, rather than treating American literature as a subset or corollary to British literature. Many research libraries may have the older editions of this work, which can be of interest to those tracing the development of a particular issue or the arc of an author's influence.

The work provides annotated bibliographies arranged by various topics ranging from general sources, research methods, and the book trade to specific genres, regions, and time periods. This source is quite selective, particularly in the sections devoted to an entire genre, but there is decent coverage of American regionalism, along with attention to "special" themes in literature, such as spiritualism, the American frontier, the Civil War, and nature. More extensive lists are offered for science fiction and literature of the sea. The work is obviously dated but can serve as a supplementary tool for locating resources.

The fourth edition of the ***Literary History of the United States: Bibliography (LHUS)*** includes corrected reprints of the original 1948 work, the 1959 supplement, and the 1972 supplement. Separate volumes subtitled "History" provide essays rather than bibliographies. *LHUS* is certainly a useful reference source in its entirety, but the focus here is on the bibliography volume. Note that the history and bibliography volumes refer to one another, but the history volumes use the bibliography sources' original pagination rather than that of the corrected volume; the pagination of the reprints should be used for the bibliographies.

LHUS offers bibliographies on genres and eras collected into broader topic areas, such as "Literature and Culture" and "Movements and Influences," as well as a section with bibliographies for individual authors. Author entries feature primary works, along with information about reprints or special editions. A "Biography and Criticism" section lists materials, such as books, articles, and reference book entries. There are 239 author entries in the edition. Coverage is complete, ranging from the Colonial era to the mid-twentieth century. Some writers considered well studied today are listed with few items of criticism. Richard Wright, for example, has only four articles presented. Sherwood Anderson is noted as having no complete studies at all in the 1963 edition. By the 1972 supplement, however, several monographs had appeared and were added to the bibliography for Anderson.

LHUS is tricky to use due to its complex organization, but it remains helpful for tracking down older materials that have been omitted in more current indexes and collections and for tracing the history and development of American literature.

Charles H. Nilon's ***Bibliography of Bibliographies in American Literature*** is dated but offers a useful overview of bibliographies through the 1960s. The work contains four sections that provide basic and general bibliographies; bibliographies of authors from the seventeenth through twentieth centuries; bibliographies arranged by genre; and an "ancillary" section that includes related topics such as science, travels, humor, language, and history.

Nilon covers a wide array of materials, such as book-length bibliographies as well as pamphlets, serials, and individual articles that feature listings of materials. Authors are arranged alphabetically within centuries, which allows for easy browsing. This is a useful source for completing an exhaustive search of an author, genre, or topic.

Woodress's work, ***American Fiction, 1900–1950***, is part of the same Gale series mentioned above in the Brier and Arthur entry. This is a straightforward bibliography, with sources arranged into topic areas such as literary history, criticism, genres, regions, and eras. Woodress also provides bibliographic essays on a range of individual authors. The work is dated but presents an interesting snapshot of scholarship at that time. One particularly valuable feature is that information in the author essays is included about manuscript collections and other special holdings at American universities and libraries.

Two sources with intriguing titles, but of little to no use to those studying American modernist writers, are Charles Evans' *American Bibliography* and *American Catalogue of Books*. The *American Bibliography* was published from 1941 to 1959 but covers only materials published through 1820. The *American Catalogue of Books* features materials through 1866, and its successor, the *Annual American Catalog*, addresses materials from 1900 through 1909. The *Annual American Catalog* was one of the first works to be published by Bowker and was eventually superseded by *Books in Print*.

Although some of the works discussed in this section are rather dated, they may prove crucial for exploring the development of scholarship over the years and may lead to sources that have been lost in newer guides or indexes. The lack of current updates for many of these sources can be explained by the expansion of online availability of search indexes as well as the ease of using these tools to search.

Bibliographies on Modernism

Davies, Alistair. *An Annotated Critical Bibliography of Modernism*. Brighton: Harvester Press; Totowa: Barnes and Noble, 1982.
Bradbury, Malcolm, and James McFarlane, eds. *Modernism 1890–1930*. New York, London: Penguin, 1991.

There is a serious lack of bibliographic scholarship on modernism itself. Some useful guides and handbooks provide source information, such as Scott

Barbour's *American Modernism*,[1] but very few proper bibliographies, and none focused on American literature entirely, are available.

Davies' work, **An Annotated Critical Bibliography of Modernism**, has an unexplained emphasis on four specific authors: W. B. Yeats, Wyndham Lewis, D. H. Lawrence, and T. S. Eliot. A fifth section of the work addresses modernism as a whole. This section annotates approximately two hundred sources arranged by topic areas, such as theory, genres, criticism, and connection to the other arts. Along with the four authors who warranted their own sections, Davies tends to focus on the works and impact of James Joyce, Virginia Woolf, and Ezra Pound. As one reviewer put it, this work "confirms the need for more extensive bibliographical work" in the topic of modernism.[2] Given its focus on British literature, this work will be of limited interest to scholars of American modernism, but given the dearth of bibliography in this area, Davies' work may provide leads for general sources that will inform your study of modernism.

The Bradbury and McFarlane work, **Modernism 1890–1930**, was first published in 1976 and has been reprinted but not expanded or revised. It is useful to those who are beginning a study of modernism and want to explore the topic broadly. Bradbury and McFarlane focus on the timeframe of 1890–1930 and offer listings of sources that deal with the definitions of modernism, literary movements within the period, poetry, drama, and the novel. Drawbacks for American modernist scholars include the focus on European literature and that the bibliography does not examine periodicals; monographs are the only type of material presented in the bibliography.

Genre Bibliographies

Another resource for scholars of American modernist literature is bibliographies that address particular genres. These works will provide general sources on American literature as well as information about materials that focus on particular authors who were active in producing certain genres. For American literature studies, works of this type tend to cover post–World War II writings. However, several resources discussed below will be of assistance to the scholar of American modernism.

Demastes, William W., ed. *American Playwrights, 1880–1945: A Research and Production Sourcebook*. Westport, CT: Greenwood, 1995

Huang, Guiyou, ed. *Asian American Short Story Writers*. Westport, CT: Greenwood, 2003.

Hanna, Archibald. *A Mirror for the Nation: An Annotated Bibliography of American Social Fiction, 1901–1950.* New York: Garland, 1985.

Mothers and Daughters in American Short Fiction: An Annotated Bibliography of Twentieth-Century Women's Literature. Comp. Susanne Carter. Westport, CT: Greenwood, 1993.

The Political Left in the American Theatre of the 1930's: A Bibliographic Sourcebook. Comp. Susan Duffy. Metuchen, NJ: Scarecrow, 1992.

Smith, Geoffrey D. *American Fiction, 1901–1925: A Bibliography.* Cambridge: Cambridge University Press, 1997.

American Playwrights, 1880–1945 and *Asian American Short Story Writers* are representative samples of a bio-bibliographical guide. Greenwood publishes a number of these volumes that typically focus on an era, an ethnic group or gender, a genre, or some combination thereof. Each entry includes a biographical sketch, information about critical reception, and a complete bibliography of primary and secondary works. *American Playwrights* presents forty entries on a range of authors, such as Langston Hughes, Zora Neale Hurston, Maxwell Anderson, Gertrude Stein, and Eugene O'Neill. *Asian American Short Story Writers* offers entries for approximately fifty writers, ranging from the late nineteenth century to present day.

Archibald Hanna's *A Mirror for the Nation: An Annotated Bibliography of American Social Fiction, 1901–1950* is culled from twenty earlier, disparate bibliographies, which Hanna organizes and annotates. This source addresses fiction published between 1901 and 1950 as a means of exploring the economic, social, and political history of the United States. This volume concludes with subject and title indexes.

Mothers and Daughters in American Short Fiction is organized by a variety of topics, including abuse, aging, alienation, death, expectation, nurturance, and portraits. Author, title, and subject indexes are provided in this annotated bibliography. Examples of modernist writers featured are Willa Cather and Djuna Barnes.

The Political Left in the American Theatre of the 1930's covers plays from the era as well as secondary sources about the times, playwrights, and works. Annotations are provided. This is another example of a source that focuses on a particular theme.

Geoffrey D. Smith's *American Fiction, 1901–1925* offers more than 13,000 records for the first printings of original adult fiction published between 1901 and 1925. The volume is arranged alphabetically by author and includes indexes for pseudonyms, illustrators, titles, and publishers. This is an exhaustive, authoritative work for identifying novels from this era of American literature.

Modernist Author Bibliographies

Scholars focusing on one particular author will want to locate all of the bibliographies that have been created about that writer. General literary resources and specialized ones such the Nilon work described earlier will identify these works. Library catalog subject heading searches using the author's name will also prove useful; items with the subheading "bibliography" will provide these types of sources. Newer bibliographies, as well as earlier bibliographies or checklists, can help locate resources about many authors that were published at the time the author was writing. Bibliographies can also offer thorough coverage of reviews and other sources that appeared earlier in the author's career. If newer bibliographies are not available for the author in question, *MLAIB*, *Humanities Index*, or other general indexes can locate updated criticisms and reviews. Author bibliographies were particularly useful at the time they were published, when searching multiple sources online simultaneously was impossible or prohibitively expensive. They remain valuable today as a means of locating minor pieces that may have been omitted from subsequent bibliographies and indexes over the years.

Listed below are examples of author-specific bibliographies for a variety of American modernist writers. Discussion of selected items follows.

Willa Cather

Arnold, Marilyn. *Willa Cather: A Reference Guide*. Boston: G. K. Hall, 1986.
Crane, Joan. *Willa Cather: A Bibliography*. Lincoln: University of Nebraska Press, 1982.

William Faulkner

Brodsky, Louis Daniel, and Robert W. Hamblin. *Faulkner: A Comprehensive Guide to the Brodsky Collection*. 5 vols. Jackson: University of Mississippi Press, 1982.
Cox, Leland H., ed. *William Faulkner, Critical Collection: A Guide to Critical Studies with Statements by Faulkner and Evaluative Essays on His Works*. Detroit: Gale, 1982.
Sweeney, Patricia E. *William Faulkner's Women Characters: An Annotated Bibliography of Criticism, 1930–1983*. Santa Barbara: ABC-Clio, 1985.

Ernest Hemingway

Catalog of the Ernest Hemingway Collection at the John F. Kennedy Library. Boston: G. K. Hall, 1982.
Hanneman, Audre. *Ernest Hemingway, A Comprehensive Bibliography*. Princeton: Princeton University Press, 1967.

Langston Hughes

Dickinson, Donald C. *A Bio-bibliography of Langston Hughes, 1902–1967*. 2nd ed. Hamden, CT: Archon Books, 1972.
Mikolyzk, Thomas A. *Langston Hughes: A Bio-bibliography*. New York: Greenwood Press, 1990.
Miller, R. Baxter. *Langston Hughes and Gwendolyn Brooks: A Reference Guide*. Boston: G. K. Hall, 1978.

Zora Neale Hurston

Newson, Adele S. *Zora Neale Hurston: A Reference Guide*. Boston: G. K. Hall, 1987.

Wallace Stevens

Edelstein, J. M. *Wallace Stevens: A Descriptive Bibliography*. Pittsburgh: University of Pittsburgh Press, 1973.
Morse, Samuel French, Jackson R. Bryer, and Joseph N. Riddel. *Wallace Stevens Checklist and Bibliography of Stevens Criticism*. Denver: Swallow Press, 1963.

Edith Wharton

Lauer, Kristin O., and Margaret P. Murray. *Edith Wharton: An Annotated Secondary Bibliography*. New York: Garland, 1990.
Melish, Lawson McClung. *A Bibliography of the Collected Writings of Edith Wharton*. Folcroft, PA: Folcroft Press, 1969.
Springer, Marlene. *Edith Wharton and Kate Chopin: A Reference Guide*. Boston: G. K. Hall, 1976.

The two items listed above for Willa Cather illustrate one major difference found in these types of sources. The item by Marilyn Arnold, **Willa Cather: A Reference Guide**, is an example of a fairly typical reference book. It offers a brief biographical outline of Cather's life, a list of her major works, and an annotated bibliography of critical works. Joan Crane's book, **Willa Cather: A Bibliography**, is much more comprehensive in terms of primary sources, but it addresses no secondary material whatsoever. Crane provides details about all of Cather's writing, including all individual newspaper articles.

The items for Wallace Stevens outline other approaches. The Morse volume, **Wallace Stevens Checklist and Bibliography of Stevens Criticism**, consists of a list of all primary works, including single poems published in newspapers, but also provides a more detailed listing of critical pieces. The Edelstein volume,

Wallace Stevens: A Descriptive Bibliography, is billed as a "descriptive" bibliography, addressing the physical characteristics of the publications such as size, binding, edging, and fonts. The Melish volume of Edith Wharton's works, *A Bibliography of the Collected Writings of Edith Wharton*, also takes this approach, noting the details of the cover art, title page, and verso as well as size, color, binding, and edgings.

Bibliographies may also focus on a particular collection of materials. Examples above include the *Catalog of the Ernest Hemingway Collection at the John F. Kennedy Library* and the guide to a special collection of Faulkner materials, *Faulkner: A Comprehensive Guide to the Brodsky Collection*. The Kennedy Library bibliography simply reprints facsimiles of the actual catalog cards. The Brodsky guide discusses the collections in more detail, with annotations and analyses of various sources. It presents facsimiles of manuscript pages and other items.

Another interesting example is Patricia E. Sweeney's work on Faulkner, *William Faulkner's Women Characters: An Annotated Bibliography of Criticism, 1930–1983*, which addresses Faulkner's treatment of women characters. The volume is arranged by novel, and in each section Sweeney traces the critical scholarship of Faulkner's works in relation to the female characters. Sweeney provides annotations and excerpts of the sources, which will allow you to determine which sources are most valuable for further research in this area.

Bibliographies devoted to a single author can offer a quick overview of major primary and secondary resources but can also be very specialized in terms of types of material or topics addressed. Explore what is available for the particular authors you are studying.

Annual Reviews

American Literary Scholarship: An Annual. Durham: Duke University Press, 1965–.

The Year's Work in English Studies. The English Association. Oxford: Oxford University Press, 1921–. Available online via subscription from Oxford University Press, ywes.oxfordjournals.org/.

Yearbook of Research in English and American Literature: REAL. Berlin: De Gruyter/Gunter Narr, 1982–.

American Literary Scholarship was first published in 1965. The volumes are organized into two parts, one for specific authors and another for genres or time periods. The first volume offered eight chapters on specific authors, namely Ralph Waldo Emerson and Henry David Thoreau, Nathaniel Hawthorne, Herman Melville, Walt Whitman, Mark Twain, Henry James, William Faulkner, and Ernest Hemingway and F. Scott Fitzgerald. Over the years, Emily Dickinson was added to the Whitman section, and two other sections were added, for Edith Wharton and Willa Cather and for Ezra Pound and T. S. Eliot. The categories devoted to time periods have also shifted and expanded over time, and sections for general reference works and scholarship in other languages have been featured.

Each section of the work addresses a year's scholarship extensively. A wide array of journals and publishers is surveyed, and the chapters offer information about the content of all the critical sources. In addition, author and subject indexes are provided to allow easy access to the various chapters. This is particularly helpful if the author studied is not one of the primary authors covered. Many references to other authors exist in the second part of the work.

The second part of the work includes sections on various genres, separated by eras as appropriate. For example, American modernist scholars might explore "Fiction 1900–1930" and "Fiction 1930–1960" or "Poetry 1900–1940" and "Poetry 1940–Present." Each "Fiction 1900–1930" segment features a number of authors. Most years there is coverage for Gertrude Stein, Jack London, Theodore Dreiser, Sinclair Lewis, Sherwood Anderson, John Dos Passos, the Harlem Renaissance, regionalist writers, and general interest materials. The regionalist section often focuses on one particular writer or one particular region, such as Mary Austin, Ellen Glasgow, or the American West. Other writers who have appeared in selected recent volumes are H. L. Mencken, W. E. B. DuBois, Edgar Rice Burrows, Upton Sinclair, and Jean Toomer. Compared with other sources, *American Literary Scholarship* is well organized and filled with readable, informative material. Volumes from 1998 to the present are accessible in *Project MUSE*.

The first volume of **The Year's Work in English Studies** was published in 1921 and covered November 1919–November 1920. After the first few volumes, the definition of "year's work" was adjusted to match the actual calendar year. Scholars of American literature should note that early volumes dealt only with British literature. The first few did not even address the twentieth century, although they began using a designation of "Nineteenth Century and Beyond." The twentieth century and American literature were both bestowed with their own separate sections beginning in 1954.

Each volume examines all periods and genres of literature written in English. The sections are written by a variety of scholars and describe major works published during the particular year under review. Within the section "American Literature: The Twentieth Century" are separate essays on poetry and fiction, 1900–1945; fiction since 1945; drama; Native, Asian American, Latino/a, and general ethnic writing; and African-American literature. The online version is updated more rapidly than the print volumes appear. The "Fiction 1900–1945" section surveys books and journal articles and is arranged by author, giving a good, comparative view of all new scholarship on each major author from the period. A scan of the section to find particular authors of interest is fairly simple. The more general categories of poetry and drama have an introductory paragraph that alerts readers to the writers who are addressed within the volume. A complete bibliography is included at the end of the American literature section.

The Year's Work not only offers an excellent overview of what was published but also provides a great deal of information about those sources, their critical approaches, and works analyzed, so that scholars can make informed judgments about which sources are most valuable. As with many sources, the essays may reflect the individual essayists' opinions and biases. You may notice differences in perspective between the various essays within one volume. The whole set is also valuable as a historical survey of the field.

The Yearbook of Research in English and American Literature (REAL) was launched in 1982. Designed to address any literature written in English, *REAL* fosters an international scope and presents a variety of topics. The initial purpose was to present original research, as opposed to literary criticism. Early volumes feature various essays on a wide array of authors, works, and themes. Recent volumes have a particular focus, such as "Theories of American Culture, Theories of American Studies" and "Literature, Literary History and Cultural Memory." American modernist writers may not be included in every volume of *REAL*, but the yearbook is certainly a source to consider because of its excellent quality, detailed analysis, and deep coverage of scholarship.

Conclusion

Scholars of American modernism have a wide array of tools at their disposal, including major indexing tools such as *MLAIB*, *Humanities Index*, and *ABELL* as well as other indexes, reviews, and bibliographies that were produced during the Modernist period and beyond. Many of these resources are available online, offering today's scholars easier access and more efficient searching techniques. Taking advantage of the great number of indexes and bibliographies available in print and electronic formats will allow the scholar to thoroughly research works, authors, genres, and issues related to this era of American literature.

Notes

1. Scott Barbour, ed., *American Modernism* (San Diego: Greenhaven, 2000).
2. Jerry A. Varsava, *The Review of English Studies*, New Series, vol. 36, no. 144 (Nov. 1985), p. 626.

CHAPTER 5

Scholarly Journals

While monographs remain important in the humanities, the scholarly journal represents a key segment of the dissemination of information in literary studies. Journals are a significant source for scholars who wish to publish their own emerging research and also remain current on issues related to their research interests. Literary periodicals are also crucial for learning about new areas of study and trends in the field. Scholarly journals often include book reviews, which can help keep you up to date on new materials. Keep in mind that due to the publishing cycle for most journals, the books under review will not be brand new, but the reviews will likely be in depth and will compare the book to other works or otherwise depict the book's relevance in the field.

While many publishers have offered tables of contents via e-mail for many years, technological advances have made it easier for scholars to keep up to date on developments. Almost all journals have websites, and many of them provide features such as RSS feeds, which provide notification when a site is updated. Even if a site does not provide free, full-text access online, researchers can use the Web to stay current much more easily than in the past.

Note that virtually all of these sources are indexed in *MLAIB*, *ABELL*, *Humanities Index*, and the other indexes listed in chapter 4. Many of these titles are available online through subscription databases or collections such as *JSTOR*, *Project MUSE*, or *Academic Search Premier*; check your library catalog or ask a reference librarian for assistance in locating electronic versions of these works. The descriptions below provide information about *JSTOR* and *Project MUSE* availability, as well as *ABELL* and *MLAIB* coverage.

Scholars can use the *MLA Directory of Periodicals* to explore available journals. The *Directory* has been published since 1978, and the range of biennial volumes is available in most research libraries. The *Directory* is also part of the online *MLAIB*; if your library's version of *MLAIB* does not offer an obvious link, ask a reference librarian for assistance. The online version provides searches by journal name, ISSN, publisher, sponsoring organization, place of publication, editorial staff, date founded, language, and subject. This tool does not include a keyword approach; instead, you should use MLA subject headings, as discussed in chapter 4. This resource can be a valuable tool for locating journals on particular subjects, especially when looking for materials in specific languages. Again, using *ABELL* or *MLAIB* will provide citations and access to specific articles rather than to journals as a whole.

In addition to the sources listed in this chapter, you can explore the library catalog for other journals devoted to a particular era, author, genre, or issue. Use a keyword search linking the word "periodicals" to other words to describe your topic, as illustrated in figure 5.1.

In the record above, "Periodicals" is an official Library of Congress subheading and will appear in the cataloging records of any magazines, newspapers, or journals. This approach retrieves any type of periodical, not just peer-reviewed journals of literary criticism. You may need to check the *MLA Directory of Periodicals* or a source such as *Ulrich's International Periodicals Directory* to determine if sources are peer reviewed.

Scholars may also want to browse histories of periodicals, such as *The Literary Journal in America, 1900–1950.*[1] This work presents citations for sources that address the publication history, scope, and accomplishments of various maga-

| Title | The Journal of **American drama** and theatre. |
| Imprint | New York, N.Y. : CASTA, CUNY Graduate School, 1989- |

Description	v. ; 23 cm.
Frequency	3 no. a year, winter 1990-
Descript.	Two no. a year, 1989
Pub date	Vol. 1, no. 1 (spring 1989)-
Note	Issued by: Center for Advanced Study in Theatre Arts.
Subject	**American drama -- Periodicals.**
	Theater -- United States -- **Periodicals.**
Other author	Center for Advanced Study in Theatre Arts.
Other title	J. Am. drama theatre
	The Journal of **American drama** and theatre
ISSN	1044-937X

Figure 5.1.   Sample catalog record for keyword search = "american drama" and periodicals
Source: Washington State University Libraries, Griffin Catalog (Innovative Interfaces)

zines and journals during the first half of the twentieth century. The scholarly journal *American Periodicals: A Journal of History, Criticism and Bibliography* is also devoted to the study of American periodicals.[2]

This chapter lists and describes the major journals that cover American literature from the first half of the twentieth century. These are the peer-reviewed journals that mainly or exclusively publish articles of literary criticism. See chapter 7 for a discussion of literary journals and popular periodicals from the Modernist era that publish primary materials and less formal essays.

The journals discussed here are grouped into three categories: modernism and the Modernist era, modernist authors, and twentieth-century American literature. The first category lists journals specifically devoted to the Modernist period or movements within that time frame, while the second category lists journals that are devoted to specific authors. The third category includes journals that broadly deal with the twentieth century and with American literature. Sources from all three categories may be useful, depending on the research topic.

Modernism and the Modernist Era

When perusing journals, remember that their use of the term "modern" often means contemporary, current, or twentieth century, rather than being connected specifically to the Modernist era. For example, *Modern Quarterly* is a journal about socialism. Several useful journals with "modern" in the title are included below in the section on American and twentieth-century literature journals.

Although this era is well studied, very few journals are devoted solely to this period. Reasons may be that the era is so diverse that it would be difficult to narrow down the field. Journals covering American literature or twentieth-century literature tend to cover the Modernist era well. Also, the period is still relatively recent; perhaps journals will emerge in the future. Below are listed the interdisciplinary journals that address the theories and history of modernism in art, literature, and aesthetics.

International Review of Modernism. Richland, WA: Department of English, Washington State University, 1997–. 2/yr. No ISSN. www.modernism.wsu .edu/.

Modernism/Modernity (MoMo). Baltimore: Johns Hopkins University Press, 1994–. 3/yr. ISSN: 1071-6068; E-ISSN: 1080-6601. www.press.jhu.edu/ journals/modernism_modernity/.

Modernist Studies: Literature & Culture 1920–1940 (MSLC). Edmonton: Department of English, University of Alberta, 1974–1982. Quarterly. ISSN: 0316-5973.

The *International Review of Modernism* is a peer-reviewed journal that focuses on European literature and history from 1890 to 1939. Although it will not offer specific information about American literature, it may be of interest as background or corollary readings. The journal was published from 1997 to 2000, and after a two-year hiatus, it planned to re-emerge as an electronic journal. That plan appears still to be in development. If the *Review* does resume publication, it will be an important source for the study of modernism. Table of contents information is available at http://www2.tricity.wsu.edu/leonardorr/.

The official journal of the Modernist Studies Association, *Modernism/ Modernity* covers film, literature, history, art, music, and architecture and is the major source for scholarship on modernism and modernist themes and issues. This journal is indexed in both *MLAIB* and *ABELL*, and *Project MUSE* provides full-text access to issues from 1994 to the present.

The University of Alberta published a relevant journal from 1974 to 1982. Entitled *Modernist Studies: Literature & Culture 1920–1940*, it featured articles about literature and other arts created between 1920 and 1940. The journal dealt with European literature primarily, but American modernist scholars may be interested in more general or comparative pieces, such as the one on modern literature and iconography. Although it had a short publishing history, some articles may be of interest in your research, particularly to offer a flavor of the types of issues discussed. This journal is indexed in *MLAIB*.

Journals on Modernist Era Authors

Several major figures of the Modernist era have journals devoted to the study of their works. Many of these are connected with scholarly societies that promote awareness of the authors' works through scholarships, conferences, and other activities. Some of these societies are also connected to a place, such as a former home, that serves as a museum or research library. This section features journals that had long runs or are still currently publishing. A number of newsletters and small periodicals, many of them devoted to Fitzgerald and Hemingway, had brief publication runs. Use the *MLA Directory of Publications*, discussed above, to locate all the sources about the author studied. Several of these journals are available freely online, while others may be more difficult to track down. Journals available online can be uncovered easily by using *Google* or another search engine. See chapter 9 for more details about searching the Web. Smaller university libraries may not subscribe to all of these specialized journals; a reference librarian can assist with interlibrary loans or consortial borrowing possibilities.

Cather Studies (CathSt). Lincoln: University of Nebraska Press, 1990–. Biennial. ISSN: 1045-9871. cather.unl.edu/scholarship/cs/index.html.

Edith Wharton Review (EWhR). Union, NJ: Kean University, 1984–. 2/yr. No ISSN. www.wsu.edu/~campbelld/wharton/ewr.htm.

The Eugene O'Neill Review. Boston: Suffolk University, 1989–. 2/yr. ISSN: 1040-9483; 1040-9843. Former title: *Eugene O'Neill Newsletter* (1977–1988) ISSN: 0733-0456. www.eoneill.com/library/review/index.htm.

F. Scott Fitzgerald Review (FSFR). Hempstead, NY: Hofstra University; Montgomery: Troy University, 2002–. Annual. ISSN: 1543-3951. www.fitzgeraldsociety.org.

Faulkner Journal (FJ). Ada: Ohio Northern University Press; Orlando: University of Central Florida Press, 1985–. 2/yr. ISSN: 0884-2949; 0882-6412. www.english.ucf.edu/faulkner/.

The Faulkner Newsletter & Yoknapatawpha Review. Oxford, MS: L. Wells, 1981–2001. Quarterly. ISSN: 0733-6357.

The Hemingway Review (HN). Ada: Ohio Northern University Press, 1981–. 2/yr. ISSN: 0276-3362; 1548-4815. www.hemingwaysociety.org/#hemingway_reviewajax.asp.

The Langston Hughes Review (LHRev). Providence, RI: Brown University Press; Athens: University of Georgia Press, 1982–. 2/yr. ISSN: 0737-0555. www.uga.edu/iaas/lhr/index.html.

Wallace Stevens Journal (WSJour). Northridge, CA: Wallace Stevens Society, 1977–. Quarterly. ISSN: 0148-7132. www.wallacestevens.com/.

William Carlos Williams Review (WCWR). Lubbock: Texas Tech University Press, 1980–. 2/yr. ISSN: 0196-6286. Former title: *William Carlos Williams Newsletter* (1974–1979) ISSN: 0099-216X. english.ttu.edu/WCWR.

Zora Neale Hurston Forum (ZNHF). Baltimore: Morgan State University, 1986–. Annual. ISSN: 1051-6867.

Cather Studies includes articles on all aspects of Willa Cather, such as biography, various critical approaches, and literary relationships and reputation, along with the artistic, historical, intellectual, religious, economic, political, and social backgrounds to her work. The journal features scholarly articles as well as briefer pieces intended to update readers on developments in Cather scholarship. The website provides complete access to all volumes published so far. The journal is published once every two or three years and is part of the larger Cather online archive project hosted by the University of Nebraska and the Cather Society. Both *MLAIB* and *ABELL* provide indexing for this journal.

The Eugene O'Neill Review began publication in 1989 as a continuation and expansion of the *Eugene O'Neill Newsletter*. The journal is published twice a year and is available online. The website has a table of contents along with links to the complete articles from the year 2000 to the present. Subject and author indexes are also made available for scholars. This journal is part of the larger *eOneill.com* site, an electronic archive of O'Neill materials comprising letters, manuscripts, and other online collections. The website also provides the complete texts of the *Newsletter* issues from 1977 to 1988 and a newer version of the *Newsletter* that features shorter, less scholarly articles, which is particularly useful since these works are not indexed in *MLAIB* or *ABELL*.

The **Faulkner Journal** is a peer-reviewed journal dedicated to the scholarly study of Faulkner's life and works. It is published quarterly, with two general issues and a double issue focused on a special theme. Previous special themes have included "Faulkner and Feminisms," "Faulkner and Latin America," and "Faulkner and Whiteness." Articles in the general issues have included analyses of translations of Faulkner's works, the treatment of female characters, race relations, homosexuality, and masculinity. Issues typically contain five articles per issue. The journal is indexed in both *MLAIB* and *ABELL*. The website has table of contents information back to issue 4 (1989).

Another source dedicated to Faulkner, *The Faulkner Newsletter & Yoknapatawpha Review* appeared from 1981 to 2001 and was published by Lawrence Wells and Dean Faulkner Wells, Faulkner's niece. This publication was designed as a newsletter and, although not a peer-reviewed journal, contained items of interest such as book reviews, articles about new editions, conference reports, biographical inquiries, and information about websites devoted to Faulkner. In addition, it covered the annual Faux Faulkner contest, sponsored by the Wells family. According to a news release about the journal's end, a bound edition of the first fifty-four issues, with a complete index, was published in 1994 under the title *The Faulkner Newsletter: Collected Issue*s.[3] Additional access is available via *MLAIB*.

The Hemingway Review publishes articles encompassing a variety of traditional and contemporary critical approaches along with notes, letters to the editor, book reviews, library information, current bibliography, and professional news. Recent articles include treatments of the multilingual dialogue in *A Farewell to Arms*, an analysis of *The Sun Also Rises* via Schopenhauer, and Afro-Cuban influences in *The Old Man and the Sea*. The journal is published twice a year, and each issue typically contains six articles. It is indexed in both *MLAIB* and *ABELL*, and full-text access is available in *Project MUSE* for issues from 2003 to the present.

The Langston Hughes Review features articles about other African-American writers, such as Richard Wright, Zora Neale Hurston, and Frank Marshal Davis, in addition to studies of Hughes' life and works. Some issues are devoted to special themes, such as one on the legacy of Negrismo/Negritude, another on Dorothy West, and an issue that featured interviews with people speaking about Hughes. The journal is published twice per year by the Langston Hughes Society, which was founded at Brown University, and is currently housed at the University of Georgia. Both *MLAIB* and *ABELL* index this journal. The website offers a table of contents.

The Stevens Society publishes the ***Wallace Stevens Journal***. The site makes available a complete listing of journal issue contents back to the first issue. Published twice a year, the journal features at least five articles per issue, reviews of books about Stevens, a bibliography of recent works about Stevens, and poems written in honor of or from the influence of Stevens. The articles cover all aspects of Stevens' work and life, including essays on his use of legal terms and on the relationships with art, music, metaphysics, and politics, as well as comparisons with other poets and explications of specific poems. The journal is indexed by *MLAIB* and *ABELL*.

The ***William Carlos Williams Review*** was called the *William Carlos Williams Newsletter* until the Williams Society changed the title and expanded the content. The journal is published twice a year and includes articles on all aspects of the life and works of William Carlos Williams and his "literary milieu," including his relationship to art, philosophy, and social and political movements of the time. Recent articles range from a discussion of the politics of literary reception to the use of the abstract in his poetry. The journal is indexed by both *MLAIB* and *ABELL*. The website offers a table of contents for the current issue and a bibliography of works about Williams from recent years.

General Twentieth-Century and American Literature Journals

Some twentieth-century and American literature journals have been created in recent decades, while some American literature journals began publishing before the twentieth century. Journals active during the Modernist era may be of particular interest to scholars. Perusing journals published during the first half of the twentieth century will allow scholars to uncover the development of scholarship surrounding particular authors or themes. Interesting editorial statements or letters may also shed light on various critical debates and emerging trends. Considering the book reviews that were produced contemporaneously may also be interesting, as some authors who are now highly esteemed were not received enthusiastically at the time they produced their works.

American Literary History (ALH). Oxford: Oxford University Press, 1989–. Quarterly. ISSN: 0896-7148. alh.oxfordjournals.org.
American Literature (AL). Durham, NC: Duke University Press, 1929–. Quarterly. ISSN: 0002-9831; E-ISSN: 1527-2117. americanliterature.dukejournals.org.
American Literary Realism (ALR). Arlington: University of Texas Press, 1967–1999. Champaign: University of Illinois Press, 1999–. 3/yr. ISSN: 0002-9823. www.press.uillinois.edu/journals/alr.html.

American Quarterly (AQ). Baltimore: Johns Hopkins University Press, 1949–. Quarterly. ISSN: 0003-0678; E-ISSN: 1080-6490. www.americanquarterly.org.

American Studies International (ASInt). Washington, DC: George Washington University Press, 1975–2005. 3/yr. ISSN: 0883-105X. Former titles: *American Studies News* (1962–1969) and *American Studies: An International Newsletter* (1969–1975). www.gwu.edu/~asi.

Journal of American Studies (JAmS). Cambridge: Cambridge University Press for the British Association for American Studies, 1967–. 3/yr. ISSN: 0021-8758. journals.cambridge.org/jid_AMS.

Journal of Modern Literature (JML). Philadelphia: Temple University Press; Bloomington: Indiana University Press, 1970–. Quarterly. ISSN: 0022-281X; E-ISSN: 1529-1464. inscribe.iupress.org/loi/jml.

Modern Fiction Studies (MFS). West Lafayette, IN: Purdue University Press, 1955–. Quarterly. ISSN: 0026-7724; E-ISSN: 1080-658X. www.cla.purdue.edu/English/mfs.

MLN (MLN). Baltimore: Johns Hopkins University Press, 1962–. 5/yr. ISSN: 0026-7910. Former title: *Modern Language Notes* (1886–1961) ISSN: 0149-6611. www.press.jhu.edu/journals/modern_language_notes.

Modern Language Quarterly (MLQ). Seattle: University of Washington Press; Durham, NC: Duke University Press, 1940–. Quarterly. ISSN: 0026-7929; E-ISSN: 1527-1943. mlq.dukejournals.org.

Modern Language Studies (MLS). Selinsgrove, PA: Northeast Modern Language Association, 1971–. Quarterly. ISSN: 0047-7729. www.nemla.org/mls.html.

PMLA: Publications of the Modern Language Association (PMLA). Chicago: Modern Language Association, 1884–. 6/yr. ISSN: 0030-8129. www.mla.org/publications/pmla.

Resources for American Literary Study (RALS). Brooklyn: AMS Press, 1971–. Annual. ISSN: 0048-7384. www.amspressinc.com/rals.html.

Sewanee Review (SR). Sewanee, TN: University of the South Press, 1892–. Quarterly. ISSN: 0037-3052. www.sewanee.edu/sewanee_review.

Studies in 20th and 21st Century Literature (StTCL). Manhattan: Kansas State University Press, 2003–. 2/yr. ISSN: 1555-7839. Former title: *Studies in 20th Century Literature* (1977–2002) ISSN: 0145-7888. www.k-state.edu/sttcl/index.html.

Texas Studies in Literature and Language (TSLL). Austin: University of Texas Press, 1959–. Quarterly. ISSN: 0040-4691. www.utexas.edu/utpress/journals/jtsll.html.

Tulsa Studies in Women's Literature (TSWL). Tulsa, OK: University of Tulsa Press, 1982–. 2/yr. ISSN: 0732-7730. www.utulsa.edu/tswl/.

Twentieth Century Literature (TCL). Hempstead, NY: Hofstra University Press, 1955–. ISSN: 0041-462X. www.hofstra.edu/Academics/Colleges/HCLAS/ENGL/engl_tcl.htm.

American Literary History provides extensive coverage of the early twentieth century. Recent articles explore topics such as Ralph Ellison and jazz, the imaginary in modernist poetry, ethnic writers in the Modernist era, and Dorothy Parker. The journal is quite interdisciplinary in approach and markets itself as open to the "various, often competing voices of contemporary literary inquiry," meaning that it does not publish in a narrow range but is more open to a broad range of theoretical approaches. The journal's website offers a variety of services, including current issue and archives, which are available to subscribers; links to the fifty "most-read" articles; and alerting services such as e-mail and RSS. Issues from 1989 to 2001 are available in *JSTOR*, while *Project MUSE* includes issues from 2000 to the present. The journal is indexed in both *MLAIB* and *ABELL*.

A major journal for the literature of the United States, **American Literature** addresses all periods of American literary production, but there is excellent coverage of twentieth-century works. Each issue typically comprises six articles plus book reviews and notes. Recent articles feature topics such as Modernist-era poets, modernism and ecology in fiction, films, modernism and American nationalism and democracy, Native American identity as related to modernism, William Carlos Williams, Djuna Barnes, F. Scott Fitzgerald, and Edith Wharton. The journal's website offers an archive and RSS services. *JSTOR* provides access to issues from 1929 to 1999, and *Project MUSE* includes issues from 1999 to 2004. *MLAIB* and *ABELL* both index the journal.

American Literary Realism focuses on the late nineteenth and early twentieth centuries, featuring a good number of Modernist-era writers. Issues contain four or five articles plus notes and book reviews. Recent articles of interest to modernist scholars have been published on Willa Cather, Kate Chopin, Edith Wharton, Upton Sinclair, and Frank Norris. Indexing is done by both *MLAIB* and *ABELL*. The journal's website offers a table of contents.

The official journal of the American Studies Association, **American Quarterly** is an interdisciplinary journal that "examines American societies and cultures, past and present, in global and local contexts." Many issues contain articles on literature from the Modernist era. The journal places an emphasis on film and inter-arts studies and offers excellent coverage of African-American, Latino/Chicano, and Native American writers and issues from all periods of American literature. The website includes a table of contents and responses to previous articles. *Project MUSE* provides access to issues from 1996 to the present. *MLAIB* and *ABELL* both index the journal.

American Studies International takes a broad, comparative approach in its coverage of early-twentieth-century writers and politics. The journal began in 1962 under the title *American Studies News* but ceased publication in 2005 and became part of the journal *American Studies*. It is not primarily a literature journal, but there may be some items of interest, especially as background or corollary material. For example, a recent article about black cultural identity in

Chicago from 1915 to 1947 may shed light on the writings of Richard Wright. The journal's website features the current table of contents and selected issues online. Indexing is provided by both *MLAIB* and *ABELL*.

The official journal of the British Association for American Studies, the *Journal of American Studies* espouses an interdisciplinary approach to American studies, with articles addressing links between film and literature and sociocultural approaches to literary study. A recent issue featured an article that compared the early works of Ernest Hemingway and Gertrude Stein. *MLAIB* and *ABELL* both index this journal. The website provides access to the current issue and offers content alerts.

Journal of Modern Literature addresses twentieth-century and contemporary literature with an international scope. Recent articles have included a comparative piece on the writings of Gertrude Stein and Laura Riding, an essay on the aspects of politics of William Carlos Williams, an article on Edith Wharton's use of epiphany and its connection to modernist themes, and an analysis of Zora Neale Hurston's ethnographic work. The journal's website does not offer any special services or information but, instead, basic subscription information. *Project MUSE* provides access to this journal from 1998 to the present. Indexing is done by both *MLAIB* and *ABELL*.

Modern Fiction Studies features a wide array of twentieth-century American literature, including new approaches and attention to new genres. Recent years' issues have provided good coverage of authors in relation to modernism and modernist themes, such as race relations and social conditions, as well as articles on Zora Neale Hurston, various Harlem Renaissance figures, and Jewish-American writers. The journal's website offers a table of contents and a complete, searchable index. *Project MUSE* provides access to issues from 1994 to the present, and both *MLAIB* and *ABELL* index the work.

MLN has been published for more than 120 years. The journal was originally called *Modern Language Notes* but has been known as *MLN* since 1962. It is strongly international in scope and publishes articles written in languages other than English. There is not much emphasis on American literature, but there are some articles of interest, such as a recent comparison of the Latin American avant-garde and the Harlem Renaissance. *MLN* is published five times per year, with four issues devoted specifically to Italian-, Spanish-, French-, and German-language literatures. The fifth issue is dedicated to comparative literature (called the "general issue" in earlier years) and includes most of the items that deal with American authors and that are of interest to American literature scholars. The website offers sample articles and an RSS feed. *JSTOR* provides access to issues from 1886 to 2001. Indexing is available in both *MLAIB* and *ABELL*.

Modern Language Quarterly offers fair coverage of Modernist-era literature. The journal focuses on literary change from the Middle Ages to the present and "welcomes theoretical reflections of literary change or historicism to feminism, ethnic studies, cultural materialism, discourse analysis, and all other forms of representation and cultural critique." Recent articles include comparisons of various authors to F. Scott Fitzgerald and studies of Langston Hughes and Gertrude Stein. Published quarterly, there are typically four to five articles per issue, along with book reviews. *Project MUSE* supplies access to issues from 1999 to 2004. *MLAIB* and *ABELL* both index this journal.

Modern Language Studies is published by the Northeast Modern Language Association (NEMLA), one of the regional chapters of the Modern Language Association. There are six regional MLA organizations across the country, and while they all host conferences and publish newsletters for their members, NEMLA publishes this major journal, which addresses all periods, genres, and national literatures and includes an average of eight to ten articles per issue. Examples of special topic issues are photography and literature and literature and science. A recent redesign organized the journal into three sections: critical essays, essays on pedagogy and the profession, and essays about "significant, intriguing or unusual" primary source materials. The journal originally appeared three or four times a year but seems to have settled into twice-yearly publication since 2000. *JSTOR* offers access to issues from 1971 to 2003. The journal is indexed in *MLAIB*.

The official journal of the Modern Literature Association, **Publications of the Modern Language Association**, began in 1884 with a few slight title variations during the first four years. Although it addresses American literature to some extent, *PMLA* is international in scope. The journal has six issues per year: four with typical content and two special issues, the annual directory for the organization and the program for the annual MLA conference. Special topic issues have addressed areas such as teaching literature, ethnicity, ethics and literary study, and globalization. In addition to critical essays, reports from MLA committees and other professional notes such as conference announcements and calls for papers are frequently published. Issues often feature a set of linked articles on a particular topic, drawn together in a forum. The website offers table of contents information, and *JSTOR* provides access to issues from 1884 to 2001. *MLAIB* and *ABELL* both index *PMLA*.

Resources for American Literary Study addresses American literature of all periods, from colonial to contemporary. The journal describes itself as "showcas[ing] enduring critical methods and lively research findings" and is well known for archival scholarship and bibliographical analysis. Originally published by the Pennsylvania State University Press, it moved to a commercial publisher in 2002. Previously a biannual, it is now an annual publication, with eight to ten essays per issue. Recent issues have featured articles on Eugene O'Neill and translations of his work into Portuguese, Willa Cather and her correspondence with a Norwegian author, and marine life in Ernest Hemingway's *The Old Man and the Sea. Project MUSE* supplies access to issues from 1999 to 2001. Indexing is done by both *MLAIB* and *ABELL*.

Sewanee Review is the longest continually published literary journal in the United States. Published by the University of the South since 1892, the journal appears quarterly and presents critical works along with fiction and poetry. The long duration of this source makes it a likely candidate for locating reviews or original short fiction or poetry published during the Modernist era. The journal often features articles about American writers from the Modernist era. A typical issue contains three to five essays or works of creative nonfiction, five to seven poems, four to six short stories, three to five essays specifically on topics related to reading and writing, four to six critical essays, and book reviews. Some issues are devoted to particular themes or genres as well. Upcoming special issues include a fiction-only issue, while others focus on war stories and travel narratives. This journal is accessible in *JSTOR* and *Project MUSE* after 2007. *MLAIB* and *ABELL* both index the journal.

Studies in 20th and 21st Century Literature, formerly known as *Studies in 20th Century Literature*, is published twice a year and is international in scope. Although it explores the years typically connected to modernism, the only recent articles related to American writers address multicultural or multilingual writers, such as Vladimir Nabokov and various Mexican-American authors. The journal's website offers a table of contents, and the journal is indexed in both *MLAIB* and *ABELL*.

Texas Studies in Literature and Language covers all periods of literature and embraces a wide range of critical and theoretical approaches. While not specifically focused on twentieth-century American literature, this is an important journal for a number of Modernist-era topics. There are four to eight articles per issue. The journal has been published quarterly by the University of Texas at Austin since 1959. Recent articles on modernism and Modernist-era authors feature F. Scott Fitzgerald, Willa Cather, Richard Wright, and Ernest Hemingway. The website offers table of contents information, and *Project MUSE* provides access for issues from 2001 to the present. *MLAIB* and *ABELL* index this journal.

Tulsa Studies in Women's Literature focuses on women's writing internationally and throughout history but does have some focus on Modernist-era writers such as Willa Cather, Rebecca West, and H. D. While feminist criticism is featured a good deal, it is not the only theoretical stance in view. The journal has been published twice a year by the University of Tulsa since 1982. *TSWL* includes a large number of book reviews in each issue, and there are occasional special issues or special sections or forums within issues. For example, a recent issue presented a forum entitled "Is There an Anglo-American Feminist Criticism?"

comprising brief essays from many major scholars. Also of note is an archives section that features articles about primary sources. A recent volume presented an article about Edith Wharton and a previously unpublished travel essay she wrote. Issues without a special section tend to have four to six articles. The website includes a table of contents and *JSTOR* access ranges from 1982 to 2001. Indexing is done by both *MLAIB* and *ABELL*.

Twentieth Century Literature provides solid coverage of American modernism, although it focuses a good deal on international and post–World War II literatures. Of interest to modernist scholars are recent articles on gender identity in Hemingway, racial identity in Nella Larsen, articles on modernism and Orientalism in Pound, analysis of Ralph Ellison, a comparative study of the image of the Lost Generation as portrayed in later works, and a comparative study of T. S. Eliot and H. G. Wells. The journal has been published quarterly by Hofstra University since 1955. Through the 1980s, issues featured three to five articles and a lengthy "current bibliography" section that traced current scholarship, including international literary criticism journals. In 1975, the journal began publishing special issues devoted to topics such as surrealism and to specific authors. This practice has continued, with recent special issues on American writers and France, literature and apocalypse, and Salman Rushdie. The special issues tend to offer more articles of shorter length than the regular issues. In the 1980s, the bibliography section was dropped, and the journal expanded the number of articles per issue, typically ranging from five to nine. The journal's website presents information about subscriptions but no other special information or services. *JSTOR* supplies access to issues from 1955 to 2003. Indexing is available in both *MLAIB* and *ABELL*.

Conclusion

This chapter provides an overview of key scholarly journals to help make researchers familiar with these resources. This information also introduces the scope and coverage of the journals.

While you may want to peruse these journals to become familiar with trends, you should also use *MLAIB* and *ABELL* to obtain complete lists of pertinent articles about various topics or authors. Some journals publish on a wide array of topics, and an article about a given author or subject may appear in a journal you would not usually consider.

New research and scholarship often appear first in journals, before book-length studies are published. To fully understand new trends in theoretical stances and to keep up to date on the development of issues or the critical reception of authors, you should periodically review the scholarly journals in your field. Sources discussed in chapter 4, such as annual reviews, will also be helpful in scanning the scholarly literature in the field. Becoming aware of the trends and directions in scholarly writing will assist in developing your own research agenda.

Notes

1. Edward E. Chielens, *The Literary Journal in America, 1900–1950* (Detroit: Gale, 1977).

2. *American Periodicals*, initiated in 1990 and published by The Ohio State University Press, is the official journal of the Research Society for American Periodicals.

3. "*Faulkner Newsletter* & *Yoknapatawpha Review* ceases publication after 20 years." Mississippi Writers Page. March 20, 2002. Available at http://www.olemiss.edu/mwp/news/2002/2002_03_20_faulknernewsletterceases.html (accessed 15 May 2007).

CHAPTER 6

Contemporary Reviews

The modern book review and literary criticism parallel the rise of English literature as a distinct academic discipline in American universities in the early period of the twentieth century. As one observer commenting on the American literary scene at the turn of the century through the 1920s remarked, "We have expressed ourselves in a literary criticism probably less perfunctory, more fresh and alert, more energetic and abundant, than that of any previous epoch in our three centuries of history."[1] In line with commercial pressures, a publication's editorial philosophy, and the biases of the book reviewer, literary criticism was seen by mid-century as a problematic hybrid of craft, abstract system, and hucksterism:

> In one direction literary criticism is bounded by reviewing, in the other by aesthetics. The reviewer, more or less, is interested in books as commodities; the critic, in books as literature or, in modern terms, as literary action or behavior; the aesthetician in literature in the abstract, not in specific books at all.[2]

In retrospect, this taxonomy is too artificial and schematic to fully account for the complexity of literary reception or literary production during the period of American modernism, but its ambivalent note was not uncommon and persisted well into the 1940s and 1950s.[3] In a historical overview of literary criticism, René Wellek rehearses this functional typology of book reviewing from a nineteenth-century perspective: the book critic, he observes, might function as a judge, a showman, or a scientific analyst, according to whether the critical act is rooted in historical principles, the sensibility of the reviewer, or the historical evolution of literary types.[4]

A major tension emerged on the American cultural scene in the first half of the twentieth century between academic literary critics, with their specialized journals and scholarly monographs, and highly influential writers and literary editors like H. L. Mencken and Edmund Wilson, who promoted literary modernism in literary periodicals and popular books. (The ambiguous connections between book reviewing and academic literary criticism can also be seen in the library subject cataloging associated with both forms of writing. See examples and discussion below.) As a cultural impresario, Ezra Pound promoted modernist writing in a variety of ways, but his role was both singular and pervasive, particularly in the early period of the twentieth century. Another tension emerged from the impact of consumer capitalism in American life. Many people read for entertainment and diversion, while the modernist publisher, editor, and author of vanguard literary texts tried to establish and promote new literary norms and foster a new readership. The cultural divide between private consumption, in which people began to define themselves in terms of commodities, and the desire to participate in a marginalized public sphere characterized by cultural acquisitiveness, suggests to some commentators a peculiarly modern crisis. In the end, the cultural dilettante and the literary mandarin from an earlier era in American culture were displaced by academic specialists and highly accomplished literary journalists whose growing audiences were becoming self-reflective consumers of classic and modernist literature. Genteel promotional schemes such as Charles Eliot's "Five-Foot Shelf of Books" (1923), Harry Scherman's Book-of-the-Month Club (1926), and Samuel Craig and Harold Guinzburg's The Literary Guild of America (1926) were symptomatic of those attempts by cultural mediators of the era to influence and profit from the book-reading public's aspirations to middle-class respectability.[5] Many publishing houses, meanwhile, pitched books through advertising campaigns, modernist dust jacket designs, and enticing blurbs. Keep in mind that book reviews of modernist American authors from 1914 to 1949 might appear in any of the period's popular, middlebrow, or highbrow periodicals. The literary reception of a work or author can partly be measured through contemporary reviews or the publication of specialized anthologies, some of which point to the eventual canonization of a particular text, author, or literary movement. Consult the section on "little magazines" in chapter 7 for the book reviews available in those periodicals.

No single reference source or periodical index offers complete coverage of contemporary reviews of American modernist writing as a whole. This limitation reflects in part the realities of particular publishing arrangements, older indexing practices, and the ephemeral nature of certain niche periodicals and magazines from that era. Unavoidable gaps and inconsistencies associated with retrospective periodicals indexing are also a hindrance, especially when this involves obscure writers or ephemeral texts. Hence, the reference sources described in this chapter should be consulted as a group to locate a wide range of bibliographic citations to literary and theatrical reviews. Various monograph series that reprint contemporary book reviews are discussed below and should be consulted for those American modernist writers who appear in these series to date. Particular reviews discussed in this chapter might be available in different formats, and increasingly so in full-text digital versions through commercial online information providers as licensing agreements and retrospective conversion projects make more copyrighted and public domain literary material available to scholars and researchers. In addition, these review sources frequently overlap in coverage. At a minimum, photocopies of criticism and reviews should be obtainable through your library's interlibrary loan department or other document delivery services if they are otherwise unavailable. JSTOR, for example, with its advanced search option to limit retrieval sets, is a convenient archive of contemporary book reviews of American modernist literature.

Contemporary Reviews from Periodicals

Annual Bibliography of English Language and Literature (ABELL). London: Modern Humanities Research Association, 1921–. Information on print and online versions of ABELL is available at http://www.mhra.org.uk/Publications/Journals/abell.html.

American Periodicals Series Online, 1740–1900. Ann Arbor, MI: ProQuest Information and Learning Company, 2000–. Available at www.proquest.com/products_pq/descriptions/aps.shtml.

Book Review Digest. New York: H. W. Wilson, 1905–. Online version from WilsonWeb as *Book Review Digest Retrospective: 1905–1982* at www.hwwilson.com/Databases/brdig.htm.

Farber, Evan Ira, Susan Hannah, and Stanley Schindler, eds. *Combined Retrospective Index to Book Reviews in Humanities Journals, 1802–1974*. 10 vols. Woodbridge, CT: Research Publications, Inc., 1982.

Johnson, Robert Owen. *An Index to Literature in the New Yorker, 1925–1940*. Metuchen, NJ: The Scarecrow Press, Inc., 1969.

———. *An Index to Literature in the New Yorker, 1940–1955*. Metuchen, NJ: The Scarecrow Press, Inc., 1970.

Leary, Lewis. *Articles on American Literature 1900–1950*. Durham, NC: Duke University Press, 1954.

Literary Writings in America: A Bibliography. 10 vols. New York: KTO Press, 1977.

National Library Service Cumulative Book Review Index, 1905–1974. 6 vols. Princeton, NJ: National Library Service, 1975.

New York Times Book Review Index 1896–1970. 5 vols. New York: Arno Press, 1973.

The New York Times Directory of the Theater. New York: Arno Press, 1973.

ProQuest Historical Newspapers. Ann Arbor, MI: ProQuest Information and Learning Company, n.d. Available at www.proquest.com/products_pq/descriptions/pq-hist-news.shtml.

Twentieth-Century Literary Criticism. Detroit, MI: Thomson-Gale, 1978–.

The Times Literary Supplement Index 1902–1939. 2 vols. Reading, England: Newspaper Archive Developments Ltd., 1978.

TLS: Times Literary Supplement Centenary Archive 1902–1990. Woodbridge, CT: Primary Source Media/Gale Group and Times Supplements Ltd. Pub., 1999–. Information about the subscription archival database is available at http://www.tls.psmedia.com/.

The ***Annual Bibliography of English Language and Literature*** (***ABELL***) is the British version of the *MLAIB* but includes bibliographic citations of book reviews, searchable in the online version by choosing "reviews" as a document type in the query interface. *ABELL* began as a printed publication under the title *Bibliography of English Language and Literature* in 1921, with coverage of material that appeared in 1920. With the 1923 edition, the title changed to *Annual Bibliography of English Language and Literature.* Early printed volumes of *ABELL* note book reviews of American modernist writers under the headings "Twentieth Century," "Literary Criticism, General," and "Literary Criticism and Appreciation." A principal author index was added with the 1922 issue, linking writers to numbered entries in the bibliography. Book review citations are recorded under the principal author/title entry. Researchers should consult the section on journal abbreviations provided in the front matter of *ABELL* to clarify the titles used in book review citations. Although cumulative coverage of twentieth-century American literature is among its classified sections, the range of book reviews in *ABELL* depends on which periodicals were indexed at any given time. The commercially licensed online version is also available on CD-ROM from Chadwyck-Healey for the years 1920–2003. Beginning with early printed issues from the 1920s, the electronic editions of *ABELL* and *MLAIB* provide enhanced retrospective indexing that permits multiple search options, though as previously noted, *MLAIB* does not include book reviews. As part of *Literature Online*, citations in the *ABELL* database are linked to digitized full-text documents when these are available.

Although its scope appears to fall outside the period of American modernist literature, ProQuest's commercially available ***American Periodicals Series Online, 1740–1900*** (***APS Online***) offers access to full-text, digitized book reviews that appeared in journals and popular magazines that began publication between 1740 and 1900, with content coverage extending to the period of World War II. Based on the *American Periodicals Series* microform collection, 1,100 periodicals in a variety of subjects are indexed, and the online search interface allows limiting to "reviews" as a document type; keyword searching by title of literary work and its author will produce fairly precise results for book reviews on American modernist writing. Citations come with a review abstract. ProQuest reports that it holds 7 million pages of digitized content in *APS Online*. Some of the periodicals containing book reviews of American modernist literature are *The Dial: A Semi-Monthly Journal of Literary Criticism, Discussion, and Information*; *Forum*; *The Bookman: A Review of Books and Life*; *Forum and Century*; *The North American Review*; *The Independent*; and *Life* (1883–1936).

The ten-volume ***Combined Retrospective Index to Book Reviews in Humanities Journals, 1802–1974*** offers convenient access to 500,000 book review citations on titles published during this period in more than 150 humanities journals. Volumes are organized in alphabetical ranges by the reviewed authors' last names; thus, volume 1 consists of "A–Bohme." Each principal author entry lists the works under review in alphabetical order, and under each title, review citations are alphabetically arranged by journal title. Where available, the reviewer's name is noted in the citation. Two separate index volumes list book titles in alphabetical order, with cross-references to principal authors' names. An alphabetical journal code list provides journal abbreviations used in citations, including the full name of the journal, year(s) of publication, publisher and place of publication, and the ISSN, when available. After identifying an author, the American modernism scholar may consult this source to find contemporary reviews in the periodicals indexed in it. Though most of these are academic journals, the set also covers literary magazines from the period.

Two volumes from Robert Owen Johnson's ***An Index to Literature in the New Yorker*** for the period 1925–1955 offer convenient access to literature that was originally published in the *New Yorker* as well as book and theatrical reviews. Both volumes are similarly arranged. Part 1 is an alphabetical listing of titles of original material and bibliographical citations; part 2 consists of book and theatrical reviews prefaced by a list of the reviewers. All entries are numbered. Perhaps the easiest way to use these tools is through the personal name index, which gives entry number citations to review material of a principal author or by a particular reviewer.

Another useful guide to contemporary book reviews of American modernist writing is Lewis Leary's ***Articles on American Literature 1900–1950***, part of a series that indexes book reviews and review articles based on various contemporary bibliographical listings of American literature. The first section lists principal authors alphabetically by last name, with the review citations arranged under each author entry by last name of the reviewer. Users should consult the list of abbreviations used in citations to ensure full understanding of the bibliographical information provided throughout the book. Another benefit of this bibliographic guide is that it provides reviews of American theater published from 1900 to 1950. Other sections cover reviews on various subjects and aspects of American culture also published during this period, such as printing, regionalism, religion, and newspapers and periodicals. Similar to the *Combined Retrospective* index described above, this book review resource indexes more than American modernist writers, so researchers should identify a particular author to locate specific review citations on them and then locate the published review text in the cited journal or in other formats.

The *New York Times Directory of the Theater* supplies synoptic coverage of American theater primarily for the period 1920–1970, as viewed by critics and writers at the *New York Times*. A section with a chronological list of major literary awards is followed by a section of the *Times*' coverage of the Pulitzer Prize and Nobel awards for the period 1920–1972 that offers related theatrical notices as they appeared in those articles in the paper. A play title index provides alphabetized access to 21,000 entries of the *Times*' theatrical reviews from 1920 to 1970. The separate personal name index is taken from these reviews and notes performers, producers, directors, playwrights, and others mentioned there. Citations are by year, month, section of newspaper, day, page, and column, with multiple citations in entries arranged in chronological order. This citation information in the *New York Times Directory of Theatre* is invaluable for those with access to the retrospective run of the *New York Times* on microfilm or in full-text digital versions of the *Times*, including the recently released *TimesSelect* edition. Another option for those with access is the ten-volume set of *New York Times Theatre Reviews, 1870–1941*. For the period 1920–1941, this set reprints the *Times*' articles on American theater that are indexed in the *Times Directory*.

The five-volume *New York Times Book Review Index 1869–1970* offers the researcher multiple access points to "a monumental archive of modern literature—the annals of creative writing as set down in contemporaneous reportage and criticism" (Introduction). The volume contents are: 1, principal author index; 2, title index; 3, byline index; 4, subject index; and 5, category index. To understand bibliographical citations and volume arrangement, users should consult the key to abbreviations and explanatory material prefacing each volume. For scholars of American modernist writing, volume 1 offers the quickest access to the *New York Times*' reportage and critical writing on American modernists, conveniently arranging book reviews under each principal author entry alphabetically by the title of book or work under review. With these citations, scholars can obtain the full-text review material in multiple formats. The *New York Times* licenses its full-text digital content and indexes to various online information providers; a reference librarian can assist in determining what is available in your library. ProQuest's commercially available *Historical New York Times* (1851–2003) provides retrospective full-text coverage of its contents with an online search interface that features "Review" as a document type limiter. Book reviews of American modernist works can be easily accessed in this resource by performing a title search coupled with the "review" document type; additional search options in the interface allow the researcher to customize lists. Full-text book reviews of American modernist writing are also available from the other digitized newspaper archives currently offered in ProQuest's **Historical Newspapers** set, such as *The Chicago Tribune* (1849–), *The Los Angeles Times* (1881–1984), and *The Washington Post* (1877–1987).

The ten-volume set *Literary Writings in America: A Bibliography* resulted from a WPA research project begun at the University of Pennsylvania in 1938. The intended purpose of the bibliography was to provide researchers with a list of American literature published between 1850 and 1940. The resulting alphabetical arrangement by author across ten volumes consists of reduced, photo-offset reproductions of 250,000 library card catalog records, some of which appear faint. The source material used in this project was based on "over 2,000 volumes of magazines, more than 500 volumes of literary history and criticism, and more than 100 bibliographies" (vii). Volume 1 in the set lists all the periodicals and abbreviations used for the compilation. Each catalog citation indicates literary genre and occasional content notes; where available, these records also provide an abbreviated citation to a literary review for the item cited in a given record.

Book Review Digest (**BRD**) is a handy, though limited, source for general reviews of American modernist literature. Entries in annual volumes are arranged alphabetically by author with review excerpts and bibliographical citations listed beneath each reviewed title, along with the approximate length of each book review. The notices excerpted from the reviews from the year of a book's original publication offer contemporaneous information about its reception prior to its subsequent canonization by the academic and cultural establishment. Thus, the notice from the 1923 edition of *BRD* taken from the *Literary Review of the New York Evening Post* on T. S. Eliot's *The Waste Land* begins, "If this is a trick, it is an inspired one." Each volume of *BRD* lists periodicals indexed and the abbreviations used for them in the citations. Though it is a general review index of fiction and nonfiction, the *Book Review Digest Author/Title Index 1905–1974*, edited by Leslie Dunmore-Leiber, offers convenient access to reviews of specific literary works and authors from the Modernist period. Finally, H. W. Wilson has made the retrospective contents of *BRD* available in the online database **Book Review Digest Retrospective: 1905–1982**. With coverage of 300,000 books and 1.5 million book reviews, the source material for the online *BRD* consists of 500 English-language magazines, newspapers, and academic journals.

The six-volume **National Library Service Cumulative Book Review Index, 1905–1974** offers bibliographic citations to books reviewed in *Saturday Review* (1924–1974), *Library Journal* (1907–1974), *Book Review Digest* (1905–1974), and *Choice* (1964–1974). Volumes 1–3 consist of principal authors arranged in alphabetical order, and volumes 3–6 arrange principal works in alphabetical order by title. In both cases, bibliographical citations to book reviews follow main entries.

Gale's multivolume set *Twentieth-Century Literary Criticism* (*TCLC*) (numbering 181 volumes as of 2006) "has covered more than 1,000 authors, representing over 120 nationalities and over 40,000 titles" (vol. 181, vii). The scope of *TCLC* was expanded after the 1999 edition to include authors who lived or died between 1900 and 1999. Articles on principal authors feature a section of reprinted review excerpts and criticism from contemporaneous and later publications, arranged in chronological order to suggest changes in the reception of an author's work. *TCLC* entries note birth and death dates, a list of principal publications, a bibliography of secondary readings, and full bibliographic citations to material previously published elsewhere. Each volume contains a title index for the main literary titles referenced in that volume. When authors appear in multiple *TCLC* volumes, the latest entry cross-indexes the earlier material in *TCLC* or to entries in other Gale literary reference sets. Volumes contain cumulative name, topic, and nationality indexes, with the most recently published volume providing retrospective indexing and cross-referencing to the entire *TCLC* series. In this vein, the Cumulative Topic Index in volume 181 of *TCLC* is worth examining. Researchers in American modernism might want to consult *Topics Volume 70* in *TCLC* (1997), which has a chapter on "Modernism" (pp. 165–277), including bibliographical references, or *Topics Volume 74* (1998) with a chapter on the history of *The American Mercury* magazine (pp. 1–80). References in *TCLC 74* provide an alphabetical list of obscure writers who appeared in *The American Mercury* from January 1924 to December 1933 as well as a list of reviews authored by its founding co-editor, H. L. Mencken. Useful short histories of American modernist publishers are available in *American Literary Publishing Houses, 1900–1980: Trade and Paperback*, volume 46, of Gale's *Dictionary of Literary Biography* series. Gale's free online *Literary Index* (http:www.galenet .com/servlet/LitIndex) conveniently provides citations to articles in the full array of Gale's published literature series through separate author, title, and custom searches, the latter permitting queries by name, birth and death dates, or nationality. This tool gives access to specific literary works and authors wherever they appear in Gale's published literature sets. Though in the process of expanding, Gale made full-text online access to articles in certain sets available only through the commercially licensed *Literature Resource Center*.

The two-volume printed retrospective *The Times Literary Supplement Index 1902–1939* (*TLS*) consists of volume I, A–K, and volume II, L–Z. The index provides access to 350,000 references to letters, reviews, leading articles, and articles that appeared in the *TLS*, which began as a self-standing publication shortly before World War I. The scope is broad: "The [cumulative] *TLS* represents an unrivalled record of literary activity and critical opinion during the past seventy-five years, a record which frequently has to be consulted by scholars, librarians, bibliographers, writers engaged on research in many different fields" (iii). The index features an alphabetical arrangement of personal names of principal authors; title entries of books, poems, journals, newspapers, and periodicals (and their authors); and subject entries. Citations are given as page number and year separated by a colon. With pages of the annual, bound issues of the *TLS* numbered consecutively for the entire year, finding a particular review is relatively easy; also, the *TLS* index has a yearly chart showing publication dates correlated to page numbers in issues. Under principal author entries, citations are alphabetically arranged by title of work under review; in the printed version of the *TLS* index, the reviewer's name is left anonymous. The scholar will find useful review material on American modernists in the *TLS*. For example, the review in the November 1, 1934, issue of the *TLS* of Pound's essay collection *Make it New* observes that "It must be admitted that Mr. Pound has serious faults. To begin with, his style can be atrocious" (751). The subscription online version **TLS: Times Literary Supplement Centenary Archive 1902–1990** has identified many of the formerly anonymous reviewers from the early years of this periodical. In addition to this enhancement, the electronic *TLS* index is searchable by article or book review title, principal author, subject, publisher, and kind of publication (book review, lead article, etc.), with additional biographical information available on selected *TLS* contributors in the archive version.

The ***Readers' Guide to Periodical Literature*** is significant since it is a relatively old index of popular magazines and journals and, as such, contains plenty of information on a variety of subjects. Although this guide may be consulted under specific author entries to locate publications by that author in contemporary periodicals, *Readers' Guide* is spotty through the Modernist period in terms of book review coverage. It may be consulted to locate some book reviews, but even using the online version of *Readers' Guide Retrospective* is not likely to turn up review material unique to these resources. The eccentric ***A Guide to Book Review Citations: A Bibliography of Sources*** by Richard A. Gray (1968) is designed to direct researchers to bibliographies and indexes where substantial book review citations are recorded. Numbered, annotated entries reflect the author's ad hoc topical arrangement for listing index sources. However, the eccentricities of this guide might be its strength; the subject index entries under "American Literature" describe certain items that may provide access to review material overlooked in more prominent indexing resources.

Author-Specific Bibliographies and Book Review Monographs

Bryer, Jackson R., ed. *F. Scott Fitzgerald: The Critical Reception*. New York: Burt Franklin & Co., Inc., 1978.

Dace, Tish, ed. *Langston Hughes: The Contemporary Reviews*. New York: Cambridge University Press, 1997.

Gallup, Donald. *Ezra Pound: A Bibliography*. Revised ed. Charlottesville, VA: Bibliographical Society of the University of Virginia and St. Paul's Bibliographies, 1983.

Martin, Mildred. *A Half-Century of Eliot Criticism: An Annotated Bibliography of Books and Articles in English, 1916–1965*. Lewisburg, PA: Bucknell University Press, 1972.

O'Connor, Margaret Anne, ed. *Willa Cather: The Contemporary Reviews*. New York: Cambridge University Press, 2001.

Ricks, Beatrice. *T. S. Eliot: A Bibliography of Secondary Works*. Metuchen, NJ: The Scarecrow Press, Inc., 1980.

———. *William Faulkner: A Bibliography of Secondary Works*. Metuchen, NJ: The Scarecrow Press, Inc., 1981.

———. *Ezra Pound: A Bibliography of Secondary Works*. Metuchen, NJ: The Scarecrow Press, Inc., 1986.

The traditional printed bibliography remains a significant aid in all areas of research, but getting the most out of these important reference tools in a literary context requires a brief discussion to clarify basic differences among the bibliographies discussed here. For a more detailed discussion of the history and different branches of bibliography and bibliographic procedures, please refer to titles listed in the appendix in the section "Bibliography and Research Guides."

Library of Congress (LC) subject headings for some of the authors listed above are:

Eliot, Thomas Stearns, 1888–1965—Bibliography
Faulkner, William, 1897–1962—Bibliography
Pound, Ezra, 1885–1972—Bibliography
Hughes, Langston, 1902–1967—Bibliography
Hurston, Zora Neale—Bibliography

Although library catalogs employ such standardized subject headings to roughly describe and collocate a large number of heterogeneous items in their collections, here they provide summary descriptions of different kinds of literary bibliographies. The primary distinction is between bibliographic guides to those works produced *by* a principal author (primary sources) and guides to secondary works *about* a principal author (secondary sources). Both collect information in a convenient location—usually in a book, periodical, or article. Some guides describe both primary and secondary material. In addition, the arrangement of content and the level of descriptive detail vary among bibliographies; some, for example, are annotated or exhibit some form of classification. Bibliographers usually describe the arrangement, scope, and criteria used in compiling bibliographies in the volume's introduction or preface. This is very useful information since it tells the scholar how best to use a specialized guide for research needs, especially in cases where the bibliographical guide exhibits a classified arrangement, provides technical details, or employs specialized terminology and symbols. Many bibliographers will indicate whether they have examined the material they describe in their bibliographic entries. Although bibliographers rarely use the words "definitive" or "complete" to describe their work, many years of conscientious labor can go into the production of a reliable bibliography, and it remains valid for many research projects even if in retrospect it falls short of the unattainable desiderata of completeness, total accuracy, or exhaustiveness. The lament of a prominent literary scholar is all too true: "It is the fate of every bibliographer to produce a work that includes errors and is outdated before the last sheet of the final draft cranks out of the computer printer."[6]

The approximate accuracy of Library of Congress subject headings is further complicated in this context because of the imprecision and inconsistency involved in how certain headings and groups of subject headings are assigned to specific books or monographic series. Thus, in addition to the Library of Congress subject headings noted above, scholars should *always* consult the following form of an author-specific subject heading (obviously varying with the author) to find monographs that might contain information on contemporary book reviews:

Cather, Willa, 1873–1947—Criticism and interpretation

Even though Cambridge's *American Critical Archives* and Burt Franklin & Co.'s *The American Critical Tradition* series collect and either reprint, excerpt, summarize, or list contemporary book reviews, most of the titles so far issued in these and similar literary sets (including those for twentieth-century authors) have been cataloged *without* any of the following Library of Congress subject headings in their bibliographic records:

American literature—20th century—Book reviews
Criticism—United States
American literature—History and criticism
Books—Reviews
American fiction—Book reviews

The same is true for titles in *The Critical Heritage Series*, currently issued by Routledge and previously by Routledge & Kegan Paul; the *Helm Information*

Critical Assessments of Writers in English Series, which appears irregularly; and the Chelsea House series *Modern Critical Views*, with various spin-offs under the editorship of Harold Bloom.[7] The Willa Cather example noted above is the *only* form of subject cataloging that appears in all the titles thus far issued in these specialized monographic series. However, since the subheading "criticism and interpretation" covers a wide range of scholarly forms and approaches, a library catalog search under the full subject string (with the author) can result in a long list of titles, making it difficult to find a particular kind of research guide such as one devoted exclusively to book reviews or criticism on a particular work. In catalog notes called "analytics," an item's contents are briefly described in more detail, but this doesn't guarantee that a typical online library catalog search will efficiently retrieve what is needed, even using a "keyword" search. More so than the other bibliographies discussed in this section, some of the titles in these specialized series offer nearly exhaustive coverage of contemporary book reviews, including notices in obscure or small publications that are often overlooked in more general secondary reference sources. As such, these particular reference tools constitute what M. Thomas Inge aptly calls "a literary chronicle"; volume notes indicate that many of the book reviews cited or reprinted in these monographs were found in the clippings files of an author's archival collection. Titles in the Cambridge *American Critical Archives* series are issued irregularly.[8] The *Critical Responses in Arts and Letters* monograph series issued by Greenwood Press offers a selection of contemporary book reviews and literary criticism of twentieth-century American authors and literary works. Similar to the library cataloging issues discussed above, the titles in this series also contain the author-specific form of subject cataloging (like the Willa Cather example). Presenting yet another variation is the G. K. Hall series *Critical Essays on American Literature*, which reprints contemporary book reviews, literary criticism and articles, original essays, and introductory chapters on the critical reception of American writers.

Jackson Bryer's **F. Scott Fitzgerald: The Critical Reception** is a volume in the short-lived *American Critical Tradition* series from Burt Franklin & Co. The introduction has contextual notes and a synoptic publication history for Fitzgerald works and summarizes trends in reception among the reviewers and critics. Prominent reviews are also discussed. Contents are arranged in chronological order according to dates of original publication, with each section prefaced by a facsimile reproduction of the title page. Where possible, each book review contains full bibliographic information, including the review's author and title, periodical title, date published, section or part, and page number. Each section has a checklist of additional reviews arranged in chronological order. An index allows the researcher to cross-reference particular publications and reviewers in the context of Fitzgerald's literary output.

Comprehensive in scope and rigorous in presentation, Tish Dace's *Langston Hughes: The Contemporary Reviews* from the Cambridge *American Critical Archives* series is a model of its kind. The chronological volume arrangement is similar to the Bryer title discussed above, without the presence of facsimile title pages. Dace collected and edited book reviews for twenty-eight works by Hughes, dating from 1926 to 1967; an appendix notes limited-edition poetry pamphlets by Hughes as well as reviews of books that he either edited or translated. Especially important for Langston Hughes scholars is the range of critical notices reprinted from the African-American press, the insightful and informative introduction to the contemporary reception of Hughes' work, and the extensive indexing of reviewers and periodicals. In addition to collecting reviews from major literary periodicals, Margaret Anne O'Conner's volume in the Cambridge series *Willa Cather: The Contemporary Reviews* offers a representative sampling of the regional newspaper reception of Cather's work from *April Twilights* (1903) to *The Old Beauty and Others* (1948). Collectively, these book reviews chart the emergence of a major literary talent and Pulitzer Prize winner. Volume format and arrangement follow the standards set for this series.

Donald Gallup's *Ezra Pound: A Bibliography* is a fine example of a comprehensive descriptive bibliography of primarily literary works by Ezra Pound that appeared in a variety of publications over the course of his lifetime. With detailed descriptive entries arranged under five broad textual headings, this bibliography offers what is probably a complete overview of Pound's published literary output in addition to ancillary works in different media or related projects authored by Pound but never published. Historical notes and publishing information accompany each bibliographical entry, adding important details about textual variants occurring in individual publications. The value of such a bibliography for literary research cannot be overestimated. With this tool, the scholar can be fairly certain that he or she has access to all of Pound's published literary texts or related projects, however obscure or ephemeral, wherever they appeared. Moreover, the comprehensive index coherently links all of the classified bibliographic entries, adding to the guide's research value by suggesting patterns and possibilities for research on Pound's writing that might not be readily apparent from a perusal of the classified sections of the bibliography.

As its title indicates, Beatrice Ricks' *Ezra Pound: A Bibliography of Secondary Works* provides access to a wide range of material about Ezra Pound that appeared in books and periodicals, from an early critical notice in English 1914 through the early 1980s. In terms of books reviews and other interpretive writing, this classified bibliography provides convenient access to a wealth of secondary material about Ezra Pound, including early book reviews from the teens, 1920s, and beyond. An alphabetical list of abbreviations and publications is supplemented with separate critic and topical indexes that enhance the usefulness of this tool. Within classified sections, numbered bibliographic citations are arranged alphabetically by author. Ricks follows the same approach and procedures in her bibliographies of William Faulkner and T. S. Eliot, listed above.

Mildred Martin's *A Half-Century of Eliot Criticism: An Annotated Bibliography of Books and Articles in English, 1916–1965* represents a sophisticated presentation of secondary criticism and reviews of T. S. Eliot. In addition to providing evaluative annotations and review excerpts with her bibliographic citations, Martin's bibliography has the advantage of presenting the numbered citations in chronological order, with critics and reviewers arranged alphabetically under each year. An alphabetical list of cited journals and newspapers is supplemented by an appendix of citations to peripheral material, also arranged chronologically. A real strength of this bibliography is the separate author, subject, and periodicals indexes. By drawing together scattered citations under these index headings, the researcher can discover specific patterns and relationships that might otherwise remain hidden. Scholars may also conveniently locate various articles by the same writer, determine how many reviews appeared in particular publications during this period, or concentrate research on particular topical areas in Eliot criticism.

Conclusion

As budgets in higher education shrink or stagnate, and with a finite amount of physical space in which to house printed collections, some research libraries have opted to spend part of their budget on electronic access to digitized full-text versions of scholarly content, particularly on digitized back files of older serials, newspapers, and periodical indexes. The online versions of these reference tools are usually updated in a timely manner to maintain currency. In addition to making archive material available on CD-ROM, some owners of scholarly content license retrospective electronic versions of their material to different online information services that allow for remote access by multiple users; as with the *New Yorker* magazine, for, example, its entire retrospective full-text digital content may be purchased on CD-ROM and DVD-ROM or on a portable computer hard drive that can be periodically updated. A reference librarian can help determine which formats are available in the library, and interlibrary loans are always an option. Locating information through different online search interfaces requires practice, but learning their basic and advanced capabilities and "controlled vocabularies" is well worth the effort, especially in formulating effective research queries. Despite the current transformations in scholarly communication and research, traditional print reference resources such as literary bibliographies and periodical indexes are still very useful reference tools. Thus, the various book review monograph series discussed in this chapter provide scholars with an invaluable source of reprinted contemporaneous material (both excerpts and entire reviews) for research in American modernist writing, even in contexts where other library resources might be unavailable. A holdings list of these specialized monographs may be easily retrieved in electronic library catalogs that allow title searches by a series title. A Boolean keyword search combining a series title and a primary author's last name is a convenient way to check availability of a specific book review monograph in your library; if it is not available, a *World-Cat* search can help determine if it may be obtained through interlibrary loan.

Notes

1. Norman Foerster, *American Criticism: A Study of Literary Theory from Poe to the Present* (New York: Russell & Russell, Inc., 1928, rprt. 1962), vii.

2. Stanley Edgar Hayman, *The Armed Vision: A Study in the Methods of Modern Literary Criticism* (New York: Vintage, 1955), 9.

3. See, for example, Robert Avrett, "Waning Art of Book Reviewing," *South Atlantic Bulletin* 14, no. 4 (March 1949): 1, 8–9, and Geoffrey Wagner, "The Decline of Book Reviewing," *The American Scholar* 26, no. 1 (Winter 1956–1957): 23–36. For a scholarly overview of literary modernism and criticism, see *Modernism and the New Criticism*, ed. A. Walton Litz, Louis Menand, and Lawrence Rainey (New York: Cambridge University Press, 2000), vol. 7 in *The Cambridge History of Literary Criticism*, and *Modern American Critics, 1920–1955* (Detroit, MI: Gale Research Company, 1988), ed. Gregory S. Jay, vol. 63 in the *Dictionary of Literary Biography*.

4. René Wellek, "Criticism, Literary," in *Dictionary of the History of Ideas*, vol. 1, ed. Philip P. Weiner (New York: Charles Scribner's Sons, 1973), 601.

5. Gary Cross, *An All-Consuming Century: Why Commercialism Won in Modern America* (New York: Columbia University Press, 2000), 120.

6. James L. Harner, *Literary Research Guide: An Annotated Listing of Reference Sources in English Literary Studies*, 4th ed. (New York: The Modern Language Association of America, 2002), 4.

7. So far, the only twentieth-century American writer to appear in the *Helm Information Series* is William Faulkner, in four volumes. Thus far, the *Critical Heritage Series* contains Dos Passos, Hemingway, Henry James, Eliot, Wallace Stevens, Pound, William Carlos Williams, Nabokov, and Sylvia Plath. From the period of American modernist writing, the *Critical Responses in Arts and Letters* series lists Tom Wolfe, Eugene O'Neill, Eudora Welty, Richard Wright, Gertrude Stein, and Ralph Ellison, among others.

8. Additional twentieth-century American authors whose collected contemporary book reviews are currently available in Cambridge's *American Critical Archives* series are John Steinbeck, T. S. Eliot, Ellen Glasgow, Eudora Welty, William Faulkner, and Edith

Wharton. Henry James is in the series, but his work spans the nineteenth and twentieth centuries. Additional twentieth-century authors in the Burt Franklin *American Critical Tradition* series are Richard Wright, Ernest Hemingway, Theodore Dreiser, Thomas Wolfe, Robert Frost, and E. E. Cummings. Both series include nineteenth-century American authors.

CHAPTER 7

Newspapers, Periodicals, and Microforms

Newspapers in the 1920s attained wider circulation in American households than at any other time in the twentieth century. Metropolitan newspapers, tabloids, and ethnic newspapers shaped the chaos and experience of urban life for millions of readers. Elements of the sensationalist, scandal-mongering yellow journalism of the late nineteenth century persisted alongside the crusading, social-reform journalism in the immediate aftermath of World War I. Garish crime stories occupied the page along with muckraking denunciations of the status quo; world, national, and local politics were also a staple. Increased literacy rates and millions of new immigrants meant a huge readership for the most varied newspaper content. With higher wages and newly enacted labor regulations, working people had more leisure to devote to cultural pursuits, including newspaper reading. The mainstream newspaper mirrored the social milieu of the emerging American *nouveau riche*, chronicling its antics and excesses. Audience-specific newspapers covered stories of interest to its communities, providing access to the sociological mélange characteristic of the period associated with modernist literature. These illustrated papers were affordable at pennies per copy because newspaper production and distribution benefited from economies of scale and lower postal rates.[1]

While advertising drove the sale of newspapers and mainstream periodicals by the 1920s, local authorities and the federal government attempted to curtail the production and distribution of modernist newspapers like the *Masses*, the *Liberator*, and the *New Masses* on the grounds that they were obscene, politically suspect, or socially degenerate. The pressure to cater to both readers and advertisers during the emergence of consumer capitalism, coupled with governmental surveillance and interference, fundamentally altered the business and marketing of periodicals during this period in American history. Some literary monthlies were exempt from overt political surveillance but were nevertheless harassed on moral grounds. (For instance, H. L. Mencken and George Jean Nathan, the editors of *Smart Set* (1900–1924), were cleared in court of charges related to questionable content in their publishing venture *The American Mercury*.) Progressive highbrow periodicals in the style of *The American Mercury* and *The New Yorker* offered a venue for new literature and book reviews (see chapter 6). Other monthlies roughly in this genre—*Atlantic*, *Scribner's*, *Harper's*—and more mainstream fare like *The Saturday Evening Post* offered short stories, poetry, and serialized longer works, but it took the emergence of the "little magazines" (see below) and the ethnic presses to provide a relatively consistent outlet for the modernist literary work that emerged in America after World War I. The American readership for modernist periodical publications and books has yet to be described with scholarly precision, but it probably differs from the readership of mass market niche publications from this period and is comparable in numbers to those who read regional and various (ephemeral) small press periodicals and newspapers. A significant contrast here is between readers of mass-produced periodical content, whose orientation became part of the consumer consumption nexus, and those literary producers and readers whose promotion of American modernist periodicals offered an alternative to the emerging consumerist ethos. As Edward Bishop notes, "Little magazines are by definition magazines that do not make money; they are trying to promote new ideas of forms of art, rather than sales."[2]

Because of provisions in American copyright law, most, if not all, of the modernist writing created or published prior to 1978 is currently (2008) under copyright and not in the public domain. Thus, publicly accessible digital or microform collections of primary literary texts associated with American modernism are at present virtually nonexistent.[3] Microform collections of some periodical literature and selected newspapers provide access to the retrospective content of original publications and thus to a wealth of material. Newspapers like *The New York Times* are available in full-run, full-text digital formats or through commercial information vendors such as ProQuest (the Times currently provides free access to selected retrospective content in the public domain). As noted in the previous chapter, for a magazine like *The New Yorker*, retrospective digitized content is available for purchase on CD-ROM, DVD-ROM, or a portable computer hard drive archive, reproduced as it originally appeared in print, including advertisements and recurring features. Unfortunately, electronic newspaper indexes to the major metropolitan dailies like the *Chicago Daily Tribune* are only available by subscription or on a per-order cost basis, though many libraries maintain the printed versions of the major newspaper indexes. *ProQuest Historical Newspapers* contains full-text, online digitized archives of the *Chicago Tribune* (1849–), *The New York Times*, and other newspapers. (See chapter 6 for more information on *ProQuest Historical Newspapers*.) Locating literature in these periodicals and newspapers might require the use of indexes or other reference sources described here and in other chapters of this book. To locate more obscure authors or pieces of literature that have escaped critical notice, perusal of the original published source material is recommended, perhaps in conjunction with a good literary bibliography or other specialized reference tool.

Finding Newspapers and Periodicals: General Resources

Black Literature, 1827–1940. Microfiche. Alexandria, VA: Chadwyck-Healey, Inc., 1987–1996.

Danky, James P., and Maureen E. Hady. *African-American Newspapers and Periodicals: A National Bibliography.* Cambridge, MA: Harvard University Press, 1998.

United States Newspaper Program Union List. 5th ed. Dublin, OH: OCLC Online Computer Library Center, 1999.

Forming part of Harvard's Black Literature Periodicals Project, the collection of roughly three thousand microfiches currently available in Chadwyck-Healey's **Black Literature, 1827–1940** documents 150,000 pieces of African-American fiction, poetry, book reviews, and literary notices selected from more than nine hundred black-owned publications from this time period. A cumulative CD-ROM index provides subscribers to this resource with electronic access to the microfiche collection. Issued with the original microfiche collection is an author–title–genre index, available in print and microfiche formats, edited by noted scholar Henry Louis Gates. This collection of primary sources from the black periodicals is worth consulting for the variety of source material assembled here. Despite the fact that much of what is available in *Black Literature, 1827–1940* falls outside the period and genre of American modernist literature, much relevant and interesting American modernist writing from 1910 through 1940 is potentially available in this special microfiche collection.

Arising from a 1989 conference at Harvard's W. E. B. DuBois Institute and based at the University of Wisconsin–Madison, James Danky and Maureen Hady's **African-American Newspapers and Periodicals: A National Bibliography** describes slightly more than 6,500 African-American periodicals and newspapers dating from 1827 to 1997. Numbered entries are arranged alphabetically by title, and each record gives complete bibliographic information along with the title's place of publication. When available, titles are linked to ISSN, OCLC control number, and Library of Congress catalog number so that the researcher has additional multiple identifiers to aid in identifying and locating materials. Bibliographic information is based on visual inspection of each title and features a section that briefly describes the subject focus or features and symbols for the holding institutions. The guide has a key to the commercial scholarly indexes cited throughout the bibliography, a list of libraries and their symbols arranged alphabetically by state, and a list of microfilm sources. The volume features separate, alphabetically arranged editor, publisher, and geographic indexes. The "Subject and Features Index" in *African-American Newspapers and Periodicals* offers possible leads on modernist writing; here the most useful entries are listed under books and reading, culture, drama, essays, fiction, history, literature, literary criticism, plays, poetry, short stories, and theater. As there is no chronological index, the researcher must examine full bibliographic entries for a given title to determine the time of publication and then consult either the original source material or possibly the microfilm set *Black Literature, 1827–1940*, described above.

Unfortunately, newspaper union lists such as Anita Miller's three-volume *Newspaper Indexes: A Location and Subject Guide for Researchers* lacks the necessary indexing to be useful in this context. The fifth edition of OCLC's **United States Newspaper Program National Union List (1999)**, available on microfiche, supersedes both Miller's work and Winifred Gregory's *American Newspapers, 1821–1936: A Union List of Files Available in the United States and Canada* (1937). The OCLC project aims to microfilm and index some 300,000 newspapers and is arranged alphabetically by title (with variants), place of publication, and date of publication, and it also contains a subject topical index and a subject geographic index. Slightly less generic in approach but no less problematic for locating modernist literature is Jean Kujoth's *Subject Guide to Periodical Indexes and Review Indexes*. Consult with a reference librarian to determine which of these resources is available in your library.

In general, access to American modernist literature that appeared in specific newspapers can be determined by searching by author in the printed or online indexes of those papers. However, some versions of literary texts published in periodicals may not accurately represent the texts of those works as intended by their authors. In some cases, the compositors made errors in setting the type, misread the copy text, or were provided with corrupt texts from which to set type. Moreover, later versions of the same published work may reflect subsequent authorial revisions.

Modernism and the Little Magazines

Doing research in American literary modernism for the period 1914 to 1949 will entail some acquaintance with highly specialized literary publications known as little magazines. Scholars have observed that roughly 80% of important American modernist writing was originally published in little magazines.[4] Little magazines are a rich primary source of modernist writing because original publications contain important textual details and contemporaneous historical information that offer additional information about the image and presentation of modernist literary production, often produced in contrast to the homogenizing tendencies of more commercial publications. The role of little magazines in publishing literature once thought to be obscene or otherwise controversial is noteworthy since court rulings from this and subsequent periods challenged ongoing censorship efforts in all media in the United States.[5]

Modernism was an international artistic phenomenon that gathered force in the early part of the twentieth century, and the little magazine embodied the iconoclastic aspirations of writers, editors, publishers, and readers for whom it functioned as both an introduction and a conduit to modernist writing during a moment of intense cultural ferment. Literary experimentation and political radicalism were prevalent in little magazines, and though they operated on small budgets, were based in urban centers, usually had small circulations, and were consciously promoted in opposition to popular culture, the little magazines "were, in large part, the center of American modernism in the early decades of the twentieth century, and they were considered vital by the men and women who were busy shaping the nation's cultural and political landscape."[6] It is somewhat ironic that mostly ephemeral little magazines introduced writing that would later be canonized and categorized as "modernist" literature, far outliving its forgotten origins in small publishing ventures. Nonetheless, one famous little magazine, *Poetry*, begun in Chicago in 1912, is still being published in the early twenty-first century, with no end in sight.[7]

Scholars have noted that little magazines were "the product of several converging social, technological, and artistic forces," including less expensive and more efficient printing methods, expansive literary markets, and a readership sufficient to sustain small-run literary periodicals.[8] Hundreds of little magazines appeared during this period, and some of their varied content is relatively obscure, if not unique, to the little magazine in which it appeared. What began in part as coterie publishing and reading, though, had a significant impact on the course of modern literature and culture. It is therefore crucial for the scholar of American modernism to have access to the contents of these specialized literary publications. In his farewell column concluding sixteen years as editor of *The Criterion*, T. S. Eliot, apprehensive about widespread social demoralization and symptoms of waning cultural literacy, observed of little reviews that

> The continuity of culture may have to be maintained by a very small number of people indeed—and these not necessarily equipped with

worldly advantages. It will not be the large organs of opinion, or the old periodicals; it must be the small and obscure papers and reviews … that will keep critical thought alive, and encourage authors of original talent.[9]   .

The resources described in this section will enable the researcher in American modernism to locate both notable and relatively obscure modernist periodicals and much of their contents, including reviews. These indexes partially overlap in their coverage, though some periodicals and literary works might only be indexed in these resources, so it is worthwhile to consult them despite their format and presentation. Published primary source material is at present primarily available in print or microform formats. Digitization projects for modernist American periodicals is restricted by current American copyright law, but the *Modernist Journals Project* co-sponsored by Brown University and the University of Tulsa is designed to "provide fully-searchable online editions of the English-language journals and magazines that were important in shaping those modes of literature and art that came to be called modernist."[10] The emphasis in this project is on British and continental periodicals, but this site might prove useful for research in American literature since literary modernism was, in many ways, an international phenomenon. In years to come, the digitization of modernist periodicals will take them out of archives and put them online. Through high-resolution images and texts, this material will be made available to anyone with a computer and access to the Internet.

Burke, John Gordon, Leon Fulton, and Ned Kehde, eds. *The Access Index to Little Magazines.* s.l.: John Gordon Burke Publisher, Inc., 1979.

Sader, Marion, ed. *Comprehensive Index to English-Language Little Magazines, 1890–1970.* Series 1. 8 vols. New York: Krause-Thomson, 1976.

Chielens, Edward E. *The Literary Journal in America, 1900–1950.* Detroit, MI: Gale Research Company, 1977.

Chielens, Edward E., ed. *American Literary Magazines: The Twentieth Century.* Westport, CT: Greenwood Press, 1992.

Hoffmann, Frederick J., et al. *The Little Magazine: A History and a Bibliography.* Princeton: Princeton University Press, 1946.

Bruccoli, Matthew J., and Robert W. Trogdon, eds. *American Expatriate Writers: Paris in the Twenties.* Detroit, MI: Gale Research, 1997.

O'Neill, Edward H., et al., compilers. *Literary Writings in America: A Bibliography.* 8 vols. Millwood, NY: KTO Press, 1977.

Granger Book Company, Inc. *Index to Poetry in Periodicals, American Poetic Renaissance 1915–1919: An Index of Poets and Poems Published in American Magazines and Newspapers.* Great Neck, NY: Granger Book Company, Inc., 1981.

————. *Index to Poetry in Periodicals, 1920–1924: An Index of Poets and Poems Published in American Magazines and Newspapers*. Great Neck, NY: Granger Book Company, Inc., 1983.

————. *Index to Poetry in Periodicals, 1925–1929: An Index of Poets and Poems Published in American Magazines and Newspapers*. Great Neck, NY: Granger Book Company, Inc., 1984.

Goode, Stephen H. *Index to American Little Magazines 1920–1939*. Troy, NY: Whitston Publishing Company, 1969.

————. *Index to Little Magazines 1940–1942*. New York: Johnson Reprint Corporation, 1967.

————. *Index to Little Magazines 1943–1947*. Denver: Alan Swallow, 1965.

Smith, Avalon, Harriet Colegrove, and Alan Swallow. *Index to Little Magazines 1948*. Denver: Alan Swallow, 1949.

Smith, Avalon, Harriet Colegrove, Alan Stephens, and Alan Swallow. *Index to Little Magazines 1949*. Denver: Alan Swallow, 1950.

The first extended scholarly treatment of the little magazine in America appeared in 1946 under the title **The Little Magazine: A History and Bibliography**. This excellent introduction enables researchers of modernism to get a sense of the scope, styles, trends, and editorial practices of literary modernism as it emerged in the pages of many of the prominent early little magazines. The broad literary context is examined in chapters on particular magazines, a decade-by-decade review of trends and themes from 1910 through the 1940s, and a lucid account of the complicated political and cultural crosscurrents that informed different phases of modernist literary production during this period. Little magazines sometimes appeared on an irregular basis, owing to financial problems or outside disruptions, and occasionally their titles were changed. *The Little Magazine* offers an annotated chronological bibliography, with periodical titles arranged alphabetically for the years 1891 to 1945. A supplementary list of related publications for the period 1892 to 1945 is similarly compiled. These lists contain place of publication, notes on editorial figures, content notes, and a brief description of publication history, including periodical title changes through the dates that are indexed. In addition to a substantial bibliography, *The Little Magazine* provides an index and an invaluable section of articles featuring a convenient listing of references contemporaneous with the emergence of little magazines.

A good supplement and update to *The Little Magazine* is **American Literary Magazines: The Twentieth Century**, a volume in Greenwood Press's series *Historical Guides to the World's Periodicals and Newspapers*. Although some of these publications fall outside the era of high modernism, many are central to the dissemination of American modernist literature. Chapters by various authors on more than seventy-five major little magazines follow a set format that contains a full profile of the publication, a section on information sources, and a valuable section on publication history that notes title changes, volume and issue data, frequency of publication, publisher, and editors. Some chapters are cross-referenced to earlier volumes in the *Historical Guides* series. An appendix on "Minor Literary Magazines" offers an annotated chronological list of ephemeral publications that contain "interesting poetry and fiction" (397). Another appendix, "A Chronology of Social and Literary Events and American Literary Magazines, 1900–1991," is a convenient summary of American publishing correlated with selected highlights from American social and cultural history. Perhaps the most valuable supplement in *American Literary Magazines* is the section "The Archives: An Analysis of Little Magazine Collections in the United States and Canada" on pages 439–58. The editor notes that this "analysis provides an overview of twenty-eight major and minor repositories of little magazines in the United States and Canada" (439). Entries record repository information, brief collection descriptions and condition, some notes on archival guides, and a section on complementary collections. This information allows researchers to locate original source material if microfilm or photocopies prove inadequate or unavailable for research. The volume has a short general index.[11]

Prior to editing the volume on little magazines for Greenwood, Edward E. Chielens produced a bibliographic guide for the Gale information series in American literature, English literature, and world literatures in English titled **The Literary Journal in America, 1900–1950: A Guide to Information Sources**. An informative analytical introduction on little magazines in terms of general overview, regionalism, political factionalism, editorial policies, and major modernist writers offers a good orientation to their role in literary production during this period. The volume's chapters consist of annotated topical bibliographies on literary periodicals including "General Studies and Views," "General Literary Periodicals of Large Circulation," "Little Magazines of Poetry, Fiction, and Art," "Regional Literary Periodicals," "Politically Radical Literary Periodicals," "Academic Quarterlies of Scholarship and Criticism," "Bibliographies and Checklists," and "Background Studies." An appendix lists articles on literary material in miscellaneous periodicals. The index, consisting mostly of titles and names, allows the researcher to trace writers and periodicals mentioned in various chapters in the guide.

Although somewhat idiosyncratic in scope and arrangement, Stephen H. Goode's **Index to American Little Magazines 1920–1939**, as well as subsequent issues simply titled *Index to Little Magazines* that were written by Goode through 1947 and others in following years, offers the researcher a combined author/subject index of selected little magazines, with an emphasis on prose and poetry. Bibliographic citations appear complete but record abbreviations for periodical titles, with a key to titles provided in the introduction. Author entries have an alphabetized listing of their contributions. Subject entries in all capital letters list articles in roughly alphabetical order. The entry for "Little Magazines" has articles by William Carlos Williams, B. A. Botkin, James Laughlin IV, and Sherwood Anderson. The subject index for "Little Magazines" also features sub-entry headings linked to periodicals such as *Poetry*, *The Little Review*, and *Seven Arts* that cite articles about their roles in literary publishing during the time period covered by the index. Subsequent volumes of this index for the period 1940–1949 essentially recap editorial procedures from the first volume with prefatory notes on changes in the journals being indexed. The years 1948–1949 are issued as individual volumes and are compiled by a team of editors. The crude typographical aspect of these volumes is in contrast to the earnest editorial statement that observes, "Because these magazines have been so important in the publication of serious creative and critical writing of our time . . . no one may study twentieth-century American literature with any exactness without consulting these magazines on all occasions" (preface). An added feature in the 1948 and 1949 indexes are headings for "Poetry by Author" and "Stories by Author," with a convenient alphabetized "see" list of indexed authors following these entries.

The ***American Expatriate Writers: Paris in the Twenties***, volume 15 in Gale's Documentary Series in the *Dictionary of Literary Biography*, contains a wealth of information on major American modernist writers, including chapters on selected little magazines. Sections of biographical and critical overviews of these writers are supplemented with facsimile copies of original source material, copious illustrations, maps, and additional contemporaneous material that provide a good context for studying American expatriate writers. A section on "Author Bibliographies" lists publications, bibliographical and biographical works, and repositories that hold the authors' papers. The section on little magazines in *American Expatriate Writers* reprints material on editorial philosophy and contemporary correspondence about publications like *The Little Review* as well as observations on the critical reception and influence of these niche periodicals.

Some reference indexes are both ephemeral and idiosyncratic but nonetheless useful for research purposes since their retrospective indexing usually remains valid if properly done. This is especially true for the obscure poetic output in a given period of literary history, and the poetry of American modernism is no exception to this rule. The editorial board of the Granger Book Company's ***Index to Poetry in Periodicals*** compiled from the early period of American modernism, covering the years 1915–1929, although not all of the poetry listed in this index is narrowly "modernist." The first volume in the series indexes 9,441 poems in 122 selected periodicals for the years 1915–1919, announcing in the introduction that the index "is intended to provide access to the great body of work published in this period which is not otherwise retrievable. As much of this poetry has never been anthologized in book form, it is not accessible through standard poetry indexes" (vii). Periodical titles are listed along with abbreviations. Bibliographic entries are arranged alphabetically by author, with poems similarly arranged by title under author entries. The second volume covers the years 1920–1925 and indexes sixteen thousand poems in 302 periodicals, while the third volume, covering the years 1925–1929, indexes twenty thousand poems in an even larger number of periodicals than its two predecessor volumes.

A massive index initially undertaken at the University of Pennsylvania under the auspices of the Work Projects Administration from 1938 to 1942, *Literary Writings in America: A Bibliography* is primarily intended "to establish bibliographical controls for materials hitherto inaccessible to researchers; specifically, to construct a complete listing of creative American literature written between 1850 and 1940" (vii). In addition to other source material, some two thousand volumes of magazines from this period are indexed, with entries alphabetically arranged by author in eight volumes. *Literary Writings in America* consists of reproductions of 250,000 typed card catalog cards with indexing data on a variety of literary genres, including novels, verse, short stories, book reviews, criticism, and others. Unfortunately, only the first volume has the list of periodicals indexed, along with their abbreviations, editorial notes, and the project history. As this set is not chronological, scholars of American modernism will have to consult other reference materials discussed in this book to identify specific authors to track down their publications in this index. What this resource loses in usability and typographical clarity is somewhat compensated for by its scope.

Providing more focus than *Literary Writings in America* is the eight-volume set *Comprehensive Index to English-Language Little Magazines, 1890–1970*, including fifty-nine periodicals that "are partly or totally American [that] are representative of the best of the various kinds of little magazines that flourished in the period 1890–1970" (xi). The introduction to volume 1 describes the criteria for inclusion and provides a list of the periodicals indexed and their abbreviations for use in bibliographic citations. The *Comprehensive Index* affirms the importance of little magazines in publishing and promoting writing that embodied various facets of American modernism. Entries are alphabetically arranged by author and are subdivided into sections of writings by and about the author. Citations in these subsections are arranged alphabetically by title. Book reviews and translations are also indexed. This set is noteworthy for the consistency and rigor evidenced in the construction of citations, with main entries taken from Library of Congress authority records when they are available. However, in an irony worthy of modernism itself, T. S. Eliot's iconic modernist poem, *The Waste Land*, is not listed under the author section for Eliot in the *Comprehensive Index to English-Language Little Magazines, 1890–1970* because the compiler excluded both the *Criterion* and the *Dial*, the periodicals in which it first appeared.

Conclusion

The diffusion of American modernist poetry and prose in ephemeral periodicals alerted scholars to the need for secondary reference resources to provide access to a unique body of writing, some of which remains obscure. As indicated above, most of American modernist writing was published in the little magazines and highbrow monthlies, with the remainder appearing mostly in books. Writing and scholarship from an earlier period are often only sourced in printed compilations and indexes, some of which are irregular or incomplete. The secondary reference works on American newspapers from the period of American modernism do not offer detailed subject access to their contents; researchers are encouraged to search for authors using electronic or printed indexes published by particular newspapers. Depending on context and the focus of study, the researcher should carefully evaluate and use all the reference resources in all the media currently available. Traditional sources like bibliographies and literary histories, including specialized studies in publishing history, are valuable guides for locating secondary sources and understanding modernist publishing and literary production. The *WorldCat* database can help locate library holdings of specific newspapers and periodicals through a Boolean query combining the "title phrase" and the type limiter "periodical." Some of the resources described in this chapter provide information on locating original materials in archives and libraries, an aspect of literary research that is more fully described in chapter 8.

Notes

1. On American newspapers and periodicals in the first half of the twentieth century, see Michael Schudson, *Discovering the News: A Social History of American Newspapers* (New York: Basic Books, 1978); John Tebbel, *The Compact History of the American Newspaper* (New York: Hawthorn Books, 1969); John Tebbel, *The Magazine in America, 1741–1990* (New York: Oxford University Press, 1991); George H. Douglas, *The Golden Age of the Newspaper* (Westport, CT: Greenwood Press, 1999); and Aurora Wallace, *Newspapers and the Making of Modern America: A History* (Westport, CT: Greenwood Press, 2005).

2. Edward Bishop, "Re: Covering Modernism: Format and Function in the Little Magazines," in *Modernist Writers and the Marketplace*, eds. Ian Wilson, Warwick Gould, and Warren Chernaik (New York: St. Martin's Press, 1996), 287.

3. For current Library of Congress holdings of microform collections in American literature, see Research Guide No. 14, "Microform Resources for the Study of American Literature," compiled by Evelyn Timberlake, at http:www.loc.gov/rr/microform/amlitmic.html (accessed October 8, 2006). The microform collection *Black Literature, 1827–1940* is discussed in the text above. Other microform collections of American

modernist writing appear as licensing agreements permit. See, for example, *Little Magazines, American: 1910/1919–1940+* (Millwood, NY: Kraus-Thomson Organization, Ltd., 1978–1979), consisting of 11 reels of 35-mm microfilm. However, the *WorldCat* record for this item indicates that only three libraries own this set (OCLC accession no. 10009376).

4. Frederick J. Hoffman, Charles Allen, and Carolyn F. Ulrich, *The Little Magazine: A History and a Bibliography* (Princeton, NJ: Princeton University Press, 1946), 1. Iconic modernist literary works that first appeared in little magazines include Eliot's *The Waste Land*, published in the *Criterion* in October 1922 and the *Dial* in November 1922, and Joyce's *Ulysses*, excerpted in installments in *The Little Review* from 1918 to 1920.

5. On literature and obscenity during the period of modernist writing, see Edward de Grazia, *Girls Lean Back Everywhere: The Law of Obscenity and the Assault on Genius* (New York: Random House, 1992).

6. Suzanne W. Churchill and Adam McKible, "Little Magazines and Modernism: An Introduction," *American Periodicals* 15, no. 1 (2005): 4.

7. In late 2002, initial reports in the media announced that *Poetry* magazine had been given a gift of $100 million by an heiress, which would amount to $120 million over the lifetime of the donation. In a subsequent account of this gift to *Poetry*, the amount is said to have been "some two hundred million dollars." See Dana Goodyear, "The Moneyed Muse," *The New Yorker* (19 & 26 February 2007): 122–35.

8. Michael Barsanti, "Little Magazines," in *The Oxford Encyclopedia of American Literature*, vol. 2 (New York: Oxford University Press, 2004), 462.

9. T. S. Eliot, "Last Words," *Criterion*, 18, no. 71 (January 1939): 274.

10. Technical glitches have slowed progress on the *Modernist Journals Project* website thus far. The quotation above is taken from its former website. The new site is at http://www.modjourn.org (accessed 31 March 2008). An April 2007 Brown University press release updates the project at http://www.brown.edu/Administration/News_Bureau/2006-07/06-143.html (accessed 11 July 2007). Information on the British Library's collection of American little magazines is available at http://www.bl.uk/collections/americas/littlemagazines.html (accessed 15 June 2007).

11. The Harry Ransom Humanities Research Center at the University of Texas also has significant archival holdings of modernist little magazines. For a description of these collections and a discussion of their significance for modernist writing, see Richard Watson, "Modernist Little Magazines: A List of Selected Holdings at the Harry Ransom Humanities Research Center," *Library Chronicle of the University of Texas at Austin* 20, no.4 n.s. (1991): 89–97, and Shari Benstock and Bernard Benstock, "The Role of Little Magazines in the Emergence of Culture," *Library Chronicle of the University of Texas at Austin* 20, no. 4 n.s. (1991): 69–87.

CHAPTER 8

Manuscripts and Archives

Archival research in original primary source material can be simultaneously exciting, frustrating, tedious, and rewarding, and it is unique. Most archival agencies and repositories have developed rules and procedures to control access to collections and monitor their use. In some cases, the amount of material for use is limited at any one time. Since travel and other expenses might be involved, the researcher should become acquainted with an archive's procedures, hours of operation, collection policies, and collection guides prior to making arrangements for an on-site visit. At a minimum, the researcher should have at least one form of official identification—and preferably two—to present when registering at an archival facility; often, this is a precondition of access and use. Since policies on copying original manuscripts or other repository material differ, access to a laptop computer can enhance the research experience, particularly if extensive notetaking or transcriptions are necessary. Fortunately, many archival agencies now make their local procedures, policies, and other pertinent information available on the Web, including personnel contact information and some description of their holdings. In some circumstances, arrangements can be made in advance to work with a particular collection, original manuscript, or rare book; you may simply want to inquire generally about collection use, facilitating research and saving time. Use of archival materials is often governed by copyright law, donor agreements and restrictions, availability, the physical condition of original materials, or other local restrictions and circumstances. Usually, for example, only pencils are allowed in research rooms, and pens or other writing utensils with indelible inks or similar marking materials are never permitted. In the case of primary source material under copyright, researchers should consult with professional staff about the best way to secure permission to publish excerpts, even if the intended publication falls under the "fair use" doctrine of copyright law. Archival research is, for the most part, trouble free, but one should keep in mind the distinctive characteristics of doing research in facilities that house original archival collections and plan accordingly. This chapter provides an overview of this process and describes some of the best tools and resources available to help locate and effectively use archival collections.

General Information on Archives

A useful general definition of an archive is a repository for housing and administering old records. If these are the records of an organization or corporate body, they are usually noncurrent, or historical, and document the agency that produced them. An archive (or archives) can also refer to a building or location, apart from its contents or availability for public use. Finally, an archive can refer to any collection of unique or rare historical materials and records, in any media or format, originating with a person, group, or public body, or an artificial collection that is assembled from various sources by an archivist, such as material relating to a historical event or to a particular subject. When an archival collection is produced by individuals, it often consists of their unique papers or manuscripts. The general terminology for all types of archives, manuscripts, historical documents, and other historical records is *primary source material*. Regardless of physical location, a public archive housing primary source material is usually administered by professionals who restrict use of these unique collections to a designated location. Moreover, original primary source material does not circulate outside the holding institution as do ordinary library books and most other library materials. It is helpful to remember that once an archival agency or library obtains an archival collection and processes and catalogs it, the collection usually remains in that public repository *in perpetuity* unless other arrangements have been made or unusual circumstances intervene. Hence, even older guides to archival collections are probably accurate in terms of repository location information, but a valuable rule of thumb is to verify such entries in newer online reference resources to avoid unexpected problems in locating a collection of primary source material. This caveat also applies to archival finding aids (see below) that may have been substantially revised and edited over time, with the latest identifiable version usually representing the physical and intellectual arrangement of the archive it describes.

In terms of literary research, the meaning of a "primary source" can be slightly confusing, and context is essential. Published editions of literary texts are often referred to as "primary sources"; works (articles, books, reference materials, etc.) about published literary texts or authors are sometimes called "secondary sources," and reference materials are sometimes called "tertiary sources." Significant literary research and scholarship are based on all these categories of materials. Thus, a published edition of *The Great Gatsby* is a primary source for a literary review, scholarly paper, or a book about the novel, while Fitzgerald's original typescript and manuscript versions of *Gatsby*, along with the publisher's galley proofs and original correspondence relating to Gatsby, can be considered primary source material. A literary biographer frequently consults all the available published and archival resources for research. Hence, different versions of *The Great Gatsby* can be considered primary source material or a primary source, depending on the context in which they are used. None of these are hard and fast definitions, but keeping these and other technical distinctions in mind can avoid confusion and provide some acquaintance with terminology encountered in the course of research.[1] The Society of American Archivists online glossary is available at <http://www.archivists.org/glossary/list.asp>.

Manuscripts can refer to documents whose texts are produced by hand, typewriter, computer, or other recording technologies. A document written entirely in the hand of a single person is called a holograph. The original signature a typed or word-processed document, such as a letter signed by a particular person, is referred to as an autograph. A published reproduction of an original document that retains all of its original typographic features is called a facsimile. Since the professional protocols for describing, organizing, and cataloging primary source material are fairly standardized (all considered part of "processing" a collection), researchers should have little trouble identifying and using archival collections in most settings. The generic term for the variety of collection-level descriptive guides and inventories of primary source material is *finding aid*. The information in finding aids supplemented with experienced professional expertise is the best way to determine the contents and research value of a given archival collection. Finding aids usually contain the collection name, primary dates, scope, provenience (collection origin and history), biographical and content notes, and series descriptions. An archival series or sub-series refers to a portion of a collection similar in format or content, often arranged in chronological order or in an order reflecting the original arrangement of the collection. Sometimes a finding aid will provide a list of subject headings (usually Library of Congress headings) that are formulated according to cataloging rules based on a controlled vocabulary.

Beginning in the 1970s, the history of the book emerged internationally as a distinct scholarly discipline. Book history usually encompasses publishing history, the history of reading and authorship, and various branches of bibliography and scholarly editing. For the literary researcher in American modernism, publishers' and authors' archives are especially rich documentary sources on literary production, including the publishing process and editing. This chapter discusses book history in terms of manuscript and archival collections.

Practicing Archival Research

Since collections of primary source material can be extensive and often comprise unique unpublished records and manuscripts, the researcher should carefully review the secondary literature in a particular area of scholarship to determine if his or her topic has previously been researched using a particular manuscript or archival collection. Most literary research will benefit from a review of the published secondary scholarship. In some cases, examining a manuscript collection in person might suggest areas of research that cannot be clearly conveyed by a finding aid or an archivist, but this procedure, though potentially very rewarding, can be time consuming and difficult. Prior consultation with a professional archivist familiar with a particular collection of primary source material can save valuable time and effort. In some cases, a formal letter to an archival agency beforehand describing the research and intended publication or scholarly plans, if any, may be necessary, and sometimes references and a letter of introduction are required.

When using primary source material, following the information patterns in a given collection and remaining open to research possibilities that were not apparent when the topic was first formulated are beneficial. Take some time to evaluate documents and records to determine the context of their creation and their subsequent use, if any, in published form. Exposure to the research in a given area will provide a feel for importance and possible relevance when sifting through an archival collection. Sometimes a theme will suggest itself in the course of doing research in different but related collections. Carefully noting and recording ideas as they occur during research can be a useful aid to your work. Follow all repository rules and procedures, and keep all primary source materials in the order and folders and containers in which they were made available. Consulting primary source material can be time consuming, since in its raw, undigested state, such material does not immediately suggest a theme or narrative as a monograph or scholarly article might.

Since reproducing primary source material is almost always done by personnel in the archival agency, clarification about how much can be copied, the cost in addition to any handling and postage fees, and expected delivery time is essential. In some cases, photocopies or microform copies of primary source materials are made available for research in lieu of the original manuscripts, which may be consulted only under special circumstances. Archival agencies are frequently understaffed and overworked, with daily in-house responsibilities and other patrons, so requests for assistance and access may occur in a stressed situation. Etiquette and courtesy are important, promoting communication and smoothing the interaction between researcher and archives personnel.

Taking notes on your research can prove extremely important later, should you choose to incorporate primary source material in written or published work. Ensure where a record, manuscript, or item is located in its archival collection context so that it may be properly cited in footnotes or endnotes and bibliography at some future point. Consult the latest edition of the appropriate style guide (*MLA, Chicago Manual,* etc.) for consistency and to construct quotes and accurate bibliographic references. For citations to primary source materials, use the collection name preferred or indicated by the holding archival agency, taking the agency's finding aid or catalog record as your source. Since some of the primary source material you cite is likely to be unique, provide clear folder and box numbers, collection names and folder titles, dates, and locally assigned call numbers (including shelf marks or item identifiers), if applicable. Standard research protocols entail that someone consulting your notes and bibliography should be able to identify and locate the primary source material cited and retrieve the originals to verify quotes and references. The same consideration applies to all the published material cited in your work, including Internet and Web sources.

Some archival institutions advertise fellowships or special stipends or grants for qualified researchers working in a specific collection or in a particular area of scholarship. These competitive monetary awards are intended to help defray some of the costs associated with archival research and normally do not entail repayment. Check with the institution you might be working with for such programs, guidelines, and application procedures. Currently published six times a year, the "Fellowships and Grants" section of the Publications of the *Modern Language Association of America* (PMLA) is a good source of information concerning research support in the humanities.

Websites and Databases for Locating Archives and Manuscript Collections

Abraham, Terry, comp. *Repositories of Primary Sources*, 1995–. www.uidaho .edu/special-collections/Other.Repositories.html (accessed 20 August 2006).

ArchiveGrid. Mountain View, CA: RLG. www.archivegrid.org (accessed 20 August 2006).

ArchivesUSA. Ann Arbor, MI: ProQuest LLC. archives.chadwyck.com/ (accessed 23 August 2006).

Garraty, John A., and Mark C. Carnes, gen. eds. *American National Biography*. New York: Oxford University Press, 1999–. www.anb.org/ (accessed 31 March 2008).

National Union Catalog of Manuscript Collections (NUCMC). Washington, DC: Library of Congress, 1997. www.loc.gov/coll/nucmc/ (accessed 27 August 2006).

Schomburg Center for Research in Black Culture. New York Public Library. www.nypl.org/research/sc/sc.html (accessed 10 September 2006).

Society for the History of Authorship, Reading & Publishing (SHARP). SHARP Web. www.sharpweb.org/ (accessed 27 August 2006).

WorldCat and *RLIN.* Dublin, OH: OCLC-RLG. www.oclc.org/ (accessed 23 August 2006).

One of the earliest and most useful aggregator resources on archival repositories on the Web, Terry Abraham's **Repositories of Primary Sources** was developed at the University of Idaho and remains an invaluable gateway to archival information through "a listing of over 5000 websites describing holdings of manuscripts, archives, rare books, historical photographs, and other primary sources for the research scholar." The site provides various geographic and topical, alphabetically arranged lists of repository websites and other related sites. Unfortunately, some external links indexed here no longer function, but this is not surprising for a website of this scope. The tremendous value of this tool resides in its international coverage, as evidenced from the directory arranged under the "Integrated Index/List" link on the *Repositories* homepage. Geographic lists go from larger to smaller regions, so searching for a particular repository is fairly easy. The *Repositories* site is especially useful if you need to contact a holding repository for contact information, policies, and procedures about identified primary source material. Other resources described in this chapter help identify *where* a particular author's manuscript collection is located. Once the holding institution is identified on the *Repositories* website, that institution's homepage can offer more detailed information about an archival collection through its online catalog, finding aid, or other site-specific information.

ArchiveGrid is an enhanced commercial resource produced by the Research Library Group (RLG) and its website for aggregating information on primary source material from thousands of archival repositories and libraries around the world. The *ArchiveGrid* database currently holds nearly 1 million item- and collection-level catalog records and provides access to approximately 60,000 full-text finding aids to specific collections, with monthly updates to the database. The search engine for locating collections of primary source material is straightforward, providing different types of search options and explanations for each kind of query, such as proximity, phrase, and keyword search queries. Search results pages are hierarchically arranged, with a head note showing the total number of hits and a list of links with collection titles and brief collection descriptions. Clicking a link takes the user to the full-text repository finding aid for a particular collection. Users can also connect to a repository's own website, quickly providing access to important information about its policies, procedures, and contact information. Convenient, reliable access to full-text finding aids and repository information represents a signal improvement over earlier methods of doing remote research in primary source material. In addition, the *ArchiveGrid* query results page offers alternate search strategies and links to related collections and resources, making this a cutting-edge resource for doing Web-based research using collections of primary source material.

Another quality commercial Web source for locating information about archival collections in the United States is ***ArchivesUSA***. Its search interface allows the user to perform Boolean, proximity, and truncation searching by either collection or repository and features a useful "Help Page" that briefly describes the functionalities of this resource. *ArchivesUSA* aggregates in full two older print guides to archival collections, the *National Union Catalog of Manuscript Collections* (*NUCMC*) and the *National Inventory of Documentary Sources in the United States* (*NIDS*). In addition, this site has information on archival collections directly submitted by archival agencies. *ArchivesUSA* is an expanding directory of collections of primary source material that currently offers information on roughly 155,000 archival collections in almost 5,600 repositories with links to nearly 5,000 full-text finding aids. Each record comes with a link to the repository website. In a few cases, some older or obscure collections may be noted only in the guides indexed by *ArchivesUSA*, so this is a valuable collection locator as well.

The ***American National Biography*** is a commercial reference database published under the auspices of the American Council of Learned Societies and originally appeared in print in 1999. The online version is updated quarterly and currently contains cross-indexed entries for more than seventeen thousand significant Americans, including important literary figures. Besides biographical, interpretive, and bibliographical material, many entries in the *American National Biography* have information on locations of major collections of authors' papers. The search page offers full-text and personal name search options, with a variety of limiter options. As such, this is a handy place to begin one's search for archival collections and to get a basic overview of a particular writer's career and work.

The Web version of the ***National Union Catalog of Manuscript Collections*** (***NUCMC***) is a free, cooperative cataloging arrangement between the Library of Congress and the Research Library Group to produce online archival records in the RLG Union Catalog for eligible United States repositories. Records created prior to 1986 are not available through this website but are available in the printed edition of *NUCMC* or through the *ArchivesUSA* commercial database. The site offers clear explanations about contents and searching strategies (see below for a more complete description of *NUCMC's* arrangement).

In 2006 OCLC and RLG, two of the largest member-based information organizations in the world, officially merged their proprietary databases (*WorldCat* and *RLIN*) as well as services and programs to provide the research community with a continuously expanding, comprehensive bibliographic catalog, in addition to an array of allied services. This combined database contains catalog records of thousands of collections of primary source material held in institutions around the world, and its *Firstsearch* information gateway features a delimiter for "archival material," making specific searches fairly straightforward. With this electronic resource, users are able to identify collection- and item-level catalog records and holding institutions for all libraries and agencies that report their holdings to *WorldCat* and *RLIN*. Since the reporting network is extensive (including major public libraries such as the New York Public Library and independent research institutions) and because many of these OCLC member institutions hold literary archives, this is an excellent place to begin research. Also in 2006, a beta version of the *WorldCat* bibliographic database, called *Open World-Cat*, was made available to the public on the Web at no cost, located at http://worldcat.org. With simplified basic and advanced search interfaces and a convenient zip code search limiter, researchers can find library and archival materials in their local libraries. Scholars may use the more sophisticated OCLC subscription database, *WorldCat*, simply by gaining access to a public computer in an OCLC member institution. Archival collections and their holding institutions may be searched in both versions of this database by doing a keyword search on an individual or corporate author and using the previously mentioned "archival material" search delimiter to narrow the search to collection-level records of primary source material.

The **Schomburg Center for Research in Black Culture** at the New York Public Library is one of the premier centers for researching the "history, literature, politics, and culture of peoples of African descent in the Americas, Africa and England, primarily in the twentieth century," including twentieth-century black writers and material on the Harlem Renaissance in particular. The Schomburg website provides information about manuscript collections and digitized finding aids and contact information for its staff. Scholars of African-American modernism should consult with the Schomburg Center to obtain information about primary source material not held by the Schomburg Center and that might be hard to find or is not listed in any of the other sources described in this chapter.

Begun in 1991 and now international in scope, the Society for the History of Authorship, Reading & Publishing (SHARP) is devoted to the history of the book which, according to its website,

> Concerns the creation, dissemination, and reception of script and print, including newspapers, periodicals, and ephemera. Book historians study the social, cultural, and economic history of authorship;

the history of the book trade, copyright, censorship, and underground publishing; the publishing histories of particular literary works, authors, editors, imprints, and literary agents; the spread of literacy and book distribution; canon formation and the politics of literary criticism; libraries, reading habits, and reader response.

As this précis indicates, for those doing research in literary history and American modernism in particular, the *SHARP Web* offers useful information on locating publishers' archives and other resources relating to book and literary history. In part an aggregator site, the *SHARP Web* contains book history projects, research syllabi, selected scholarly journals, and publishers' series on book history. Depending on the context and level of the literary research, the *SHARP* site might offer useful research information and further avenues for publication and public presentation of your work.

If the commercial databases or Web resources described above are not accessible, search engines such as *Google* can help track down information about collections of primary source material. Posting queries to specialist electronic literature or archive Internet listserves may also elicit informed responses with direction to relevant collections. Writing or calling an archival repository can lead to good results. Some archival repositories now post "accession lists" of unprocessed collections of primary source material on their websites. These collections may still be consulted for research, but more often than not they do not come with a finished finding aid; at most, a rudimentary collection inventory might be available for use. Finally, verification of the information on archival collections from sites like *Google* is essential to help ensure accuracy and currency.

Locating Relevant Archives and Manuscripts: Print Sources

Ash, Lee, and William G. Miller, comps. *Subject Collections: A Guide to Special Book Collections and Subject Emphases as Reported by University, College, Public, and Special Libraries and Museums in the United States and Canada.* 7th ed., rev. and enl., 2 vols. New York: R. R. Bowker Co., 1993.

DeWitt, Donald L., comp. *Articles Describing Archives and Manuscript Collections in the United States: An Annotated Bibliography.* Westport, CT: Greenwood Press, 1997.

———. *Guides to Archives and Manuscript Collections in the United States: An Annotated Bibliography.* Westport, CT: Greenwood Press, 1994.

Dictionary of Literary Biography. Detroit: Gale Research Company, 1978.

Garraty, John A., and Mark C. Carnes, gen. eds. *American National Biography*. 24 vols. New York: Oxford University Press, 1999.

Hamer, Philip M. *A Guide to Archives and Manuscripts in the United States*. New Haven, CT: Yale University Press, 1961.

Index to Personal Names in the National Union Catalog of Manuscript Collections, 1959–1984. Alexandria, VA: Chadwyck-Healey, 1988.

Index to Subjects and Corporate Names in the National Union Catalog of Manuscript Collections, 1959–1984. Alexandria, VA: Chadwyck-Healey, 1994.

National Union Catalog of Manuscript Collections (NUCMC), 1959–1993. Washington, DC: Library of Congress.

Robbins, J. Albert. *American Literary Manuscripts: A Checklist of Holdings in Academic, Historical, and Public Libraries, Museums, and Authors' Homes in the United States*. 2nd ed. Athens, GA: University of Georgia Press, 1977.

Your library might have specially published reproductions of original literary manuscripts. By using the truncated term *facsimile** in a search string that includes the author's name you may be able to locate facsimile versions of a writer's papers. Thus, the Boolean keyword query *william faulkner* and *facsimile** might turn up Garland's multi-volume edition of Faulkner's literary archives, the *William Faulkner Manuscripts Series*.

Published resources for locating collections of primary source material often rely on answers to questionnaires, not all of which reflect the same level of accuracy or completeness. Lee Ash and William Miller's **Subject Collections: A Guide to Special Book Collections and Subject Emphases as Reported by University, College, Public, and Special Libraries and Museums in the United States and Canada** went through several editions through 1993 and is based on answers to questionnaires. Though dated, this two-volume directory of various special collections and institutions is useful as a supplement to the electronic resources discussed above, particularly in terms of small or obscure collections unrecorded elsewhere. *Subject Collections* is arranged topically by Library of Congress subject headings. Entries consist of collection descriptions and contact and repository information that were submitted at the time these volumes were compiled in the early 1990s. The entry for "American Language and Literature" and for individual authors from the Modernist period might prove useful. The entry for "Eliot, Thomas Stearns, 1888–1965" indicates holdings at various institutions, but in certain cases determination of the extent or importance of some of these collections is difficult. By contrast, the entries for the writer "Faulkner, William" (not the current authority heading for this Faulkner) are fuller and give a good idea of what is available in different institutions.

The archival reference sources compiled by Donald DeWitt for Greenwood exhibit the strengths and limitations of older printed tools. **Articles Describing**

Archives and Manuscript Collections in the United States: An Annotated Bibliography is necessarily limited in scope to those manuscript collections that have been described and interpreted in special articles published from the late nineteenth century to the mid-1990s. The strength of this reference work is that it consolidates much useful information in a clearly organized text. The bibliography consists of thirteen general headings and forty-six topical subcategories. Full bibliographic entries are mostly numbered and arranged alphabetically by the author's surname in each section, with accompanying brief annotations. The American modernism researcher will want to consult entries under "Literary Collections" for possible leads. The volume's index further consolidates secondary themes or subjects by grouping them in entries. The value of what DeWitt rightly calls a "subgenre of historical literature" (ix) is that such examinations are usually informed by a close, accurate knowledge of important documentation in a given collection of primary source material, often illuminating it in ways not readily apparent from consulting a library catalog record or even the repository's finding aid. To locate additional analytical articles on manuscript and archival collections, the researcher might want to consult H. W. Wilson's *Library Literature*, a commercial scholarly index to library and archival literature that is available in online and print versions, with full-text articles available from *WilsonWeb* from 1994 onward. Regular bibliographies published in *American Archivist* have these specialized articles as well. Other important sources of information on manuscript and special collections are the in-house publications issued by some archival repositories that describe particular collections, revolving exhibits, or significant new acquisitions. *The Library Chronicle* of the University of Texas at Austin is an excellent example of such a publication, and many research libraries subscribe to these serials.

Donald DeWitt's companion volume, *Guides to Archives and Manuscript Collections in the United States: An Annotated Bibliography*, likewise consists of numbered annotated entries for archival guides and finding aids arranged alphabetically by author, covering thirteen general categories that are divided into fifty-eight topical subcategories. These normally unpublished guides are produced by the holding repository and made available to researchers on request. "Literary Collections" is a general category with eighty-nine entries. DeWitt explains that the index to this volume brings together "guides that might be separated due to different authors, multiple themes, or arbitrary placement. It lists authors, repositories, and subjects and is keyed to entry numbers" (x). While a reference work like this might be useful in certain situations, references to archival collections can occasionally be found in bibliographies and book reviews and in the notices and announcements found in professional and scholarly literature.

The bibliographic notes accompanying many articles in the *Dictionary of Literary Biography* offer information about important collections of primary source material concerning the authors treated in the *DLB* series thus far. (See, for example, the *DLB* volumes discussed in chapter 2 on John Dos Passos and American expatriate writers from the Modernist period.) A benefit of these archival notes is that they provide information on major manuscript collections as well as smaller collections scattered in different archival repositories.

The print version of ***American National Biography*** (***ANB***) is a handy place to look up important American writers. Many of the alphabetically arranged entries contain information about significant collections of primary source material in the bibliographic notes at the end of each article. Major American modernist writers are listed in *ANB*, so the fact that this edition was published in 1999 does not limit its usefulness in this context. For a discussion of the online version of the *ANB*, see above and the "Biographical Sources" section in chapter 2. Notes for entries in *The African American National Biography* (2008), similar in arrangement to the ANB, also indicate repositories where a writer's original manuscripts are held.

Philip Hamer's ***A Guide to Archives and Manuscripts in the United States*** is an eclectic guide chiefly to historical papers alphabetically arranged by state and then by location in that state. Entry annotations consist of individual names, general notes on repository holdings, featured special topics and subjects, and contact information current at time of publication. The strength of Hamer's book is its incorporation of various guides, lists, and inventories of manuscript collections around the United States, many of which are "in-house" publications. Those consulting *A Guide to Archives and Manuscripts in the United States* are advised to use the book's extensive index to locate pockets of literary manuscripts relating to their research.

The print version of the ***National Union Catalog of Manuscript Collections*** (***NUCMC***) ceased with the 1993 edition, but it might be available where the electronic edition is lacking. The entire printed set of *NUCMC* describes 72,300 collections in 1,406 different repositories. The volumes accumulate information gathered from reports by the Library of Congress and consist of entries of collections of original primary source material that may be found in a "public or quasi-public repository that regularly admits researchers." Entries are transposed library card catalog records that record the principal name around which the collection is formed (either an individual or corporate author), the collection name, collection dates, extent of collection, name of holding repository, collection notes describing primary subjects, Library of Congress subject headings, and an MS (manuscript) symbol consisting of the last two numbers of the year in which the entry (or card) was published and a serial number. Since the entries in these volumes are arranged according to the manuscript number and not alphabetically, users should consult the name index, subject index, or repository index in each volume to efficiently locate entries in a given volume. Some volumes in *NUCMC* cumulate indexes for a number of years; certain annual volumes were issued with their own index. Check the library catalog to verify which volumes contain indexes. Chadwyck-Healey issued the two-volume *Index to Personal Names in the National Union Catalog of Manuscript Collections, 1959–1984* in 1988 and the three-volume *Index to Subjects and Corporate Names in the National Union Catalog of Manuscript Collections, 1959–1984* in 1994. In the print edition of *NUCMC*, these cumulative indexes offer quicker access to volume contents, particularly in terms of subjects that may be found in various volumes in the *NUCMC* series.

The second edition of *American Literary Manuscripts* (1977) is a guide to collections of primary source material relating to 2,750 American authors and six hundred holding institutions or libraries. Use of this resource requires brief study of its conventions and symbols. Entries are arranged alphabetically by author, followed by the symbols assigned to the holding library or libraries and a brief description of collection contents, also abbreviated according to the book's conventions. The alphabetical symbols for holding libraries are listed in the introduction and are based on *Symbols of American Libraries* (1969) and those then authorized by the Library of Congress. Another list describes the abbreviations assigned to different kinds of primary source material and their physical extent. Through these editorial devices, the compilers of *American Literary Manuscripts* have been able to collect a significant amount of information in one volume and concisely describe in individual entries where material relating to an author may be scattered. The caveat relating to older printed reference sources holds here as well: an academic Web source such as *Repositories of Primary Sources* should be used to verify current contact and collection information, if available.

Conclusion

Recent technological developments with digitization and the Web have greatly enhanced access to primary source material and the repositories and libraries that house these collections. Websites offer digitized finding aids, policies, selected digitized content, and contact information to help scholars communicate with libraries about their archival collections; in archival research, clear communication between patron and staff is especially important throughout the entire process. Older printed reference sources that describe major archival collections are probably still current in terms of the holding library information. Where possible, the electronic and print resources described in this chapter should be used together to provide a solid foundation for the complex process of archival research. Quality archival Web sources offer a valuable supplement to printed guides to collections of primary source materials, both in terms of content and timeliness since reputable scholarly and commercial sites are constantly updated, edited, and maintained for their end users. Many of the publicly accessible manuscript collections associated with American literary modernism are currently under copyright for a period determined by Congress. Manuscript collections might have other use restrictions, such as the amount of original material that can be copied or additional donor or repository restrictions. The *Willa Cather Archive* at the University of Nebraska-Lincoln is a good example of use restrictions imposed by an author on work held in copyright, in this case on Cather's personal correspondence, though other Willa Cather manuscripts will eventually be available online (http:cather.unl.edu/). These collections may be researched, but their use in publications must either conform to the "fair use" provisions of copyright law or require that a good faith effort is made to obtain permission from the copyright holder prior to publication. Researchers might want to consult the online *WATCH* database (Writers, Artists, and Their Copyright Holders) run jointly by the Harry Ransom Center at the University of Texas and the University of Reading, available at http:tyler.hrc.utexas.edu/, or the *Copyright Clearance Center* site available at http://www.copyright.com/. These Web resources provide information on works in copyright, including contact information for those holding copyrights. The U.S. Copyright Office offers additional information on American copyright law at http://www.copyright.gov/help/faq/.

Finally, since archival research differs in important ways from regular library research, clarify policies about access and use in the early planning stages of your work with original manuscripts and other primary source material. A reference librarian or archives professional can help answer questions about your archival research.

Notes

1. For an overview of archival terminology, see Richard Pearce-Moses et. al., *A Glossary of Archival and Records Terminology* (Chicago: Society of American Archivists, 2005), and the shorter, and older, *A Glossary for Archivists, Manuscript Curators, and Records Managers* by Lewis and Lynn Bellardo (Chicago: Society of American Archivists, 1992). For special collections terminology, see *ABC for Book Collectors* by John Carter, revised by Nicholas Barker, 8th ed. (New Castle, DE: Oak Knoll Press, 2004).

CHAPTER 9

Web Resources

Along with the other resources discussed in this volume, the Web can provide additional, valuable sources for researching American modernism. There are websites available that offer biographies of writers, critical interpretations of their works, and useful information about the historical and cultural contexts of the period. Given the copyright laws in the United States, a great deal of the literature published during this time is still under copyright protection and not available freely online. However, materials that are out of copyright are becoming increasingly available in digital format. The Web also offers access to e-mail lists and discussion boards that can be of interest to advanced students, as well as a growing number of electronic open-access journals and other sites that provide bibliographies of works. Although the Web cannot deliver all the sources needed for research, it can certainly be an effective tool. This chapter will identify an array of currently available, helpful, and free Web resources for studying American modernism.

Searching the Web is different from searching a library catalog or a database like *MLAIB*. Websites are not subject to standardized cataloging practices, such as use of the MARC record, although there is great interest in standards for ways of bringing more efficiency to the structure of the Web, including uniform use of metadata or other means of consistently describing content. At this time, all searches are basically keyword searches and are usually executed against the full text of the documents. Also, given the freedom of the Web, some materials published there may be inappropriate for research. In particular, online class projects from high schools or other colleges should not be cited. Remember that given the for-profit structure of the publishing business, many books and journals will not be freely available online. Do not pay fees to access materials that your library may be able to provide free of charge in either print or electronic format.

In using the Web for research, there is a greater need to evaluate the sources you locate since there is no guarantee that there has been a peer review or editing process. The researcher must determine whether the source is credible. Consider the following criteria as you evaluate websites:

1. Authority. Be sure you can identify the author of the page and determine whether he or she is qualified or has expertise in the field.
2. Currency. Check when the site was last updated and if it is being maintained. This is particularly important if the topic is time sensitive.
3. Audience. Determine whom you think the page is for in assessing its use for you. For instance, if the page is intended for sixth-grade students, it should not be used for a university-level paper. Evaluate the depth of coverage.
4. Bias. Look for levels of objectivity or bias in the page and consider how that affects the source.
5. Accuracy. Try to determine whether the information provided is correct. Consider whether the material can be verified by other sources. Look for whether the author cites his or her sources.

These criteria can be used to evaluate any resource, in any format.

Scholarly Gateways

Given the number of links that are often returned, searching the entire Web with *Google* can be daunting. You may want to begin research by using one of these gateway sites, which collect and present useful websites:

Liu, Alan. *Voice of the Shuttle*, n.d., at vos.ucsb.edu (accessed 12 July 2007).
Lynch, Jack. *Literary Resources—American,* n.d., at andromeda.rutgers.edu/~jlynch/Lit/american.html (accessed 12 July 2007).
Ishikawa, Akihito. *American Literature on the Web*, 2001, at www.nagasaki-gaigo.ac.jp/ishikawa/amlit/ (accessed 12 July 2007).

Voice of the Shuttle is one of the best-known and most respected humanities gateways on the Web. Led by Alan Liu, a team from the English Department at the University of California, Santa Barbara, maintains and updates the site. In the section "Literature in English," there is a link to American literature. Along with a list of general resources, including links to multimedia poetry sites, the section "Modern American Authors, Works, Projects" is available. This section is most relevant for research of the American Modernist era. The section begins with general information and then offers options for specific authors. Approximately fifty authors are listed, with links to online texts as well as biographical and critical materials.

Jack Lynch of Rutgers University maintains a large website entitled *Literary Resources—American* that provides access to an array of valuable online materials. Lynch does not separate American materials by time periods, but he does include sections for women writers, Native American literature, and various genres and regions, which may prove helpful to researchers focusing on works from a particular region, such as the American South. In addition, he offers extensive listings by author, providing access to online texts and critical materials.

Akihito Ishikawa's *American Literature on the Web* offers a choice of time periods, including 1914–1945, one of the common time frames for defining the Modernist period. Ishikawa connects readers to timelines, individual author pages, and sources that focus on music, art, and the social history of the era. Ishikawa's site is particularly valuable for locating those kinds of contextual sources about the period.

While there will certainly be some overlap between these three gateways, each offers a distinct arrangement and some unique content. Depending on the specific research question or focus, one gateway may serve better than another, but all three are highly recommended to help delve into information about American modernist literature and authors that is available freely online.

Your library's website may also provide important information. In many cases, the librarian who handles collection development and liaison work for American literature will have created an online guide that highlights resources available at your university as well as freely available websites.

Electronic Text Archives

As noted above, the copyright laws of the United States limit the amount of material from the Modernist period that will be freely available online, but several universities and libraries have made great strides in making available as many materials as possible. Along with the pioneering *Project Gutenberg*, key players in this area are the University of Virginia, which has taken a leading role in providing access to digitized collections online, and the Library of Congress *American Memory* project.

Digital Book Index, 2007, at www.digitalbookindex.org (accessed 12 July 2007).

Library of Congress. *American Memory Project*, at memory.loc.gov/ammem/index.html (accessed 1 August 2006).

Morgan, Eric Lease. *Alex Catalogue of Electronic Texts*, 19 May 2007, at infomotions.com/alex (accessed 12 July 2007).

Ockerbloom, John Mark. *The Online Books Page*, 2007, at digital.library.upenn
.edu/books/ (accessed 12 July 2007).

Project Gutenberg, 4 May 2007, at www.gutenberg.org (accessed 12 July 2007).

University of Virginia. *Electronic Text Center*, 2 November 2006, at etext.lib.vir-
ginia.edu (accessed 12 July 2007).

A good place to start searching for electronic texts is the **Digital Book In-dex**. The site requires name and e-mail registration but is otherwise free to use. This tool indexes a number of digital collections, including several discussed below. In many cases, multiple copies of texts, including free HTML or plain text versions, are available, with other options to pay for downloads to readers or portable computing devices.

Project Gutenberg was begun in 1971 by Michael Hart, and there are currently 18,000 items available. Search features allow users to quickly identify works by author or title, with some advanced searching available. This is an excellent place to begin if you are searching for a free electronic book. John Mark Ockerbloom's **Online Book Page** provides access to a wide array of e-book projects that are made available freely online through projects that are similar to Gutenberg. The **Alex Catalogue of Electronic Texts**, created and maintained by Eric Lease Morgan, is a smaller catalog devoted to English and American literature and Western philosophy. These three sites overlap, but researchers may choose to peruse all three to locate all possible unique content. A variety of editions may have been used by people involved with the different projects.

The University of Virginia has undertaken huge efforts to provide digital access to literature in their **Electronic Text Center**, ranging from old English to contemporary works in England and the United States, as well as international works. American modernist scholars will be most interested in the "Modern English Collection," which covers all English language works from 1500 to the present. Many American modernist writers are covered here. Special collections such as "Best Sellers, 1900–1930" may also be fresh information for some researchers. The University of Virginia has worked to provide access to the materials in more formats, including new compatibility with various e-book reader software packages.

The **American Memory Project** has more to offer scholars of nineteenth-century literature, but two projects devoted to particular authors or genres are available for modernist writers. For example, ten unpublished plays by Zora Neale Hurston were rediscovered in 1997 and have been made available online through the Library of Congress **American Memory** project. Another project, The New Deal Stage: Selections from the Federal Theatre Project, provides access to scripts, posters, photographs, and other materials related to works performed during 1935–1939.

Author Sites

As noted above, the gateways offer access to hundreds of sites that focus on general topics as well as a wide array of individual authors. The American Literature Association also provides a listing of author society websites at www.calstatela.edu/academic/english/ala2/affiliates.html.

This section discusses a small sample of author-related materials, designed to provide an idea of the range of materials available. Effective use of the evaluation criteria discussed above is perhaps most crucial when searching for websites about individual authors due to the large number of student projects posted online. The quality and quantity of information available at these sites vary greatly. In many cases, the pages will be useful merely because they are the only ones available for a particular author, but the breadth and depth of content may leave much to be desired.

Sample sites are discussed below for Willa Cather, William Faulkner, Ernest Hemingway, Langston Hughes, Wallace Stevens, and Edith Wharton.

Willa Cather

University of Nebraska at Lincoln. *The Willa Cather Archive*, July 2007, at cather.unl.edu (accessed 12 July 2007).

Willa Cather Pioneer Memorial and Educational Foundation, 2007, at www.willacather.org (accessed 12 July 2007).

The ***Willa Cather Archive*** is hosted at the University of Nebraska, sponsored by the English Department and the Center for Digital Research in the Humanities. It includes access to online editions of Cather's writings, including fiction, manuscripts, and letters. Information about Cather's life, photographs, and multimedia products, as well as resources for teachers, is also provided.

The ***Willa Cather Pioneer Memorial and Educational Foundation***, located in Red Cloud, Nebraska, is an independent organization devoted to promoting Cather and her works. The organization hosts national and international conferences on Cather, administers writing competitions and scholarships for students, and runs the Cather museum and archives located in Red Cloud. The organization's website provides information about all of its programs and also presents a wide variety of Cather-related websites, news items, and event notices.

William Faulkner

University of Mississippi. *William Faulkner: American Writer, 1897–1962*, 2007, at www.mcsr.olemiss.edu/~egjbp/faulkner/faulkner.html (accessed 12 July 2007).

University of Mississippi. *The William Faulkner Society*, 2007, at www.faulkner-society.com/ (accessed 12 July 2007).

William Faulkner: American Writer, 1897–1962 is hosted at the University of Mississippi and is part of a collection of pages about Mississippi writers. The site provides a complete bibliography of Faulkner's works, including novels, short stories, letters, essays, and speeches. Access to online, full-text versions of the sources is made available when possible. The site includes information about Faulkner and his life, the region, and films based on his works.

The William Faulkner Society is also located at the University of Mississippi, and its website offers facts about the society as well as events and services, including conferences, scholarships, publication opportunities, and a mailing list for discussion of Faulkner. The site connects to other webpages devoted to the study of Faulkner and his works.

Ernest Hemingway

The Ernest Hemingway Foundation of Oak Park, 2006, at www.ehfop.org (accessed 12 July 2007).

The Ernest Hemingway Home and Museum, 2002, at www.hemingwayhome.com (accessed 12 July 2007).

Hulse, Caroline. *Ernest Hemingway*, 2007, at www.ernest.hemingway.com (accessed 12 July 2007).

The **Hemingway Home and Museum** site provides information about the Hemingway museum in Key West, with details about its collections and services. The **Hemingway Foundation**, located in Oak Park, Illinois, also has a museum and educational events. Its website offers details about those services as well as links to other sites about Hemingway.

Caroline Hulse's **Ernest Hemingway** illustrates the need for careful evaluation and consideration of websites. The author provides her credentials, but regardless of the domain name she has secured, she does not appear to have any official connection with the Ernest Hemingway Foundation or other official entity. The site contains a great deal of information, with links to works by other scholars, but a typographical error on the front page serves as an alert to be cautious of the content. Good advice for sites such as this one is to verify the factual data through another source.

Langston Hughes

Langston Hughes National Poetry Project, at www.continuinged.ku.edu/hughes (accessed 12 July 2007).

Langston Hughes, 2007, at www.poets.org/poet.php/prmPID/83 (accessed 12 July 2007).

The Langston Hughes National Poetry Project was started in 2002 as part of a project to commemorate the centennial of Hughes' birth and raise awareness among the general public of his contributions and works. The project included readings and discussions, and the website provides continuing information about Hughes and his life and works.

Langston Hughes is one site of a series at Poets.org and is maintained by the American Academy of Poets. The site offers biographical data, options for further reading, and links to poems available online. Although not a comprehensive site in terms of background, it does provide access to online texts.

Wallace Stevens

Hartford Friends and Enemies of Wallace Stevens, at www.wesleyan.edu/wstevens/ (accessed 12 July 2007).
Wallace Stevens Society, at www.wallacestevens.com/ (accessed 12 July 2007).

Hartford Friends and Enemies of Wallace Stevens hosts events in Hartford and also provides a good deal of content online, including selected poems, recordings of Stevens's readings, an online discussion group, and information about artists who were influenced by Stevens. Scholars may be particularly interested in Stevens's recordings of his own works and in making contacts with other researchers via the discussion group.

The **Wallace Stevens Society**, housed at Clarkson University in New York, publishes an online journal, as discussed in chapter 5. The site also presents materials for teachers, a concordance, a listing of journal issue contents, and related items. The concordance is particularly well done, providing a searchable index of words and themes in Stevens's work.

Edith Wharton

The Edith Wharton Society, at www.edithwhartonsociety.org/index.html (accessed 12 July 2007).
The Mount Estate and Gardens, at www.edithwharton.org/ (accessed 12 July 2007).

The **Edith Wharton Society** provides a wealth of information about Wharton, her life, and her works. It tracks secondary materials about Wharton and offers details about conferences and other events. The Society also publishes a journal and a blog for news and discussion.

The **Mount Estate and Gardens** is located in Lenox, Massachusetts, and conducts tours of Wharton's home and garden. Like other museums and foundations discussed here, it has an educational mission including tours, readings, events, and scholarships.

Current Awareness Resources

American Literature Association, at www.calstatela.edu/academic/english/ala2 (accessed 12 July 2007).

American Studies Association, *American Studies Web,* at lamp.georgetown .edu/asw/ (accessed 12 July 2007).

Kirk, Brian, ed. *Calls for Papers,* at cfp.english.upenn.edu (accessed 12 July 2007).

H-NET: Humanities and Social Sciences Online, at www.h-net.org (accessed 12 July 2007).

Modernist Studies Association, at msa.press.jhu.edu (accessed 12 July 2007).

Sauer, Geoff, ed. *Calls for Papers,* at calls.eserver.org (accessed 12 July 2007).

The Space Between: Literature and Culture 1914–1945, at www.precursors.org/ index.htm (accessed 12 July 2007).

Researching sources for this section was quite frustrating, illustrating the pitfalls of the Internet. A number of sites that are still linked on various pages and would have certainly been recommended here no longer exist, including the part of Jack Lynch's website that specifically listed e-mail discussion groups. Many people who once maintained lists of discussion groups or lists of links appear to have moved on to other pursuits. Locating discussion groups is easier than in the past, however, by visiting sites like H-NET or using search engines like *Google* or *Yahoo.*

H-NET, along with the "Calls for Papers" sites listed above, allows easy tracking of opportunities to present at conferences or write essays for journals or books. These notices can be instructive for researchers to keep track of new trends in literary research and to see what approaches other scholars are exploring in connection with particular writers or genres. The professional associations also deliver this kind of information, along with such services as connections to tables of contents or current issues of the journals they publish or sponsor.

The Space Between: Literature and Culture, 1914–1945 website reports on The Space Between society, its activities, and its journal. The society was formed by participants of a 1997 conference on the Modernist era and has been active in fostering scholarly communication about the era. The site also provides information about its annual conferences, including past themes and speakers and instructions for participating in the next conference. This is a good example of a specialized society that is directly related to the modernist movement.

Contemporary Journals and Magazines

Modern Culture & Media, Brown University. *The Modernist Journals Project*, at www.modjourn.org (accessed 31 March 2008).

Scholars of American modernism are fortunate to have at their fingertips the **Modernist Journals Project**, a joint venture between Brown University and the University of Tulsa. The project offers online, searchable editions of journals and magazines published during the years that the modernist movement took shape. Currently, three journals are available: *Dana*, *The New Age*, and *Blast*. *Dana* was published in 1904–1905, *The New Age* began in 1907, and *Blast* was in print during 1914–1915. The site includes all issues of *Dana* and *Blast* and the 1907 issues of *The New Age* as well as a selection of full-text books.

Cultural and Historical Resources

Barnes, Michael. *The Authentic History Center*, at www.authentichistory.com (accessed 12 July 2007).
Digital Library Federation. *Digital Collections Registry*, at dlf.grainger.uiuc .edu/DLFCollectionsRegistry/browse/GEMCoverage.asp (accessed 12 July 2007).
Fordham University. *Internet Modern History Sourcebook*, at www.fordham.edu/ halsall/mod/modsbook.html (accessed 12 July 2007).
New York Public Library. *NYPL Digital Gallery*, at digitalgallery.nypl.org (accessed 12 July 2007).
Smithsonian National Museum of American History, at americanhistory.si.edu (accessed 12 July 2007).
Whitley, Peggy, et al. *American Cultural History: The Twentieth Century*, at kclibrary.nhmccd.edu/decades.html (accessed 12 July 2007).

The Authentic History Center is organized into various decades and offers online access to political speeches, songs, political cartoons, sheet music, posters, and other multimedia items. Fordham University's **Internet Modern History Sourcebook** is also arranged chronologically and provides access to various documents. The New York Public Library's **Digital Gallery** is arranged by topic area. The art and literature section connects readers with digitized collections of art prints, photographs, sheet music, book dust jackets, bindings, and other materials. The *Digital Library Federation* site allows users to search by subject, place, or time period, offering access to a number of digital text and media collections. Many scholars will benefit from these collections of primary materials to enhance their study of literary works.

Peggy Whitley and others at Kingwood College Library maintain *American Cultural History: The Twentieth Century.* Visitors can choose a decade and read brief overviews of art, architecture, literature, music, fashion, fads, events, education, and media of that time. Links are provided to several other websites, and the site also offers brief bibliographies of print sources and suggested library databases for further research. This site serves as a significant starting point for beginning research into the cultural history of the Modernist era.

Print Guides to Websites

Books about websites run the risk of being obsolete as they roll off the presses. Nevertheless, they can be an effective way to quickly locate certain resources that have been recommended by a scholar or an expert in the field. Listed below are two recent, helpful guides.

Brogan, Martha L., and Daphnée Rentfrow. *A Kaleidoscope of Digital American Literature.* Washington, DC: Digital Library Federation, 2005.
Bracken, James K., and Larry G. Hinman. *The Undergraduate's Companion to American Writers and Their Web Sites.* Englewood, CO: Libraries Unlimited, 2001.

Martha L. Brogan researched the landscape of American literature in the digital realm for *A Kaleidoscope of Digital American Literature*, a report she wrote for the Digital Library Federation. She discusses a number of the broader issues related to digital access to materials while focusing on a wide array of resources for the humanities, specifically American literature. Brogan covers American literature from colonial times onward, but her work provides information about many resources available online for the modernist scholar.

As the title of James K. Bracken and Larry G. Hinman's *The Undergraduate's Companion to American Writers and Their Web Sites* indicates, their intended audience is undergraduate students, although other researchers may find the guide valuable. The source is arranged chronologically by author and includes listings of free websites, along with brief lists of print resources that will also be useful. The print resources are arranged by topic, such as biographies and criticism, journals, and bibliographies. Several modernist writers are covered in this source, including William Faulkner, F. Scott Fitzgerald, Ernest Hemingway, and Wallace Stevens.

Conclusion

This chapter discusses Web resources that were available at the time of writing. Given the fluidity of the Web, some of these resources may have disappeared and other new, essential sites may have been launched. Along with search engines, gateway sites such as *Voice of the Shuttle* can be useful for tracking these developments. Many primary and secondary materials are not available online due to copyright law, so print sources and online subscription databases will be necessary to fulfill research needs. Nevertheless, the Web can be a valuable additional source of materials. Evaluate online resources carefully, and they can certainly enrich your research process.

CHAPTER 10

Researching a Thorny Problem

Throughout this book we have covered a variety of research tools and best practices for conducting research on American literature from the Modernist period or, more broadly, the first half of the twentieth century. Although these tools and approaches answer many questions, you may have some research questions that do not have obvious answers or a clear approach. In these cases, you may have to try several different approaches and gather a range of sources that may not offer a conclusive answer but, rather, provide enough information to use in making a solid case.

Among the areas of literary research where finding direct, clear answers proves to be difficult is tracing the influence of a particular author or group of authors. For example, you might want to explore the reception and reputation of the writers of the Harlem Renaissance at the time the movement emerged, in addition to tracing the influence of those writers on others who came after. A first step would be to locate information on the history and emergence of the Harlem Renaissance, along with key participants. Finding recent secondary sources that would provide an overview is fairly simple, but locating sources from the time, such as newspaper articles, reviews, publication records, and other archival materials can prove more difficult. Locating correspondence between writers and others can offer additional insights into influence and reception. After gaining background knowledge on the broader topic, you might narrow the research question to focus on a particular author.

For this example, consider Nella Larsen, often touted as a key figure of the Harlem Renaissance. She was the first African-American woman to be awarded a Guggenheim Fellowship for creative writing. She wrote two novels, *Quicksand* (1928) and *Passing* (1929), that were well received among her peers and by critics, but after being accused of plagiarism; undergoing a messy, public divorce; and having her third novel rejected, she fell into obscurity and did not publish again. Her books were out of print for many years until the 1970s or 1980s, depending on the source.[1] In addition, there is little consistency in the biographical details of her life, and only recently has there been extensive research conducted on Larsen.

Larsen's mother was a Danish immigrant, and her father was a West Indian or perhaps an African-American. Whether her parents were married or if she ever knew her father is unclear, but several years later, her mother married a white man and had another child. Although one scholar[2] contends that her mother was with the same man, who changed his name and passed for white, other evidence indicates that Larsen indeed was the only person of mixed race in her family. Details of her childhood are extremely sketchy and, as well-known scholar and educator Charles R. Larson points out, were embroidered by Larsen herself.[3] She was trained as a nurse and later worked at the New York Public Library, earning certification at Columbia University's library school, becoming the first African-American known to be a professional librarian. She married Elmer Imes, a prominent physicist, in 1919 and they became part of educated society circles that included many of the people known for being part of the Harlem Renaissance, most notably Carl Van Vechten.

Renewed interest in Larsen's work came at a time when African-American women's writings were gaining increased scholarly attention. Yet an article about Larsen in one of Ms. Magazine's "Lost Women" features perpetuated several items thought to be long-standing errors, including information that her husband's last name was Innes, that she lived in Denmark for several years as a student, and that she died in 1963.[4] However, a recent biography by George Hutchinson shows that at least one of these items was indeed true.[5] Hutchinson did further research into the possibility of Larsen's having traveled to Denmark, a notion dismissed by Larson and others, as she stated on her 1930 passport application that it was her first. Hutchinson learned that at the time Larsen would have traveled, passports were not required, and further research uncovered ship manifests showing Larsen, her mother, and her sister as passengers.[6] Hutchinson's work sheds a great deal more light on the circumstances of Larsen's early life, along with the time she spent after falling out of the literary spotlight. Scholar Charles Larson was introduced to Larsen as part of a course at Howard University in the 1960s, where everyone had to read the copies of her work that were on reserve in the library or locate used copies if possible.[7]

Larsen published her novels under her maiden name while she was married, and no one apparently expected her to have used her married name after her divorce; until Charles Larson, other scholars never found her death certificate or other facts about her life in New York because they were not looking for Nella Imes. Although the revived interest in her work is strong, and warranted for many reasons, how can one measure her influence when her books were unavailable for many years? How did she come to be rediscovered? When did her books return to print? Were people studying her works during those years? Another question also becomes compelling, although not entirely related to her literary influence: what happened to her after she stopped writing?

The purpose of this chapter is not to disclose specific answers to these questions but, rather, to develop a plan for researching the life and works of Nella Larsen as a representative of the Harlem Renaissance. It is unlikely that any single source will have the definitive answer, and it is always possible that no source will answer a particular question. The following are steps that reference librarians would recommend for tackling the topic.

One angle of this research problem involves the publishing history of Larsen's two novels. You could search for materials about her publisher that might shed light on its practices, and you could also search for data on book sales and print runs through sources such as *Publishers Weekly*. Since the book was out of print for decades, you could use the *National Union Catalog (NUC)*, discussed in chapter 3, to determine how many libraries held copies of the original editions of her novels; this information would allow you to make some judgments about the amount of access people had to her novels from the 1930s through the 1960s. Checking the *NUC* reveals that sixteen libraries owned *Passing* and twelve libraries owned *Quicksand*. The books were available in major metropolitan public libraries, including New York, Boston, Toronto, and Cleveland, and they were held by universities across the United States, including University of Kansas, Duke University, University of Colorado, and University of Virginia. You could also consult reference works such as *Books in Print* or online union catalogs like *Open WorldCat* to gather data about various editions and publication dates of Larsen's novels. Because she won the Harmon Award, research of the Harmon Foundation and its literary awards could open another door to information about Larsen and her colleagues. To locate facts about the award, you could search the indexes for the *New York Times* and also reference sources such as *The Encyclopedia of Associations* or *The Foundations Directory*.

To learn more about the impact of Larsen's works, you might search library catalogs for materials that discuss her and her writing. Try different search techniques; keyword searching will return the broadest range of results, although some of those may be works in anthologies rather than critical treatments of her work. You may also search more broadly for materials on the Harlem Renaissance or, alternately, on her colleagues such as Carl Van Vechten. In addition to obtaining the actual materials that scholars have produced, tracing the quantity of scholarship and the timeline of publication could shed light on the question of her influence. If her works were not broadly studied prior to their reissue but were apparently taught in African-American literature courses, you could be on the path of an interesting exploration of issues of race and of canonical status of literary works.

In addition to monographs, use the indexes discussed in chapter 4 to trace scholarship related to Larsen's works published in journals. Tracing critical appraisal is also crucial, and given the dates of Larsen's novels, online indexes may not provide deep-enough coverage. Take advantage of print indexes as needed. In addition to scholarly journals, newspapers will offer glimpses into Larsen's life and the reaction to her works. Many libraries deliver online access to various historical newspapers, including ProQuest's collection of *The New York Times, Los Angeles Times,* and *Chicago Defender.* For example, a search in the *Chicago Defender* revealed a brief piece about Larsen, accompanied by a photo, published in September 1933, noting that she was visiting Chicago and that her third novel would be published in the spring.[8]

Refer to the sources and strategies in chapters 6 and 7 for delving into reviews written at the time Larsen was publishing and to locate magazines and newspapers of her time. In this case, it will be important to pursue not only mainstream periodicals but also the robust body of work that appeared in African-American newspapers, such as the *New York Amsterdam News, Baltimore Afro-American,* and *Chicago Defender.* For example, a review of *Quicksand* in the *Chicago Defender* from 1928 praises Larsen for her "gradual development of character over lengthy periods of time and under varied circumstances."[9] To assist in locating more African-American papers and indexes, most libraries will have in their collections the reference book *African American Newspapers and Periodicals: A National Bibliography.*[10]

Information about and access to some African-American newspapers are also available freely on the Web. Locating copies of articles from the 1920s and 1930s may require use of interlibrary loan services. Check with a reference librarian for more details. Be sure to search the Web using search engines such as *Google* to locate materials similar to those discussed in chapter 9. Among the Web resources that may be particularly informative are the *Schomberg Center for Research in Black Culture* website, part of the Digital New York Public Library, and the University of Virginia's *Electronic Text Center.*[12] In addition to online digital archives, review chapter 8 for strategies in using manuscripts and archives collections.

When you cannot locate sources or tools that answer your questions, consult a reference librarian, who can recommend other sources or help formulate your search strategy. While you may be happy to find nothing when researching unique but potentially difficult dissertation topics, in other cases you may be frustrated. A reference librarian can help determine whether there are other sources to consider. In addition, refer to colleagues in your field for advice or guidance. Even though you may be embarking on a unique research quest, librarians and other scholars can assist you in the journey.

Conclusion

Throughout this volume we have discussed sources and processes for the best approaches to researching literary topics related to American modernism. Print sources and webpages will be updated, database and search engine interfaces will be modified, and digital projects will continue to emerge. However, the basic skills needed for conducting research efficiently and effectively apply to all types of sources. As soon as this volume is printed, there will undoubtedly be new resources that would have been included here if the timing were different. Information is being produced at such a rapid pace that scholars must be flexible and willing to deal with changes. Many of the changes will be positive, increasing access to materials online. Reference librarians spend a great deal of time keeping current on new developments; consult with them as you progress in your research, so that you can also remain current on developments in essential collections. By honing research skills and considering the best practices for literary research discussed in this volume, scholars of American literature can confidently address any research problem and the resources available to solve it.

Notes

1. In reality, both novels were reissued by the Negro Universities Press in 1969. *Passing* was reprinted by Collier in 1971 and *Quicksand* by Knopf in 1973. Many other editions have appeared since then.

2. Thadious Davis, *Nella Larsen, Novelist of the Harlem Renaissance: A Woman's Life Unveiled* (Baton Rouge: Louisiana State University Press, 1994), pp. 21–50.

3. Charles R. Larson, *Invisible Darkness: Jean Toomer and Nella Larsen* (Iowa City: University of Iowa Press, 1993), pp. 185–88.

4. Mary Helen Washington, "Nella Larsen: Mystery Woman of the Harlem Renaissance," *Ms. Magazine* 9 (December 1980): 44–50.

5. George Hutchinson, *In Search of Nella Larsen: A Biography of the Color Line* (Cambridge, MA: Harvard University Press, 2006).

6. Ibid., pp. 4–5.

7. Larson, Charles R., ed. *An Intimation of Things Distant: The Collected Fiction of Nella Larsen* (New York: Anchor, 1992), pp. xi. (Note that this collection includes *Passing, Quicksand,* and the three stories she published. The first two were published under the pseudonym Allen Semi, and the third is the one she was accused of plagiarizing.)

8. "Novelist Here." *Chicago Defender* 23 September 1933, p. 4. ProQuest *Historical Newspapers*, 27 May 2007. Note that the third novel referred to in the article is the one that she wrote during her Guggenheim fellowship and was rejected by Knopf.

9. Barefield Gordon, "The Bookshelf," *The Chicago Defender* 25 August 1928: A1.

10. James P. Danky and Maureen E. Hady, eds., *African American Newspapers and Periodicals: A National Bibliography* (Cambridge, MA: Harvard University Press, 1999). This work covers sources published from 1827 to 1998.

11. The URLs for the *Schomberg Center for Research in Black Culture* and the *Electronic Test Center* are http://www.nypl.org/research/sc/sc.html and http://etext.virginia.edu/subjects/African-American.html, respectively.

Appendix

Selected Resources in Related Disciplines

This selection of resources is designed to supplement the research material discussed throughout this book with topical sections on literature and other academic disciplines. Although somewhat specialized, they may help clarify specific issues and problems or suggest research possibilities that are not contained in conventional literary reference tools. Some of these titles will convey the broad range of reference tools that have been developed for specific disciplines, including literature. Researchers might want to examine the titles in their libraries that are shelved near the printed resources listed here to broaden their knowledge of secondary and allied research material. Another option consists in searching for additional titles using the Library of Congress subject headings assigned to an especially useful book or in an article citation. The notes and bibliographies found in research sources may also yield valuable additional material. To round out our overview of scholarly works that treat literature, literary texts, and books as objects of specialized study, we also provide a section on general research guides and bibliography and another section on literary terms and related topics.

As noted in chapter 2, for literary research the guides by Michael Marcuse and James Harner generally remain the best place to start. Both of these reference works contain sections with annotated entries on supplemental material for literary research. Harner plans further revisions and updates to his *Literary Research Guide: An Annotated Listing of Reference Sources in English and Literary Studies* with a revised fifth edition scheduled for release in 2008

For convenience, annotated entries in each topical section are grouped together in alphabetical order regardless of format. Consult a reference librarian if you have questions about these or other reference resources that might be useful for your research in American modernism. Some online reference tools are only available through commercial subscriptions, and licensing agreements for their use will vary among institutions.

General

Balay, Robert, ed. *Guide to Reference Books.* 11th ed. Chicago: American Library Association, 1996.

Comprehensive annotated listing of 15,875 reference titles in all disciplines published primarily in North America. The indispensable starting point to get an overview of the general contours of research reference material published by 1993. The chapter on "Literature" contains useful information on sources for the study of twentieth-century American literature.

Art

Cummings, Paul. *Dictionary of Contemporary American Artists.* 6th ed. New York: St. Martin's Press, 1994.

Alphabetically arranged guide to twentieth-century American artists consisting of summary entries containing birth and death dates, birthplace, education, teaching appointments, professional memberships, commissions, awards, exhibitions, retrospectives, and museum collections. In this edition, deleted artists who appeared in previous editions are cross-referenced to those guides. Also features illustrations, an index to artists, a subject bibliography, and a general bibliography.

RILA (International Repertory of the Literature of Art). New York: College Art Association of America, 1975–1989.
Bibliography of the History of Art. Santa Monica, CA: J. Paul Getty Trust and Institut de l'Information Scientifique et Technique du Centre National de la Recherche Scientifique (INIST-NRS).

Indexes to the literature of art from ancient to modern times. The printed edition of *RILA* has subject and author indexes and is superseded and absorbed by the *Bibliography of the History of Art*, a commercial RLG product, with database sources in France and the United States, that covers thousands of art periodicals from all time periods. Information about electronic editions of the *Bibliography* is available at http://www.getty.edu/research/conducting_research/bha/.

Turner, Jane, ed. *The Dictionary of Art*. 34 vols. New York: Grove's Dictionaries, Inc., 1996.

Consists of 45,500 signed alphabetical entries on artists, national art, movements, schools, groups, and techniques in art and related disciplines, from antiquity to the present. Illustrated throughout. Entries consist of a combination of biographical information, unpublished sources, primary published writings, and bibliographies. A comprehensive index provides detailed access to *Dictionary* contents, with multiple entries on "modernism" and closely related terms. Available online at http:www.groveart.com/.

Bibliography and Research Guides

Altick, Richard D., and John J. Fenstermaker. *The Art of Literary Research*. 4th ed. New York: W. W. Norton & Company, 1993.

A deeply informed, nuanced humanistic treatment of literary scholarship and research just prior to the rise of the Internet and the World Wide Web. Wide-ranging narrative chapters on composition, libraries, finding materials, making notes, textual editing, areas of literary scholarship, and traditional scholarly protocols involving evidence and document evaluation. The volume features a chapter of literary exercises and a useful classified bibliography of additional readings.

Barzun, Jacques, and Henry F. Graff. *The Modern Researcher*. 6th ed. Belmont, CA: Thomson/Wadsworth Learning, 2004.

Barzun and Graff's *The Modern Researcher* was first published in the 1950s and reflects the authors' academic background in the discipline of history. Chapters on library research, composition, and the publishing process are informed by long experience and provide useful guidance and advice for the beginning researcher.

Booth, Wayne C., Gregory G. Colomb, and Joseph M. Williams. *The Craft of Research*. 2nd ed. Chicago: University of Chicago Press, 2003.

Clear introductory research guide by literature professors with chapters on the context and value of research, writing for specific audiences, forming topical questions and research problems, structuring arguments, and gathering and evaluating reasons and evidence. Also contains good chapters on the writing and editorial process for expository writing. An appendix has a classified bibliography of research resources that provides examples of different kinds of reference materials in each discipline.

Greetham, D. C. *Textual Scholarship: An Introduction.* New York: Garland Publishing, Inc., 1994.

A standard text on the history of textual scholarship and contemporary trends in the field. Describes the evolution of printing, books, and publishing; types of bibliography; the construction of texts and textual editing; and types of scholarly editions. Well illustrated, with an extensive classified bibliography and index. Because of its scope and detail, this book is recommended for advanced scholars.

Harner, James L. *On Compiling an Annotated Bibliography.* 2nd ed. New York: The Modern Language Association of America, 2000.

Short pamphlet offering practical guidance on compiling an annotated bibliography that emphasizes individual literary authors. Examines preparation, organization, and research, with notes, a section of bibliographies by type, a list of cited works, and a useful appendix of "annotation verbs."

Krummel, D. W. *Bibliographies: Their Aims and Methods.* New York: Mansell Publishing Limited, 1984.

Clear historical and analytical treatment of bibliography as a distinct discipline in library science. Contains sections on research, preparation, arrangement, and editing and insightful notes on annotating. Appendixes describe criteria for evaluating bibliographies and a list of significant national bibliographies. Also lists selected resources on subjects related to bibliography.

Mann, Thomas. *The Oxford Guide to Library Research.* 3rd ed. New York: Oxford University Press, 2005.

Solid overview of library research, including types of reference materials, database searching and search strategies, American library classification and arrangement, and chapters on finding source material in different media in research libraries. This guide is especially good at describing important connections between research sources and strategies.

Williams, William Proctor, and Craig S. Abbott. *An Introduction to Bibliographical and Textual Studies*. 3rd ed. New York: Modern Language Association of America, 1999.

A concise introductory guide to reference bibliography, historical bibliography, analytical bibliography, and descriptive bibliography; texts and textual criticism; and editing and editorial procedures. The volume has a glossary of bibliographical and textual terms as well as an index.

Literary Terms and Topics

Groden, Michael, Martin Kreiswirth, and Imre Szeman, eds. *The John Hopkins Guide to Literary Theory & Criticism*. 2nd ed. Baltimore: The John Hopkins University Press, 2005.

Featuring 241 signed entries by 270 contributors, this guide covers literature and literary theory in a cross-disciplinary context from the classical period through the early twenty-first century. Alphabetical entries have cross-references and bibliographies. Indexes consist of an alphabetical list of the entries; an alphabetized list of contributors, including their academic affiliations and entry topic; an index of proper names and their occurrence in the *Guide*'s text; and an alphabetical index of major and subsidiary topics, linked to their appearance in the text. The *Guide* is a useful reference source on contemporary literary theory and is also available electronically from the Johns Hopkins University Press, with information available at http://www.press.jhu.edu/.

Harmon, William, and Hugh Holman. *A Handbook to Literature*. 10th ed. Upper Saddle River, NJ: Pearson Prentice Hall, 2006.

This is the latest update on a classic guide to literary terms, literary facts and movements, linguistics, rhetoric, literary criticism, and terms in information technology. Entries are alphabetically arranged, with useful cross-references to related entries. A dual chronological outline summarizes British and American literary history from 82 to 2005 A.D., with brief publishing information organized by year and literary movements. Appendixes feature sections on British and American monetary terms and values from 1275 to 1975 A.D., a list of Nobel laureates in literature through 2004, and the Pulitzer Prize winners in poetry, fiction, and drama through 2005. Also contains a proper name index linked to *Handbook* entries.

Preminger, Alex, and T. V. F. Brogan, eds. *The New Princeton Encyclopedia of Poetry and Poetics.* Princeton, NJ: Princeton University Press, 1993.

This is a comprehensive single-volume reference on poetry, poetics, literary terms and literary theories, criticism, schools, and national traditions from all time periods. Initialed entries are arranged in alphabetical order and offer cross-references and bibliographical notes. An alphabetical contents list and list of contributors make this a user-friendly source. This title is also available electronically through *Literature Online* from ProQuest, with subscription information available at http://proquest.com/.

History and Social Sciences

America: History and Life. Santa Barbara, CA: ABC-CLIO, 1964–.

This commercial online database offers extensive coverage of secondary scholarly literature on United States and Canadian history. Searches may be limited to particular time periods and subjects. Citations have informative article abstracts. The database also features CLIO Notes, consisting of brief overviews and chronologies of historical periods and suggestions for class papers. For ease of use and access to content, the electronic version of this resource is recommended instead of the older print version. For research in world history from 1450 to the present, consult the electronic edition of *Historical Abstracts*, a commercial database available from the same vendor.

Cayton, Mary Kupiec, and Peter W. Williams, eds. *Encyclopedia of American Cultural and Intellectual History.* 3 vols. New York: Charles Scribner's Sons, 2001.

Signed articles cover the entire range of American history from the Colonial Period through the year 2000 and include the arts, sciences, social sciences, economics, politics, and cultural history. Part 5 in volume 1 covers different phases of early American modernism. Volume 3 contains synoptic articles and the index to the entire set. Excellent source of information for American modernism and related cultural information, with useful bibliographies in each article.

Fritze, Ronald H., Brian E. Coutts, and Louis A. Vyhnanek. *Reference Sources in History: An Introductory Guide.* 2nd ed. Santa Barbara, CA: ABC-CLIO, 2004.

Covering all time periods and geographic regions, *Reference Sources* consists of 930 numbered and annotated items arranged in fourteen chapters, along with an extensive index. Scope comprises all media and formats of historical source material and auxiliary resources for doing historical research. Recommended for beginning and advanced scholars.

Hornblower, Simon, and Antony Spawforth, eds. *Oxford Classical Dictionary.* 3rd ed., revised. Oxford: Oxford University Press, 2003.

"An authoritative one-volume guide to all aspects of the classical world" (1st ed.). The latest edition consists of 6,250 alphabetical entries authored by 364 international scholars. Entries indicate supplemental secondary materials. Provides a good overview of classical sources in American modernist writing. This resource is also available electronically from Oxford University Press, with information at http://www.oup.com/online/oro/.

Kutler, Stanley I. *Dictionary of American History.* 3rd ed., 10 vols. New York: Charles Scribner's Sons, 2003.

Updated edition of standard reference source in American history. Manageable, signed articles with short bibliographies. The index in volume 10 provides detailed access to contents, with entries on modernism and literature as well as short articles on social and cultural history covering the Modernist period.

Rose, Cynthia, ed. *American Decades Primary Sources.* 10 vols. Detroit, MI: Thomson-Gale, 2004.

Coverage of twentieth-century America in two thousand "primary sources," or from contemporary contextual material used to supplement the decade-by-decade thematic approach of the series. Articles have chronologies and bibliographies and sometimes feature useful websites and other illustrative information. Volumes 2 through 5 cover the American Modernist era from 1910 to 1949. In addition to the arts, standardized volume topics take in medicine and health, science and technology, religion, the media, and lifestyles and social trends, among others. Each volume contains a section on general resources and an index. This resource is also available as an e-book from Gale, with information available at http://www.gale.cengage.com/servlet/ItemDetailServlet?region=9&imprint=000&titleCode=ADC1E&cf=e&type=4&id=226375.

Philosophy

Borchert, Donald M., ed. *Encyclopedia of Philosophy.* 2nd ed., 10 vols. Detroit, MI: Thomson-Gale, 2006.

All geographic areas, time periods, and major schools are represented in signed articles that are arranged by topic in alphabetical order with references to related material and selected bibliographies. Entries on individuals note birth and death dates. Volume 1 contains alphabetical lists of contributors and topics covered in the set. Volume 10 has an appendix of supplemental material, bibliographical essays on reference works in philosophy, and a comprehensive index to the set. The article on modernism and postmodernism may be found in volume 4. An e-book version of this source is also available from Thomson-Gale, with information at http://www.gale.com/catalog/facts.htm.

Craig, Edward, ed. *Routledge Encyclopedia of Philosophy.* 10 vols. New York: Routledge, 1998.

Standard reference set alphabetically arranged by topics, with signed entries. Articles have a section with references and suggestions for further reading. Volume 1 features a complete list of alphabetized entries and contributors for the entire set; other volumes contain the alphabetical list of all topics only. The article on modernism may be found in volume 6. An electronic edition is also available, with subscription information at http://www.rep.routledge.com/about.

Horowitz, Maryanne Cline, ed. *New Dictionary of the History of Ideas.* 6 vols. New York: Charles Scribner's Sons, 2005.

Thorough update of classic reference work in intellectual history covering all time periods, major thinkers, and significant texts. Signed articles feature bibliographies and references to related articles in other sections of the *New Dictionary.* Volume 1 has alphabetical list of articles for entire set as well as a reader's guide that groups entries thematically and chronologically. Materials on modernism, modernity, modernization, and modernization theory are available.

Shook, John R., ed. *Dictionary of Modern American Philosophers.* 4 vols. Bristol, England: Thoemmes, 2005.

Contains 1,082 signed entries by five hundred contributors covering philosophical thought from 1860 to the early 1960s. Each entry contains known birth and death dates; a discussion of the subject's writings, teachings, and thought; cross-references to other entries; a bibliography section; and a section that lists selected readings. Volume 4 contains the personal name index to the entire set. The researcher can identify thinkers and philosophers relevant to the Modernist period from birth and death dates as well as from the citations in article bibliographies.

The Philosopher's Index: An International Index to Philosophical Periodicals and Books. Bowling Green, OH: Philosopher's Information Center.

Available in print and in commercial electronic versions offered by different vendors, the first printed cumulative edition appeared in 1967. This is the primary index in the field of philosophical literature, with coverage of roughly five hundred journals from 1940 to the present. Libraries may have different licensing agreements for the online version of this index, but for convenience it is preferable to the printed version.

Articles dealing with intellectual history and with philosophical themes relating to literature may be found in the *Modern Language Association International Bibliography* (*MLAIB*).

Religion

Jones, Lindsay, ed. *Encyclopedia of Religion.* 2nd ed., 15 vols. Detroit, MI: Thomson-Gale, 2006.

Updated edition of the standard reference source in the field that was first published in 1987 and edited by Mircea Eliade. Signed articles arranged in alphabetical order indicate whether they are from the older or newer edition and feature cross-references and short bibliographies. Volume 15 contains the comprehensive index, an appendix of referenced articles, and a synoptic outline of contents describing the conceptual scheme of the encyclopedia. This set is also available as an e-book from Thomson-Gale, with information at http://www.gale.com/index.htm.

Lippy, Charles H., and Peter W. Williams, eds. *Encyclopedia of the American Religious Experience.* 3 vols. New York: Charles Scribner's Sons, 1988.

Broad topical articles on different aspects of American religion. Signed, alphabetically arranged articles contain bibliographies, with an index to the set in volume 3. Parts 5 and 7 contain material relevant to the period of American modernist writing.

Queen, Edgar L. II, Stephen R. Prothero, and Gardiner H. Shattuck, eds., *Encyclopedia of American Religious History.* Revised ed., 2 vols. New York: Facts on File, Inc., 2001.

Signed topical articles arranged in alphabetical order, with bibliographies. The synoptic index in volume 2 arranges articles under specific subject headings. Volume 2 also includes a general index.

Additional material on the role of religion in America may be found in the historical database *America: History and Life* and in the *MLAIB* as well as in the titles by Cayton and Rose cited above under "History and Social Sciences."

Music

Crabtree, Phillip D., and Donald H. Foster, revised and expanded by Allen Scott. *Sourcebook for Research in Music*. 2nd ed. Bloomington: Indiana University Press, 2005.

More focused and up to date than Duckles, this guide to music research is divided into eight chapters covering different historical periods, geographic regions, musical genres, and reference sources in various media. Entries are annotated, and the volume has name and title indexes, but lack of a subject index means the researcher must consult the contents pages in order to locate relevant material.

Duckles, Vincent H., Ida Reed, and Michael A. Keller. *Music Reference and Research Materials: An Annotated Bibliography*. 5th ed. New York: Schirmer Books, 1997.

Begun as a class syllabus, this is now the standard comprehensive reference guide for resources in music research. Thirteen general topic chapters list annotated entries numbered in decimal notation covering types of sources, genres, guides, chronologies and histories, bibliographies, specialized reference sources, catalogs, discographies, yearbooks and directories, and electronic information resources. A large index provides detailed access to volume contents, including material on modernism in music.

RILM Abstracts of Music Literature. New York: RILM, 1967–.

Comprehensive index of citations and abstracts from core and primary music periodicals. Features research materials in all formats covering critical literature and other resources about music and music source material from 1967 to the present. This title is available in a commercial electronic version at http://www.rilm.org.

Sadie, Stanley, ed. *The New Grove Dictionary of Music and Musicians*. 2nd ed., 29 vols. New York: Grove, 2001.

Latest update of standard reference source on all phases of music and musicians. In addition to an article on modernism in volume 16, the index to the set contains an extensive list of entries for the United States and another list under the heading "Modernism." This reference source is commercially available in electronic format at http://www.grovemusic.com.

Sciences and Medicine

Cartwright, John H., and Brian Baker. *Literature and Science: Social Impact and Interaction.* Santa Barbara, CA: ABC-CLIO, 2005.

Historical survey of science and literature chronologically arranged in thematic chapters from the Medieval period through the twentieth century. Literary periods include the Elizabethan era, the Romantic era from 1790 to 1840, and the time of Darwinism and Gothic literature in the nineteenth century. Researchers in American modernism will find chapters 10–12 pertinent in its coverage of major scientific advances and their impacts in the twentieth century. An appendix of primary source documents reprints material originally published during the time periods covered. A bibliography of secondary sources gathers additional readings in science and literature.

Heilbrfon, J. L. ed. *The Oxford Companion to the History of Modern Science.* New York: Oxford University Press, 2003.

Focuses primarily on the sciences in modernity as embedded within cultural and social contexts. The thematic listing of signed entries emphasizes modernity and postmodernity, art and science, literature and science, and other topics current during the period of American modernist writing.

Hessenbruch, Arne, ed. *Reader's Guide to the History of Science.* Chicago: Fitzroy Dearborn Publishers, 2000.

Broad thematic coverage in short articles of roughly five hundred topics in the history of science, primarily dealing with individuals, disciplines, and institutions. Ample bibliographies offer coverage of secondary literature, and signed articles have cross-references and specific reference lists. A comprehensive index and an alphabetic list of entries by category further subdivided into topical entries are available, with various index entries for literature, the novel, the United States, culture, etc.

Isis: An International Review Devoted to the History of Science and Its Cultural Influences. Chicago: University of Chicago Press/History of Science Society, 1912–.
Isis Current Bibliography of the History of Science and Its Cultural Influences. Chicago: University of Chicago Press, Journals Division, 1913–.

Isis covers all periods and fields in the history of science and its cultural influences. Issues feature signed book reviews, with an annual cumulative index in issue 4 and an annual cumulative bibliography for the field in issue 5. Reflecting expansion in coverage over the run of *Isis*, supplemental volumes of cumulative *Isis* bibliographies offer more convenient access to journal contents, with the *Isis Cumulative Bibliography, 1913–1965*, edited by Magda Withrow, of potential interest to scholars of American modernism.

Lindberg, David C., and Ronald L. Numbers, eds. *The Cambridge History of Science.* New York: Cambridge University Press, 2003–.

Volume 5, *The Modern Physical and Mathematical Sciences*, edited by Mary Jo Nye, is composed of short narrative chapters on physical science and Western religion in the nineteenth and twentieth centuries; literature and the modern physical sciences, physics and cosmology during the early twentieth century; and science, ideology, and the state in the twentieth century. Volume 7, *Modern Social Sciences*, edited by Theodore M. Porter and Dorothy Ross, covers the nineteenth century and the subsequent rise of anthropology and sociology, psychology, and political science, among other areas. Each short chapter features a different synoptic treatment by an expert or experts in the field and has bibliographical notes. Parts 3 and 4 feature material on modernization, including its role in an American context. The index entry for the United States draws various themes together. Volume 6 in this series, *The Modern Biological and Earth Sciences*, had not been published as of this writing.

Olby, R.C., et al, eds. *Companion to the History of Modern Science.* New York: Routledge, 1990.

Useful narrative account of different facets of modern science. Researchers in American modernism will find section IIC, "Themes," of particular value.
    For additional information on the sciences and medicine in the period of American modernism, see Mary Kupiec Cayton and Peter W. Williams, eds., *Encyclopedia of American Cultural and Intellectual History*, and Cynthia Rose, ed., *American Decades Primary Sources*, both described above under "History and Social Sciences." The index *America: History and Life* also contains historical material on the sciences and medicine in American history.

Theatre

Bordman, Gerald. *The Oxford Companion to American Theatre*. 2nd ed. New York: Oxford University Press, 1992.

Alphabetical listing of people and institutions associated with American theatre, with extensive cross-references.

Wheatley, Christopher J., ed. *Twentieth-Century American Dramatists. Dictionary of Literary Biography*. Vol. 228. Detroit, MI: The Gale Group, 2000.

This volume in the *Dictionary of Literary Biography* series offers essays on selected American dramatists, including women and minority writers. The volume comes with an introductory historical essay by the editor and signed articles arranged in alphabetical order. Entries feature sections on primary texts and selected secondary sources and information on manuscript collections. A list of books for further reading cites references books on drama from the period of American modernist writing.

Wilmeth, Don B. *Cambridge Guide to American Theatre*. New York: Cambridge University Press, 1993.

An introductory historical survey of American theatre, with signed alphabetical entries on plays, playwrights, actors, critics, and others associated with American theatre. A list of topical entries is supplemented with a select classified bibliography and an alphabetical biographical index.

Additional material on American theater is available in the *MLAIB*.

Bibliography

Armstrong, Tim. *Modernism*. Malden, MA: Polity Press, 2005.

Avrett, Robert. "Waning Art of Book Reviewing." *South Atlantic Bulletin* 14, no. 4 (March 1949): 1, 8–9.

Barbour, Scott, ed. *American Modernism*. San Diego: Greenhaven, 2000.

Barsanti, Michael. "Little Magazines." p. 462 in *The Oxford Encyclopedia of American Literature*. Vol. 2. New York: Oxford University Press, 2004.

Bellardo, Lewis, and Lady Lynn Bellardo. *A Glossary for Archivists, Manuscript Curators, and Records Managers*. Chicago: Society of American Archivists, 1992.

Benstock, Shari, and Bernard Benstock. "The Role of Little Magazines in the Emergence of Modernism." *Library Chronicle of the University of Texas at Austin* 20, no. 4 n.s. (1991): 69–87.

Bishop, Edward. "Re: Covering Modernism: Format and Function in the Little Magazines" p. 287 in *Modernist Writers and the Marketplace*, eds. Ian Wilson, Warwick Gould, and Warren Chernaik. New York: St. Martin's Press, 1996.

Botshon, Lisa, and Meredith Goldsmith, eds. *Middlebrow Moderns: Popular American Women Writers of the 1920s*. Boston: Northeastern University Press, 2003.

Bradshaw, David, and Kevin J. H. Dettmar. *A Companion to Modernist Literature and Culture*. Malden, MA: Blackwell Publishing, Ltd., 2006.

Carter, John. *ABC for Book Collectors*. Revised by Nicholas Barker. 8th ed. New Castle, DE: Oak Knoll Press, 2004.

Chielens, Edward E. *The Literary Journal in America, 1900–1950*. Detroit: Gale, 1977.

Churchill, Suzanne W., and Adam McKible, "Little Magazines and Modernism: An Introduction." *American Periodicals* 15, no. 1 (2005): 4.

Cohen, M. J. *The Penguin Dictionary of Epigrams*. New York: Penguin Putnam, Inc., 2001.

Cross, Gary. *An All-Consuming Century: Why Commercialism Won in Modern America*. New York: Columbia University Press, 2000.

Danky, James P., and Maureen E. Hady, eds. *African American Newspapers and Periodicals: A National Bibliography*. Cambridge, MA: Harvard University Press, 1999.

Davis, Thadious. *Nella Larsen, Novelist of the Harlem Renaissance: A Woman's Life Unveiled*. Baton Rouge: Louisiana State University Press, 1994.

Douglas, George H. *The Golden Age of the Newspaper*. Westport, CT: Greenwood Press, 1999.

Eliot, T. S. "Last Words." *The Criterion* 18, no. 71 (January 1939): 274.

"*Faulkner Newsletter* & *Yoknapatawpha Review* ceases publication after 20 years." *Mississippi Writers Page*. (20 March 2002). www.olemiss.edu/mwp/news/2002/2002_03_20_faulknernewsletterceases.html (Accessed 15 May 2007).

Gates, Henry Louis, Jr. and Evelyn Brooks-Higginbotham, eds. *The African American National Biography*. 8 Vols. New York: Oxford University Press, 2008.

Foerster, Norman. *American Criticism: A Study of Literary Theory from Poe to the Present*. New York: Russell & Russell, Inc., 1928, rprt. 1962.

Golden, Marita. "Foreword." *An Intimation of Things Distant: The Collected Fiction of Nella Larsen*. New York: Anchor, 1992.

Goodyear, Dana. "The Moneyed Muse." *The New Yorker* (19 & 26 February 2007): 122–35.

Gordon, Barefield. "The Bookshelf." *Chicago Defender* (25 August 1928): A1.

Grazia, Edward de. *Girls Lean Back Everywhere: The Law of Obscenity and the Assault on Genius*. New York: Random House, 1992.

Harner, James L. *Literary Research Guide: An Annotated Listing of Reference Sources in English Literary Studies*. 4th ed. New York: The Modern Language Association of America, 2002.

Hayman, Stanley Edgar. *The Armed Vision: A Study in the Methods of Modern Literary Criticism*. New York: Vintage, 1955.

Hoffman, Frederick J., Charles Allen, and Carolyn F. Ulrich. *The Little Magazine: A History and a Bibliography*. Princeton, NJ: Princeton University Press, 1946.

Hutchinson, George. *In Search of Nella Larsen: A Biography of the Color Line*. Cambridge, MA: Harvard University Press, 2006.

Jay, Gregory S., ed. *Modern American Critics, 1920–1955*. Detroit: Gale Research Company, 1988.

Lawson, Charles R. *Invisible Darkness: Jean Toomer and Nella Larsen*. Iowa City: University of Iowa Press, 1993.

Little Magazines, American: 1910/1919–1940+. Millwood, NY: Kraus-Thompson Organization, Ltd., 1978–79.

Litz, A. Walton, Louis Menand, and Lawrence Rainey, eds. *Modernism and the New Criticism*. New York: Cambridge University Press, 2000.

"Novelist Here." *Chicago Defender* (23 September 1933): 4. ProQuest Historical Newspapers (Accessed 27 May 2007).

Peacock, John. *The Complete Fashion Sourcebook*. New York: Thames & Hudson, 2005.

Pearce-Moses, Richard, et al. *A Glossary of Archival and Records Terminology*. Chicago: Society of American Archivists, 2005.

Schudson, Michael. *Discovering the News: A Social History of American Newspapers*. New York: Basic Books, 1978.

Tebbell, John. *The Compact History of the American Newspaper*. New York: Hawthorn Books, 1969.

———. *The Magazine in America, 1741–1990.* New York: Oxford University Press, 1991.

Timberlake, Evelyn, comp. Research Guide No. 14, "Microform Resources for the Study of American Literature." Library of Congress. www.loc.gov/rr/microform/amlitmic.html (Accessed 8 October 2006).

Turner, Catherine. *Marketing Modernism Between the Two World Wars.* Amherst: University of Massachusetts Press, 2003.

Wagner, Geoffrey. "The Decline of Book Reviewing." *The American Scholar* 26, no. 1 (Winter 1956–1957): 23–36.

Wallace, Aurora. *Newspapers and the Making of Modern America: A History.* Westport, CT: Greenwood Press, 2005.

Washington, Mary Helen. "Nella Larsen: Mystery Woman of the Harlem Renaissance." *Ms. Magazine* 9 (December 1980): 44–50.

Watson, Richard. "Modernist Little Magazines: A List of Selected Holdings at the Harry Ransom Humanities Research Center." *Library Chronicle of the University of Texas at Austin* 20, no.4 n.s. (1991): 89–97.

Watson, Steve. *Strange Bedfellow: The First American Avant-Garde.* New York: Abbeville Press, 1991.

Wellek, René. "Criticism, Literary." p. 601 in *Dictionary of the History of Ideas*, ed. Philip P. Weiner. Vol. 1. New York: Charles Scribner's Sons, 1973.

Index

ABELL. See Annual Bibliography of English Language and Literature
Abraham, Terry, *Repositories of Primary Sources, 1995–*, 113, 114
The Access Index to Little Magazines (Burke, Fulton, & Kehde), 102
Adams, Stephen, J., *The Ezra Pound Encyclopedia*, 28, 30–31
African-American Newspapers and Periodicals: A National Bibliography, 99–100, 138
AL. See American Literature
Alex Catalogue of Electronic Texts (Morgan), 125, 126
ALH. See American Literary History
ALR. See American Literary Realism
American Cultural History: The Twentieth Century (Whitley), 131, 132
American Expatriate Writers: Paris in the Twenties (Bruccoli & Trogdon), 102, 105
American Fiction, 1900–1950: A Guide to Information Sources (Woodress), 57, 59
American Fiction, 1901–1925: A Bibliography (Smith), 61
American Literary History (ALH), 73, 75
American Literary Magazines: The Twentieth Century (Chielens), 102, 103–4

American Literary Manuscripts (Robbins), 118, 121
American Literary Realism (ALR), 73, 75
American Literary Scholarship: An Annual, 64–65
American Literature (AL), 73, 75
American Literature Association, 127, 130
American literature, journals on, 73–79
American Literature on the Web (Ishikawa), 124, 125
American Memory Project, 125, 126
American Modernism (Barbour), 17, 18
American National Biography (ANB), 24, 25–26, 113, 115, 118, 120
American Periodicals Series Online, 1740–1900 (APS Online), 83, 84–85
American Playwrights, 1880–1945: A Research and Production Sourcebook (Demastes), 60, 61
American Prose and Criticism, 1900–1950 (Brier & Arthur), 57
American Quarterly (AQ), 74, 75
American Studies Association, *American Studies Web*, 130
American Studies International (ASInt), 74, 75–76
American Studies Web (American Studies Association), 130

American Writers: A Collection of Literary Biographies, 24, 25

ANB. *See American National Biography*

and (Boolean operator), 5–6, *5f, 6f*

An Annotated Critical Bibliography of Modernism (Davies), 59, 60

Annual Bibliography of English Language and Literature (ABELL), 49, 51, 52–55, *54f*, 83, 84; versus *MLAIB*, 52–55

annual reviews, 50, 64–66

APS Online. *See American Periodicals Series Online, 1740–1900*

AQ. *See American Quarterly*

ArchiveGrid, 113, 114–15

archives, 109–22; definition, 110–11; electronic text, 125–26; primary sources in, 110–11; print sources for locating, 117–21; research in, best practices for, 112–13; websites and databases for locating, 113–17

ArchivesUSA, 113, 115

Arnold, Marilyn, *Willa Cather: A Reference Guide*, 62, 63

art, resources on, 142–43

Arthur, Anthony, *American Prose and Criticism, 1900–1950*, 57

Articles Describing Archives and Manuscript Collections in the United States: An Annotated Bibliography (DeWitt), 117, 118–19

Articles on American Literature 1900–1950 (Leary), 83, 85–86

Ash, Lee, *Subject Collections: A Guide to Special Book Collections and Subject Emphases*, 117, 118

Asian American Short Story Writers (Huang), 60, 61

ASInt. *See American Studies International*

The Authentic History Center (Barnes), 131

authors: bibliographies of, 62–64, 89–94; book review monographs on, 89–94; journals on modernist, 70–73; library

catalog searches on, 34–37, *35f, 36f, 37t*; resources on, 28–31; websites on, 127–30

Barbour, Scott, *American Modernism*, 17, 18

Barnes, Michael, *The Authentic History Center*, 131

Baughman, Judith S., *Modern African American Writers*, 19, 21; *Modern Women Writers*, 19, 21

Bendixen, Alfred, *Encyclopedia of American Literature*, 20, 23

Bercovitch, Sacvan: *The Cambridge History of American Literature. Vol. 5: Poetry and; Criticism 1900–1950*, 19, 22–23; *The Cambridge History of American Literature. Vol. 6: Prose Writing 1910–1950*, 19, 22–23

Bibliographical Guide to the Study of the Literature of the USA (Gohdes & Marovitz), 57, 58

bibliographies, 49–66; American literature, 56–59; authors, 62–64; author-specific, 89–94; general, 51–56, *52f, 53f, 54f*; genre, 60–61; modernism, 59–60; resources on, 143–45. *See also* indexes

Bibliography of American Literature, 56, 57

Bibliography of American Literature: Epitome (Winship, Eppard, & Howarth), 57

Bibliography of American Literature: A Selective Index (Winship), 57

Bibliography of Bibliographies in American Literature (Nilon), 57, 58–59

A Bibliography of the Collected Writings of Edith Wharton (Melish), 63, 64

Bibliotheque Nationale de France, 46; *Catalogue Collectif de France*, 46

A Bio-bibliography of Langston Hughes, 1902–1967 (Dickinson), 63

biographical sources, 24–26

Black Literature, 1827–1940, 99

Book Review Digest, 83, 87; *Book Review Digest Retrospective: 1905–1982*, 87

Boolean searching, search strategies, 4–8, 5f, 6f, 7f

Bracken, James K., *The Undergraduate's Companion to American Writers and their Web Sites*, 132–33

Bradbury, Malcolm, *Modernism 1890–1930*, 59, 60

Bradshaw, David, *A Companion to Modernist Literature and Culture*, 19, 20–21

BRD. *See Book Review Digest*

Brier, Peter A., *American Prose and Criticism, 1900–1950*, 57

British Library, 47; *British Library Integrated Catalogue*, 46, 47

Brodsky, Louis Daniel, *Faulkner: A Comprehensive Guide to the Brodsky Collection*, 62, 64

Brogan, Martha L., *A Kaleidoscope of Digital American Literature*, 132

Bruccoli, Matthew J.: *American Expatriate Writers: Paris in the Twenties*, 102, 105; *Modern African American Writers*, 19, 21; *Modern Women Writers*, 19, 21

Bryer, Jackson R.: *F. Scott Fitzgerald: The Critical Reception*, 89, 92; *Wallace Stevens Checklist and Bibliography of Stevens Criticism*, 63

Burke, John Gordon, *The Access Index to Little Magazines*, 102

Burt, Daniel S., *The Chronology of American Literature: America's Literary Achievements from the Colonial Era to Modern Times*, 27

Calls for Papers (Kirk), 130

Calls for Papers (Sauer), 130

The Cambridge Companion to American Modernism (Kalaidjian), 17, 18

The Cambridge Companion to Modernism (Levenson), 19, 21

The Cambridge History of American Literature. Vol. 5: Poetry and Criticism 1900–1950 (Bercovitch), 19, 22–23

The Cambridge History of American Literature. Vol. 6: Prose Writing 1910–1950 (Bercovitch), 19, 22–23

Carnes, Mark C., *American National Biography* (*ANB*), 24, 25–26, 113, 115, 118, 120

Carter, Susanne, *Mothers and Daughters in American Short Fiction: An Annotated Bibliography of Twentieth-Century Women's Literature*, 61

Catalog of the Ernest Hemingway Collection at the John F. Kennedy Library, 62, 64

catalog searches: author, 34–37, 35f, 36f, 37t; subject, 39–42, 40ff; title, 37–39, 38f, 39f

catalogs, library, 33–48

Catalogue Collectif de France, 46

Cather Studies (*CathSt.*), 70, 71

CathSt. *See Cather Studies*

Cather, Willa: *Cather Studies* (*CathSt.*), 70, 71; *The Willa Cather Archive* (University of Nebraska at Lincoln), 127; *Willa Cather: A Bibliography* (Crane), 62, 63; *Willa Cather: The Contemporary Reviews* (O'Connor), 90, 93; Willa Cather Pioneer Memorial and Educational Foundation, 127; *Willa Cather: A Reference Guide* (Arnold), 62, 63

Chielens, Edward, E.: *American Literary Magazines: The Twentieth Century*, 102, 103–4; *The Literary Journal in America, 1900–1950*, 102, 104

A Chronological Outline of American Literature (Rogal), 27 chronologies, 27

The Chronology of American Literature: America's Literary Achievements from the Colonial Era to Modern Times (Burt), 27.

Colegrove, Harriet: *Index to Little Magazines 1948*, 103, 104–5; *Index to Little Magazines 1949*, 103, 104–5

Columbia Literary History of the United States (Emory), 19, 23

Combined Retrospective Index to Reviews in Humanities Journals, 1802–1974 (Farber, Hannah, & Schindler), 83, 85

A Companion to Faulkner Studies (Peck & Hamblin), 28, 30

A Companion to Modernist Literature and Culture (Bradshaw & Dettmar), 19, 20–21

A Companion to Twentieth-Century Poetry (Roberts), 20

companions, 17–19

companions, literary, 19–22, 24

Comprehensive Index to English-Language Little Magazines, 1890–1970 (Sader), 102, 106

A Concordance to the Complete Poems and Plays of T.S. Eliot (Dawson & Holland & McKitterick), 28, 30

contemporary journals, online, 131

contemporary magazines, online, 131

contemporary reviews, 81–96

Cox, Leland H., *William Faulkner, Critical Collection: A Guide to Critical Studies with Statements by Faulkner and Evaluative Essays on His Works*, 62

Crane, Joan, *Willa Cather: A Bibliography*, 62, 63

Croft, Robert W., *A Zora Neale Hurston Companion*, 28, 29

cultural resources, online, 131–32

Curnutt, Kirk, *A Historical Guide to F. Scott Fitzgerald*, 28, 29–30

current awareness resources, 130–31

Dace, Tish, *Langston Hughes: The Contemporary Reviews*, 90, 93

Danky, James P., *African-American Newspapers and Periodicals: A National Bibliography*, 99–100, 138

Databases, choosing, search strategy, 12–13, *12t*

Davies, Alistair, *An Annotated Critical Bibliography of Modernism*, 59, 60

Dawson, J. L., *A Concordance to the Complete Poems and Plays of T.S. Eliot*, 28, 30

Demastes, William W., *American Playwrights, 1880–1945: A Research and Production Sourcebook*, 60, 61

Dettmar, Kevin J. H., *A Companion to Modernist Literature and Culture*, 19, 20–21

DeWitt, Donald L.: *Articles Describing Archives and Manuscript Collections in the United States: An Annotated Bibliography*, 117, 118–19; *Guides to Archives and Manuscript Collections in the United States: An Annotated Bibliography*, 117, 119

Dickinson, Donald C., *A Bio-bibliography of Langston Hughes, 1902–1967*, 63

Dictionary of Literary Biography (DLB), 24, 26, 117, 119–20

Digital Book Index, 125, 126

Digital Collections Registry (Digital Library Federation), 131, 132

Digital Library Federation, *Digital Collections Registry*, 131, 132

DLB. *See Dictionary of Literary Biography*

Dos Passos, John: *John Dos Passos's U.S.A.: A Documentary Volume* (Pizer), 28, 29

Duffy, Susan, *The Political Left in the American Theatre of the 1930's: A Bibliographic Sourcebook*, 61

Edelstein, J. M., *Wallace Stevens: A Descriptive Bibliography*, 63–64

Edith Wharton: An Annotated Secondary Bibliography (Lauer & Murray), 63

Edith Wharton and Kate Chopin: A Reference Guide (Springer), 63

Edith Wharton Review (EWhR), 71

The Edith Wharton Society, 129

electronic records, structure of, 2–4

electronic text archives, 125–26

Electronic Text Center (University of Virginia), 126

Elliott, Emory, *Columbia Literary History of the United States*, 19, 23

Encyclopedia of American Literature, 19, 23

Encyclopedia of American Literature (Serafin & Bendixen), 20, 23
Encyclopedia of Literary Modernism (Poplawski), 20, 22
encyclopedias, 19–20, 22–23
Eppard, Philip B., *Bibliography of American Literature: Epitome*, 57
Ernest Hemingway (Hulse), 128
Ernest Hemingway: A Comprehensive Bibliography (Hanneman), 62
The Ernest Hemingway Foundation of Oak Park, 128
The Ernest Hemingway Home and Museum, 128
Essential Bibliography of American Fiction, 21
The Essentials of Literature in English Post-1914 (Mackean), 18–19
The Eugene O'Neill Review, 71–72
EWhR. See Edith Wharton Review
Ezra Pound: A Bibliography (Gallup), 90, 93
Ezra Pound: A Bibliography of Secondary Works (Ricks), 90, 93–94
The Ezra Pound Encyclopedia (Tryphonopoulos & Adams), 28, 30–31

Farber, Evan Ira, *Combined Retrospective Index to Book Reviews in Humanities Journals, 1802–1974*, 83, 85
Faulkner: A Comprehensive Guide to the Brodsky Collection (Brodsky & Hamblin), 62, 64
Faulkner Journal (FJ), 71, 72
The Faulkner Newsletter & Yoknapatawpha Review, 71, 72
Faulkner, William: *A Companion to Faulkner Studies* (Peck & Hamblin), 28, 30; *Faulkner: A Comprehensive Guide to the Bordsky Collection* (Brodsky & Hamblin), 62, 64; *Faulkner Journal (FJ)*, 71, 72; *The Faulkner Newsletter & Yoknapatawpha Review*, 71, 72
William Faulkner: American Writer, 1897–1962 (University of Mississippi), 127, 128; *William Faulkner: A Bibliography Secondary Works* (Ricks), 90, 94; *William Faulkner, Critical Collection: A Guide to Critical Studies with Statements by Faulkner and Evaluative Essays on His Works*, (Cox), 62; The William Faulkner Society (University of Mississippi), 128; *William Faulkner's Women Characters: An Annotated Bibliography of Criticism, 1930–1983* (Sweeney), 62, 64
Fitzgerald, F. Scott: *F. Scott Fitzgerald: The Critical Reception* (Bryer), 89, 92
F. Scott Fitzgerald Review (FSFR), 71
A Historical Guide to F. Scott Fitzgerald (Curnutt), 28, 29–30
Fordham University, *Internet Modern History Sourcebook*, 131
FSFR. See F. Scott Fitzgerald Review
F. Scott Fitzgerald: The Critical Reception (Bryer), 89, 92
F. Scott Fitzgerald Review (FSFR), 71
Fulton, Leon, *The Access Index to Little Magazines*, 102

Gallup, Donald, *Ezra Pound: A Bibliography*, 90, 93
Garraty, John A., *American National Biography (ANB)*, 24, 25–26, 113, 115, 118, 120
general research, resources on, 142
Gertrude Stein and Alice B. Toklas: A Reference Guide (White), 28, 31
Gohdes, Clarence, *Bibliographical Guide to the Study of the Literature of the USA*, 57, 58
Goode, Stephen H.: *Index to American Little Magazines 1920–1939*, 103, 104–5; *Index to Little Magazines 1940–1942*, 103, 104–5; *Index to Little Magazines 1943–1947*, 103, 104–5
Granger Book Company, Inc.: *Index to Poetry in Periodicals, American Poetic Renaissance 1915–1919: An Index of*

Poets and Poems Published in American Magazines and Newspapers, 102, 105–6; *Index to Poetry in Periodicals, 1920–1924: An Index of Poets and Poems Published in American Magazines and Newspapers*, 103, 106; *Index to Poetry in Periodicals, 1925–1929: An Index of Poets and Poems Published in American Magazines and Newspapers*, 103, 106

Gray, Richard A., *A Guide to Book Review Citations: A Bibliography of Sources*, 89

A Guide to Archives and Manuscripts in the United States (Hamer), 118, 120

A Guide to Book Review Citations: A Bibliography of Sources (Gray), 89

Guides to Archives and Manuscript Collections in the United States: An Annotated Bibliography (DeWitt), 117, 119

Hady, Maureen E., *African-American Newspapers and Periodicals: A National Bibliography*, 99–100, 138

A Half-Century of Eliot Criticism: An Annotated Bibliography of Books and Articles in English, 1916–1965 (Martin), 90, 94

Hamblin, Robert W.: *A Companion to Faulkner Studies*, 28, 30; *Faulkner: A Comprehensive Guide to the Brodsky Collection*, 62, 64

Hamer, Philip M., *A Guide to Archives and Manuscripts in the United States*, 118, 120

Hanna, Archibald, *A Mirror for the Nation: An Annotated Bibliography of American Social Fiction, 1901–1950*, 61

Hannah, Susan, *Combined Retrospective Index to Book Reviews in Humanities Journals, 1802–1974*, 83, 85

Hanneman, Audre, *Ernest Hemingway: A Comprehensive Bibliography*, 62

Harlem Renaissance: A Gale Critical Companion (Witalec), 20, 24

Harner, James L., *Literary Research Guide: An Annotated Listing of Reference Sources in English and Literary Studies*, 15, 16–17, 141

Hartford Friends and Enemies of Wallace Stevens, 129

Hemingway, Ernest: *Catalog of the Ernest Hemingway Collection at the John F. Kennedy Library*, 62, 64; *Ernest Hemingway* (Hulse), 128; *Ernest Hemingway: A Comprehensive Bibliography* (Hanneman), 62

The Ernest Hemingway Foundation of Oak Park, 128

The Ernest Hemingway Home and Museum, 128

The Hemingway Review (*HN*), 71, 72

The Hemingway Review (*HN*), 71, 72

Hinman, Larry G., *The Undergraduate's Companion to American Writers and their Web Sites*, 132–33

A Historical Guide to F. Scott Fitzgerald (Curnutt), 28, 29–30

history, resources on, 146–47; online, 131

HN. See The Hemingway Review

H-NET: Humanities and Sciences Online, 130

Hoffman, Frederick J., *The Little Magazine: A History and a Bibliography*, 102, 103

Holland, P. D., *A Concordance to the Complete Poems and Plays of T.S. Eliot*, 28, 30

Howarth, Rachel J., *Bibliography of American Literature: Epitome*, 57

Huang, Guiyou, *Asian American Short Story Writers*, 60, 61

Hughes, Langston: *A Bio-bibliography of Langston Hughes, 1902–1967* (Dickinson), 63; *Langston Hughes*, 129; *Langston Hughes and Gwendolyn Brooks: A Reference Guide* (Miller), 63

Langston Hughes: A Bio-bibliography (Mikolyzk), 63

Langston Hughes: The Contemporary Reviews (Dace), 90, 93

Langston Hughes National Poetry Project, 128, 129

The Langston Hughes Review (*LHRev*), 71, 72

Hulse, Caroline, *Ernest Hemingway*, 128

Humanities and Social Science Index Retrospective, 49, 51, 55

Humanities Index, 49, 51, 55, *56f*

Hurston, Zora Neale: *A Zora Neale Hurston Companion* (Croft), 28, 29; *Zora Neale Hurston Forum* (*ZNHF*), 71; *Zora Neale Hurston: A Reference Guide* (Newson), 63

Hutchinson, George, *In Search of Nella Larsen: A Biography of the Color Line*, 136

indexes, 49–66; general, 51–56, *56f*; literature, 83, 85, 86–87, 88–89. *See also* bibliographies

Index to American Little Magazines 1920–1939 (Goode), 103, 104–5

An Index to Literature in the New Yorker, 1940–1955 (Johnson), 83, 85

An Index to Literature in the New Yorker, 1925–1940 (Johnson), 83, 85

Index to Little Magazines 1940–1942 (Goode), 103, 104–5

Index to Little Magazines 1948 (Smith, Colegrove, & Swallow), 103, 104–5

Index to Little Magazines 1949 (Smith, Colegrove, Stephens, & Swallow), 103, 104–5

Index to Little Magazines 1943–1947 (Goode), 103, 104–5

Index to Personal Names in the National Union Catalog of Manuscript Collections, 1959–1984, 118, 120–21

Index to Poetry in Periodicals, American Poetic Renaissance 1915–1919: An Index of Poets and Poems Published in

American Magazines and Newspapers (Granger Book Company, Inc.), 102, 105–6

Index to Poetry in Periodicals, 1920–1924: An Index of Poets and Poems Published in American Magazines and Newspapers (Granger Book Company, Inc.), 103, 106

Index to Poetry in Periodicals, 1925–1929: An Index of Poets and Poems Published in American Magazines and Newspapers (Granger Book Company, Inc.), 103, 106

Index to Subjects and Corporate Names in the National Union Catalog of Manuscript Collections, 1959–1984, 118, 120–21

In Search of Nella Larsen: A Biography of the Color Line (Hutchinson), 136

International Review of Modernism, 69, 70

Internet Modern History Sourcebook (Fordham University), 131

Ishikawa, Akihito, *American Literature on the Web*, 124, 125

JAmS. See Journal of American Studies

JML. See Journal of Modern Literature

John Dos Passos's U.S.A.: A Documentary Volume (Pizer), 28, 29

Johnson, Robert Owen: *An Index to Literature in the New Yorker, 1940–1955*, 83, 85; *An Index to Literature in the New Yorker, 1925–1940*, 83, 85

Johnson, Thomas, H., *Literary History of the United States: Bibliography* (*LHUS*), 57, 58

Journal of American Studies (*JAmS*), 74, 76

Journal of Modern Literature (*JML*), 74, 76

journals: American literature, 73–79; scholarly, 67–80

JSTOR: The Scholarly Journal Archive, 50

Kalaidjian, Walter B., *The Cambridge Companion to American Modernism*, 17, 18

A Kaleidoscope of Digital American Literature (Brogan & Rentfrow), 132

Kehde, Ned, *The Access Index to Little Magazines*, 102

keywords, search strategy: brainstorming, 2, *2t*; in field searching, 4; locating manuscripts using, 118; versus subject searching, 9–11

Kirk, Brian, *Calls for Papers*, 130

Langston Hughes, 129

Langston Hughes and Gwendolyn Brooks: A Reference Guide (Miller), 63

Langston Hughes: A Bio-bibliography (Mikolyzk), 63

Langston Hughes: The Contemporary Reviews (Dace), 90, 93

Langston Hughes National Poetry Project, 128, 129

The Langston Hughes Review (*LHRev*), 71, 72

Larsen, Nella, 135–40

Lauer, Kristin O., *Edith Wharton: An Annotated Secondary Bibliography*, 63

LCSH. See Library of Congress Subject Headings

Leary, Lewis, *Articles on American Literature 1900–1950*, 83, 85–86

Levenson, Michael, *The Cambridge Companion to Modernism*, 19, 21

LH Rev. See The Langston Hughes Review

library catalogs, 33–48; national, 46–47; union, 42–46

Library of Congress (LOC), 47; *American Memory Project*, 125, 126; *Library of Congress Online Catalog*, 46, 47; Library of Congress Subject Headings (LCSH), 9

Library of Congress Online Catalog, 46, 47

limiting, search strategy, 11–12

LION. See Literature Online

Literary History of the United States: Bibliography (*LHUS*), (Spiller, Thorp, Johnson, & Ludwig), 57, 58

The Literary Journal in America, 1900–1950 (Chielens), 102, 104

literary reference sources, general, 15–31; resources on, 145–46

Literary Research Guide: An Annotated Listing of Reference Sources in English and Literary Studies (Harner) 15, 16–17, 141

Literary Resources-American (Lynch), 124, 125

Literary Writings in America: A Bibliography (O'Neill), 83, 87, 102, 106

Literature Online (*LION*), 53–54

The Little Magazine: A History and a Bibliography (Hoffmann), 102, 103

little magazines, 100–106; modernism and, 100–106

Liu, Alan, *Voice of the Shuttle*, 124–25

Ludwig, Richard M., *Literary History of the United States: Bibliography* (*LHUS*) 57, 58

Lynch, Jack, *Literary Resources-American*, 124, 125

Machine Readable Cataloging. *See* MARC records

Mackean, Ian, *The Essentials of Literature in English Post-1914*, 18–19

manuscripts, 109–22; definition, 111; print sources for locating, 117–21; websites and databases for locating, 113–17

MARC records, structure of, 2–4, *3f, 4f*

Marcuse, Michael J., *A Reference Guide for English Studies*, 15, 16–17, 141

Marovitz, Sanford E., *Bibliographical Guide to the Study of the Literature of the USA*, 57, 58

Martin, Mildred, *A-Half Century of Eliot Criticism: An Annotated Bibliography of Books and Articles in English, 1916–1965*, 90, 94

McFarlane, James, *Modernism 1890–1930*, 59, 60

McKitterick, D. J., *A Concordance to the Complete Poems and Plays of T.S. Eliot*, 28, 30

medicine, resources on, 151–52

Melish, Lawson McClung, *A Bibliography of the Collected Writings of Edith Wharton*, 63, 64

MFS. See Modern Fiction Studies

microforms, 97–108

Middleton, Tim, *Modernism: Critical Concepts in Literary and Cultural Studies. Vol. I: 1890–1934*, 19, 21–22

Mikolyzk, Thomas A., *Langston Hughes: A Bio-bibliography*, 63

Miller, R. Baxter, *Langston Hughes and Gwendolyn Brooks: A Reference Guide*, 63

Miller, William G., *Subject Collections: A Guide to Special Book Collections and Subject Emphases*, 117, 118

A Mirror for the Nation: An Annotated Bibliography of American Social Fiction, 1901–1950 (Hanna), 61

MLAIB. See Modern Language Association International Bibliography

MLN, 74, 76

MLQ. See Modern Language Quarterly

MLS. See Modern Language Studies

Modern African American Writers (Bruccoli & Baughman), 19, 21

Modern Culture & Media, Brown University, *The Modernist Journals Project*, 131

Modern Fiction Studies (*MFS*), 74, 76

modernism: bibliographies on, 59–60; definitions of, ix–x; journals on, 69–70; little magazines and, 100–106

Modernism: Critical Concepts in Literary and Cultural Studies. Vol. I: 1890–1934 (Middleton), 19, 21–22

Modernism 1890–1930 (Bradbury & McFarlane), 59, 60

Modernism/Modernity (*MoMo*), 69, 70

The Modernist Journals Project (Modern Culture & Media, Brown University), 131

Modernist Studies Association, 130

Modernist Studies: Literature & Culture 1920–1940 (*MSLC*), 69, 70

Modern Language Association International Bibliography (*MLAIB*), 49, 51–52, *52f*, *53f*, 53–55; versus *ABELL*, 52–55

Modern Language Quarterly (*MLQ*), 74, 76–77

Modern Language Studies (*MLS*), 74, 77

Modern Women Writers (Bruccoli & Baughman), 19, 21

MoMo. See Modernism/Modernity

Morgan, Eric Lease, *Alex Catalogue of Electronic Texts*, 125, 126

Morse, Samuel French, *Wallace Stevens Checklist and Bibliography of Stevens Criticism*, 63

Mothers and Daughters in American Short Fiction: An Annotated Bibliography of Twentieth-Century Women's Literature (Carter), 61

The Mount Estate and Gardens, 129, 130

MSLC. See Modernist Studies: Literature & Culture 1920–1940

Murray, Margaret P., *Edith Wharton: An Annotated Secondary Bibliography*, 63

music, resources on, 150–51

national library catalogs, 46–47

National Library Service Cumulative Book Review Index, 1905–1974, 83, 87

National Union Catalog of Manuscript Collections (*NUCMC*), 114, 115, 118, 120–21

National Union Catalog, Pre-1956 Imprints (*NUC*), 42, 43, 46, 137

nesting, search strategy, 8

Newson, Adele S., *Zora Neale Hurston: A Reference Guide*, 63

newspapers, 97–108; finding in general resources, 99–100

New York Public Library, Schomburg Center for Research in Black Culture, 114, 116; *NYPL Digital Gallery*, 131–32

New York Times Book Review Index 1896–1970, 83, 86

The New York Times Directory of the Theater, 83, 86

New York Times Theatre Reviews, 1870–1941, 86

Nilon, Charles H., *Bibliography of Bibliographies in American Literature*, 57, 58–59

not (Boolean operator), 6–8, *7f*

NUC. See National Union Catalog, Pre–1956 Imprints

NUCMC. See National Union Catalog of Manuscript Collections

NYPL Digital Gallery (New York Public Library), 131–32

Ockerbloom, John Mark, *The Online Books Page*, 126

O'Connor, Margaret Anne, *Willa Cather: The Contemporary Reviews*, 90, 93

O'Neill, Edward H., *Literary Writings in America: A Bibliography*, 83, 87, 102, 106

The Online Books Page (Ockerbloom), 126

online searching, basics of, 1–14

OpenWorldCat, 42, 43, *46f*, 116

or (Boolean operator), 6, *7f*

The Oxford Encyclopedia of American Literature (Parini), 24, 25

Parini, Jay, *The Oxford Encyclopedia of American Literature*, 24, 25

Peck, Charles A., *A Companion to Faulkner Studies*, 28, 30

periodicals, 97–108; contemporary reviews from, 83–89; finding in general resources, 99–100; searching library catalogs for, 68, *68f*

philosophy, resources on, 147–49

phrase searching, search strategy, 8–9

Pizer, Donald, *John Dos Passos's U.S.A.: A Documentary Volume*, 28, 29

PMLA: Publications of the Modern Language Association, 74, 77

The Political Left in the American Theatre of the 1930's: A Bibliographic Sourcebook (Duffy), 61

Poplawski, Paul, *Encyclopedia of Literary Modernism*, 20, 22

Pound, Ezra: *Ezra Pound: A Bibliography* (Gallup), 90, 93

Ezra Pound: A Bibliography of Secondary Works (Ricks), 90, 93–94

The Ezra Pound Encyclopedia (Tryphonopoulos & Adams), 28, 30–31

primary sources, definition of, 110–11

Project Gutenberg, 126

Project Muse, 50

ProQuest Historical Newspapers, 84, 87

ProQuest Historical New York Times, 86–87

proximity operators, search strategy, 8–9

Publications of the Modern Language Association. See PMLA

RALS. See Resources for American Literary Study

The Readers' Guide to Periodical Literature, 89

REAL. See Yearbook of Research in English and American Literature

A Reference Guide for English Studies (Marcuse), 15, 16–17, 141

relevancy searching, search strategy, 11

religion, resources on, 149–50

Rentfrow, Daphnée, *A Kaleidoscope of Digital American Literature*, 132

Repositories of Primary Sources, 1995– (Abraham), 113, 114

research guides, general, 15–17, 143–45

Resources for American Literary Study (RALS), 74, 77–78

reviews, contemporary, 81–96

Ricks, Beatrice: *Ezra Pound: A Bibliography of Secondary Works*, 90, 93–94; *T.S. Eliot: A Bibliography of Secondary Works*, 90, 94; *William Faulkner: A Bibliography of Secondary Works*, 90, 94

Riddel, Joseph N., *Wallace Stevens Checklist and Bibliography of Stevens Criticism*, 63

RLIN, 114, 116

Robbins, J. Albert, *American Literary Manuscripts*, 118, 121

Roberts, Neil, *A Companion to Twentieth-Century Poetry*, 20

Rogal, Samuel J., *A Chronological Outline of American Literature*, 27

Rood, Karen L., *Southern Women Writers: Flannery O'Connor, Katherine Anne Porter, Eudora Welty. Dictionary of Literary Biography, Documentary Series, vol. 12*, 20, 23–24

Sader, Marion, *Comprehensive Index to English-Language Little Magazines, 1890–1970*, 102, 106

Sauer, Geoff, *Calls for Papers*, 130

Schindler, Stanley, *Combined Retrospective Index to Reviews in Humanities Journals, 1802–1974*, 83, 85

scholarly journals, 67–80

Schomburg Center for Research in Black Culture (New York Public Library), 114, 116

sciences, resources on, 151–52

search engines, *12t*, 13

Serafin, Steven R., *Encyclopedia of American Literature*, 20, 23

Sewanee Review (*SR*), 74, 78

SHARP. *See* Society for the History of Authorship, Reading & Publishing

Smith, Avalon: *Index to Little Magazines 1948*, 103, 104–5; *Index to Little Magazines 1949*, 103, 104–5

Smith, Geoffrey D., *American Fiction, 1901–1925: A Bibliography*, 61

Smithsonian National Museum of American History, 131

Society for the History of Authorship, Reading & Publishing (SHARP), 114, 116–17

Southern Women Writers: Flannery O'Connor, Katherine Anne Porter, Eudora Welty. Dictionary of Literary Biography, Documentary Series, vol. 12 (Wimsatt & Rood), 20, 23–24

The Space Between: Literature and Culture 1914–1945, 130–31

Spiller, Robert E., *Literary History of the United States: Bibliography* (*LHUS*), 57, 58

Springer, Marlene, *Edith Wharton and Kate Chopin: A Reference Guide*, 63

SR. See Sewanee Review

Stein, Gertrude: *Gertrude Stein and Alice B. Toklas: A Reference Guide* (White), 28, 31

Stephens, Alan, *Index to Little Magazines 1949*, 103, 104–5

Stevens, Wallace: Hartford Friends and Enemies of Wallace Stevens, 129; *Wallace Stevens Checklist and Bibliography of Stevens Criticism* (Morse, Bryer, & Riddel), 63; *Wallace Stevens: A Descriptive Bibliography* (Edelstein), 63–64; *Wallace Stevens Journal* (*WSJour*), 71, 73; *Wallace Stevens Society*, 129

StTCL. See Studies in 20th and 21st Century Literature

Studies in 20th and 21st Century Literature (*StTCL*), 74, 78

Subject Collections: A Guide to Special Book Collections and Subject Emphases (Ash & Miller), 117, 118

subject searches, search strategy, 9–11, *10f*; in library catalogs, 39–42, *40f*

surveys, literary, 19–24

Swallow, Alan: *Index to Little Magazines 1948*, 103, 104–5; *Index to Little Magazines 1949*, 103, 104–5

Sweeney, Patricia E., *William Faulkner's Women Characters: An Annotated Bibliography of Criticism, 1930–1983*, 62, 64

TCL. *See Twentieth-Century Literature*
TCLC. *See Twentieth–Century Literary Criticism*
Texas Studies in Literature and Language (*TSLL*), 74, 78
theatre, resources on, 153
Thorp, Willard, *Literary History of the United States: Bibliography* (*LHUS*), 57, 58
The Times Literary Supplement Index 1902–1939, 84, 88–89
title searches, 37–39, *38f, 39f*
TLS. *See The Times Literary Supplement Index 1902–1939*
TLS: *Times Literary Supplement Centenary Archive 1902–1990*, 84, 89
Trogdon, Robert W., *American Expatriate Writers: Paris in the Twenties*, 102, 105
truncation, search strategy, 8
Tryphonopoulos, Demetres P., *The Ezra Pound Encyclopedia*, 28, 30–31
T.S. Eliot: A Bibliography of Secondary Works (Ricks), 90, 94
TSLL. *See Texas Studies in Literature and Language*
TSWL. *See Tulsa Studies in Women's Literature*
Tulsa Studies in Women's Literature (*TSWL*), 74, 78–79
Twentieth Century, journals on, 73–79
Twentieth-Century Literary Criticism, 84, 88
Twentieth-Century Literature (*TCL*), 74, 79

The Undergraduate's Companion to American Writers and their Web Sites (Bracken & Hinman), 132–33
union catalogs, 42–46, *44f, 45f*
United States Newspaper Program Union List, 99, 100

University of Mississippi, *William Faulkner: American Writer, 1897–1962*, 127, 128
University of Mississippi, The William Faulkner Society, 128
University of Nebraska at Lincoln, *The Willa Cather Archive* 127
University of Virginia, Electronic Text Center, 126

Voice of the Shuttle (Liu), 124–25

Wallace Stevens Checklist and Bibliography of Stevens Criticism (Morse & Bryer & Riddel), 63
Wallace Stevens: A Descriptive Bibliography (Edelstein), 63–64
Wallace Stevens Journal (*WSJour*), 71, 73
Wallace Stevens Society, 129
WCWR. *See William Carlos Williams Review*
web resources, 123–33; evaluation of, 124; gateways sites as, 124–25; print guides to, 132
Wharton, Edith: *A Bibliography of the Collected Writings of Edith Wharton* (Melish), 63, 64; *Edith Wharton: An Annotated Secondary Bibliography* (Lauer & Murray), 63; *Edith Wharton and Kate Chopin: A Reference Guide* (Springer), 63; *Edith Wharton Review* (*EWhR*), 71; The Edith Wharton Society, 129
White, Ray Lewis, *Gertrude Stein and Alice B. Toklas: A Reference Guide*, 28, 31
Whitley, Peggy, *American Cultural History: The Twentieth Century*, 131, 132
The Willa Cather Archive (University of Nebraska at Lincoln), 127
Willa Cather: A Bibliography (Crane), 62, 63
Willa Cather: The Contemporary Reviews (O'Connor), 90, 93

Willa Cather Pioneer Memorial and Educational Foundation, 127
Willa Cather: A Reference Guide (Arnold), 62, 63
William Carlos Williams Review (*WCWR*), 71, 73
William Faulkner: American Writer, 1897–1962 (University of Mississippi), 127, 128
William Faulkner: A Bibliography of Secondary Works (Ricks), 90, 94
William Faulkner, Critical Collection: A Guide to Critical Studies with Statements by Faulkner and Evaluative Essays on His Works (Cox), 62
The William Faulkner Society (University of Mississippi), 128
William Faulkner's Women Characters: An Annotated Bibliography of Criticism, 1930–1983 (Sweeney), 62, 64
Williams, William Carlos: *William Carlos Williams Review* (*WCWR*), 71, 73
Wimsatt, Mary Ann, *Southern Women Writers: Flannery O'Connor, Katherine Anne Porter, Eudora Welty. Dictionary*

of Literary Biography, Documentary Series, vol. 12, 20, 23–24

Winship, Michael: *Bibliography of American Literature: Epitome*, 57; *Bibliography of American Literature: A Selective Index*, 57
Witalec, Janey, *Harlem Renaissance: A Gale Critical Companion*, 20, 24
Woodress, James, *American Fiction, 1900–1950: A Guide to Information Sources*, 57, 59
WorldCat, 42–43, *44f, 45f,* 114, 115–16
WSJour. See *Wallace Stevens Journal*

Yearbook of Research in English and American Literature (*REAL*), 64, 66
The Year's Work in English Studies, 64, 65–66

ZNHF. See *Zora Neale Hurston Forum*
A Zora Neale Hurston Companion (Croft), 28, 29
Zora Neale Hurston Forum (*ZNHF*), 71
Zora Neale Hurston: A Reference Guide (Newson), 63

About the Authors

Elizabeth Blakesley Lindsay is the Assistant Dean for Public Services and Outreach at the Washington State University Libraries, where she was previously the head of Library Instruction and the liaison librarian for English. She has a B.A. in English and Spanish from the University of Dayton and an M.L.S. and an M.A. in comparative literature from Indiana University, Bloomington. Her previous book, *Great Women Mystery Writers (2nd edition)*, was published by Greenwood Press in 2006.

Robert Matuozzi is an associate professor and humanities bibliographer in English and American literature, philosophy, religion, and art and photography at Washington State University Libraries. He holds a B.A. in history from Indiana University, an M.S. in library and information science from the University of Illinois at Urbana–Champaign, and an M.A. in history from Ohio State University.